Ageing and Economic Welfare

D1100027

Ageing and Economic Welfare

Paul Johnson
and
Jane Falkingham

SAGE Publications
London · Newbury Park · New Delhi

SAGE Publications Ltd
6 Bonhill Street
London EC2A 4PU

SAGE Publications Inc
2455 Teller Road
Newbury Park, California 91320

SAGE Publications India Pvt Ltd
32, M-Block Market
Greater Kailash – I
New Delhi 110 048

British Library Cataloguing in Publication data

Johnson, Paul
  Ageing and Economic Welfare
  I. Title II. Falkingham, Jane
  362.6

  ISBN 0–8039–8248–8
  ISBN 0–8039–8249–6 pbk

Library of Congress catalog card number 92–050169

Typeset by Photoprint, Torquay, Devon
Printed in Great Britain by Billing and Sons Ltd, Worcester

Contents

List of Tables   vii
List of Figures   ix
Acknowledgements   xi

1 Introduction: Ageing and the Social Sciences   1
2 The Demography of Ageing   18
3 Income, Wealth and Health in Later Life   49
4 Work and Retirement   84
5 Public Pensions, Government Expenditure and
   Intergenerational Transfers   124
6 Ageing and the Macroeconomy   152
7 Ageing and Public Policy   177

Bibliography   189
Index   203

List of Tables

2.1 Trends in the relative size of the 65 and over age group in 14 advanced countries 21

2.2 Expectation of life at birth for generations born 1841–1991, United Kingdom 23

2.3 Ratio of females to males in the elderly population 1881–1981, Great Britain 27

2.4 Proportion of elderly men and women reported as head of household, 1599–1985 33

2.5 Proportion of elderly men and women reported as living alone, 1684–1985 33

2.6 Local authorities with the highest and lowest fractions of their population aged over pensionable age 38

2.7 Selected statistics for the UK population aged 60 or above, 1991–2031 41

2.8 Number of persons aged 60 or over 47

3.1 Ratio of public pensions to average wages in manufacturing 56

3.2 Sources of pensioners' gross incomes, Great Britain 59

3.3 Sources of pensioner households' gross incomes, Canada, Japan, USA 60

3.4 Pensioners' income by source, 1987 63

3.5 Selected characteristics of the Woopies and all persons aged over 65 64

3.6 Equity by income for households with head over retirement age, England 1986 68

3.7 Disability level of elderly men and women by age group 72

3.8 Elderly persons unable to perform certain tasks at all or without help 77

3.9 Use of services by the Woopies 77

4.1 Long-term development of labour force participation rates for older men and women in France, Germany, UK and USA 90

4.2 Index of occupational concentration, males aged 65 and over England and Wales 94

4.3 Correlation coefficients between changes in the unemployment rate and labour force participation rates of older men, 1970–89 104

4.4   Membership of occupational pension schemes in
      Britain, percentage of total workforce, excluding un-
      employed   115
4.5   Retirement pension as percentage of average male
      earnings, UK 1948–2050   118
5.1   The contributions and benefits of successive cohorts
      in a hypothetical pay-as-you-go pension system   130
5.2   Influence of demographic change on the share of
      pension expenditure in national income, 1984–2040   134
5.3   Impact of demographic change on social expenditure
      and financing burdens, 1980–2040   136
5.4   Pensions at award for men and women on average
      earnings as a proportion of earnings before
      retirement on the assumption of a growth in real
      earnings of 1.5 per cent per year, 1990–2050   143
5.5   Projected joint employer/employee National
      Insurance contribution rates   144

List of Figures

2.1 Proportion of the population aged 60/65 or over, Great Britain, 1871–2021   19

2.2 Age structure of the population, Great Britain, 1871–2021   20

2.3 Crude birth and death rates, England and Wales, 1840–1980   24

2.4 Age structure of the population of pensionable age, Great Britain, 1901–2021   25

2.5 Marital status of the population aged 65 and over by gender, 1985   29

2.6 Marital status of persons of pensionable age, Great Britain, 1901–81: (a) males; (b) females   30

2.7 Dependency ratios, Great Britain, 1871–2021   44

3.1 Supplementary benefit (and income support) recipients, 1970–89   54

3.2 Standard rate of pension as a proportion of average male weekly earnings, 1975–90   55

3.3 Benefits in kind to five-year age groups, 1987   58

3.4 Income distribution for persons aged 65 plus, 1987   61

3.5 Cumulative income distributions, 1987   62

3.6 Tenure by equivalent income quintile group: (a) 1974; (b) 1985   70

3.7 Disability level of elderly men and women, 1985   72

3.8 Projection of the number of moderately and severely disabled elderly men and women, 1991–2031   74

4.1 Labour force participation rates for males and females, England and Wales, 1881–1989   86

4.2 Labour force participation rates for men aged 65 plus, 1885–1989   88

4.3 Labour force participation rates for women aged 65 plus, 1885–1989   88

4.4 Labour force participation rates by age for successive birth cohorts of English men   93

4.5 Labour force participation rates by age for successive birth cohorts of English women   93

4.6 Labour force participation rates in selected OECD countries, males 55–64   104

4.7 Hypothetical income and consumption profiles of a
      life cycle saver   110
5.1 Index of working age (15–64) population   139
6.1 Percentage change by age group 1990–2000,
      populations of: (a) United States; (b) United
      Kingdom; (c) France; (d) Germany   154
6.2 Hypothetical age–earnings profiles for successive birth
      cohorts and for a population cross-section   162
6.3 Pension income for a hypothetical worker in 'defined
      benefit' and 'defined contribution' pension schemes   169

Acknowledgements

This book is the outcome of research funded by the Economic and Social Research Council (ESRC). The initial work was carried out as part of a project to investigate the economics of retirement and old age in twentieth-century Britain (grant reference G00 23 2344), and has been continued under the Welfare State Programme at the London School of Economics (LSE) (grant reference X206 32 2001). Paul Johnson completed part of the manuscript while holding a Senior Research Fellowship at the Institute of Advanced Studies of the Australian National University. All this support is gratefully acknowledged.

We would like to thank our colleagues at LSE and elsewhere for their advice and assistance, particularly Maria Evandrou, Chris Gordon, John Hills, Carli Lessof, Peter Scott and Christina Victor. Many others have heard and reacted to our ideas at seminars; we have benefited greatly from comments made by our critics, though we continue to disagree on many issues.

In this book, as with any collaborative project, there has been some division of labour. Jane Falkingham took primary responsibility for Chapters Two and Three, Paul Johnson for Chapters Four, Five and Six, but the overall interpretation is very much a joint product.

1

Introduction: Ageing and the Social Sciences

The age structure of a country's population – that is the relative proportions of children, working-age adults and elderly people – can have an enormous impact on the performance of the economy and the welfare of individuals. Many dependent children means many mouths to feed and the commitment of a large part of a nation's income to consumption expenditure rather than to investment. The endemic malnutrition and low rates of economic growth typical of many less developed countries are, in part, a result of rapid population growth and a large dependent child population. But this does not mean that a population with few children and many elderly people will necessarily experience faster growth or higher living standards. An ageing society – one where the ratio of elderly to non-elderly people (and therefore the average age of the population) is rising – may impose economic costs on all its members. In 1949 an official inquiry into demographic trends in the United Kingdom warned that:

> Older people excel in experience, patience, in wisdom and breadth of view; the young are noted for energy, enterprise, enthusiasm, the capacity to learn new things, to adapt themselves, to innovate. It thus seems possible that a society in which the proportion of young people is diminishing will become dangerously unprogressive, falling behind other communities not only in technical efficiency and economic welfare, but in intellectual and artistic achievement as well. (Royal Commission on Population, 1949: 121)

The aim of this book is to assess whether, or to what extent, this doom-laden speculation of more than forty years ago is relevant today. This is a vital question for contemporary developed economies because almost all of them have rapidly ageing populations, and the process of societal ageing now under way will continue well into the twenty-first century. The 'baby-boom' that occurred in the aftermath of the Second World War has been followed in most developed countries by a 'baby-bust' since the late 1960s as birth rates have fallen below the level needed to maintain the population at its current size. When the baby-boomers enter retirement in the second decade of the next century they may be succeeded by a working population that is ageing and diminishing in size. This scenario of a rising number of pensioners and a declining number of workers has been widely described as 'a demographic time bomb', an economic disaster simply waiting to happen (Teitelbaum and Winter, 1985: 1–4; McLoughlin, 1991: ch. 1) .

Unlike other predictions of long-term catastrophe, such as global warming, the depletion of energy reserves, or harvest failure and mass famine (predictions which often depend on contentious assumptions and questionable inferences), the idea of a demographic time bomb *appears* to rest on firmer foundations. We know to within very close limits how many people of working and pensionable age will be alive in the year 2010, because nearly all of them have already been born. Population projections that extend further into the future must involve some degree of uncertainty because future decisions people take about whether to have children, or how large a family to aim for, may be very different from decisions taken by people now and in the past. In practice, however, demographers do not anticipate dramatic changes in fertility patterns in the immediate future. Even if birth rates do suddenly rise or fall, this cannot alter the fact that the large cohorts of baby-boomers who are found in nearly all the advanced industrial countries will be retiring between 2010 and 2025. The 'demographic time bomb' has a long fuse but the length is known. What is uncertain is whether the time bomb will go off with a whimper or a bang.

The outlook may be profoundly pessimistic, with population ageing leading to lower growth rates, higher taxes, reduced living standards and pronounced social tension throughout the developed economies; or it may be pleasantly benign, with ageing initiating gradual, almost imperceptible and ultimately beneficial changes to the existing economic and social order. The fact that different observers can anticipate such disparate outcomes from the same social process indicates the complexity of the link between population, society and economic performance, but it also illustrates how important it is for social scientists and policy-makers to have a firm understanding of the causes and of the economic and social consequences of demographic change in the developed economies. The issue of population ageing is too often regarded as the preserve of demographers interested in the mechanics of population dynamics or of actuaries concerned with the financial implications of changes in life expectancy. Although there was considerable interest in both the causes and anticipated consequences of ageing during the low fertility years of the 1930s (Thane, 1990), contemporary social science has had relatively little to say about the impact of demographic change in developed societies. For instance, the

Journal of Economic Literature, which produces quarterly listings of articles published in leading economics periodicals, introduced the category 'economics of ageing' only in 1982, and seldom finds more than a small handful of works to include under this heading.

This relative neglect of the role of population change is in marked contrast to the way it was viewed 200 years ago by one of the founding fathers of economics, Thomas Malthus, who argued that there was an intimate relationship between the rate of growth of the economy and the size and rate of growth of the population. In 1798 Malthus published his *Essay on the Principle of Population* in which he asserted that population growth would be limited by the productive capacity of the economy. He believed that whereas the size of a population could expand geometrically (1, 2, 4, 8, 16 . . .), food supply could expand only arithmetically (1, 2, 3, 4, 5 . . .), and therefore demand for food would periodically and inevitably out-strip supply, resulting in recurrent famine. Malthus's dire predictions proved to be wrong; in practice people limited their rate of reproduction to something well below the physiological maximum, and agricultural productivity expanded far faster than anyone could have anticipated in the late eighteenth century. The restrictive link between population growth and economic growth appeared to have been broken.

Yet it had not been broken everywhere; the experience of many less developed countries over the last thirty years shows that very rapid population growth can still inhibit the overall rate of economic growth (by which we mean the rate of growth of national income per capita). The twentieth-century experience for the industrialized countries, on the other hand, has been quite different. They have witnessed positive but very modest population growth rates which have acted as a gentle economic stimulus through a slow but relatively stable growth in the size of the domestic market and through having a slightly larger number of young, recently-trained workers coming into the labour force each year than of older workers withdrawing from it. But negative population growth rates in the future may reverse this optimistic outlook. Malthus argued that the productive capacity of the economy would restrict popula-tion growth; the questions for the future are whether an ageing and shrinking population will restrict the productive capacity of the economy, and if it does, how will the social costs of this restriction be distributed.

Before addressing these questions directly it is instructive to see how the subject of population ageing has been treated in the social science literature. Interpretations that have emerged from the different social science disciplines have been partial and to some extent conditioned by the prevailing orthodoxies within these disciplines. Economists have tended to measure costs and consider how they are distributed, social policy analysts have emphasized welfare outputs and the rights of older people, sociologists have begun to take note of the way a changing age profile affects key elements of the social structure, and political scientists have been concerned with the way older people vote.

Ageing and Economics

Classical economists such as Malthus and Adam Smith ascribed a central role in their models of economic development to the size and rate of growth of the population, but this emphasis has not been continued in more recent writings. Whereas for Malthus population growth was endogenous to his economic system, both acting on and reacting to changes in the performance of the economy, in standard neo-classical growth theory population growth is typically treated as an exogenous variable, one that impinges on the workings of the economy but which is determined by non-economic criteria (van Praag, 1988). This assumption in macroeconomic growth models is at odds both with rationalist microeconomic theory which sees all decisions about marriage, family formation and size of family as essentially economically determined (Becker, 1981), and with the conclusions of modern econometric studies which show that decisions about the timing and number of births are related to the opportunity cost of lost income (Cigno, 1984; Ermisch, 1988a, 1989).

Even the limited attempts that have been made to incorporate population change as an endogenous element in growth models have concentrated on the *rate of growth* of the population rather than on changes in the population *age structure*. These two phenomena are clearly related, because the prime determinant of both is the fertility rate (see Chapter Two), and a population that is declining in size will also typically exhibit an increasing average age, but the economic effect can be distinct. For instance, a fall in the size of the population will increase the capital/labour ratio (more machines per worker) but a rise in the average age of the workforce may reduce average labour productivity (if older workers are less productive than younger ones). These two forces might by chance neutralize each other, but there is no particular reason why they should do so. Although this book will consider the consequences of both population ageing and population decline for the developed economies, the main stress will be on ageing because, as will be explained in detail in the next chapter, this is the more immediate and general phenomenon. The macroeconomic implication of this general ageing of western populations will be returned to in Chapter Six once a more complete picture of the ageing process has been assembled.

A second, and more successful, way in which economists have considered the consequences of population ageing lies in a general concern with the distribution of economic resources. It is a truism that we bring nothing into the world with us when we are born and take nothing with us when we die, but at every point in between our actions are to some extent conditioned and motivated by our access to economic resources. A stylized description of the way in which individuals accumulate and use resources from birth to death has been incorporated in modern economics under the generic name of 'life cycle theory'. At its simplest, the life cycle theory postulates that any individual will accumulate resources (savings) during prime working years of peak earnings, and will then live on these savings during the years of later life which may be characterized by low or zero earnings because of retirement or disability. In other words, an individual redistributes economic resources across his or her own life cycle (Hurd, 1990).

If this stylized description of individual behaviour is generalized to a whole population, then it implies that an ageing population will undertake progressively less saving as a growing proportion of society realizes its assets to finance the non-earning years of later life. But the analogy between the ageing of an individual and the ageing of society is not perfect. An ageing individual who enters retirement no longer contributes to the measured output of the economy, but instead draws on savings in order to purchase goods and services produced by others. An ageing society, however, has no one else, no 'younger society' to turn to for the production of goods and services, but instead has access only to its own current national product. If the proportion of non-working elderly people to working-age adults rises, then a larger share of the measured output of the working population will have to be transferred to the retired population if the relative consumption levels of individuals in these two groups are to be maintained. This transfer, which is typically brought about through a combination of private savings and social security systems, is effectively a redistribution of economic resources between generations, from young to old. An action such as participation in a pension scheme may be seen not only as part of a *life cycle* redistribution from the perspective of the individual, but also as part of an *intergenerational* transfer from a broader social perspective. Whether such transfers should be viewed as benign or problematic will be discussed more fully in Chapter Five.

Economists interested in questions of distribution have also examined how population ageing has affected the distribution of economic resources *between* the young and the old and *within* the elderly population (Smeeding, 1990; Atkinson and Sutherland, 1992). Older people are no more homogeneous in terms of income, wealth or social class than are people of working age, but they do not necessarily exhibit the same distribution of these characteristics as do the rest of the adult population. Age is itself a very important determinant of economic distribution, since it is a close correlate of average level of disability and labour force participation. Generation (or birth cohort) is also of particular influence, since small differences in date of birth can produce enormous differences in lifetime experiences. For instance, a man born in Britain in 1915 was an infant during the privations of the First World War, entered the labour market during the mass unemployment of the 1930s, spent the whole of the Second World War in military service, and was approaching middle age by the time the British economy was prospering in the mid-1950s. A man born ten years later did not suffer from rationing during infancy, served in the armed forces only in the latter stages of the Second World War, and was demobilized in his early 20s into the booming labour market of the immediate post-war years. This younger man is much more likely to have reached retirement age in good health and with adequate savings than is the man who was born just ten years earlier. This cohort effect may act in combination or in opposition to the age effect as a population ages, so it is not obvious whether population ageing will increase or decrease the economic inequalities within the elderly population, or between the old and the young. Some of the basic data on the distribution of resources between younger and older people and among the elderly population will be examined in Chapter Three.

A third area of interest for economists has been the way in which population ageing affects the supply of labour (Quinn and Burkhauser, 1990). As people move into old age they tend to undertake less paid work. This may be a consequence of an increased frailty in old age, or of restricted demand on the part of employers for the services of older workers, or it may be the result of a positive choice on the part of the older workers to opt for increased leisure at the expense of lost earnings. In practice there has been a common trend in developed economies for this purely demographic restriction on labour supply to be exacerbated by a behavioural trend towards increased early retirement by people in their 50s. Population ageing, therefore, can have a direct impact on the size of the labour force below normal pension age, but even if the size of this potential working population remains constant, population ageing may induce a decline in the actual labour force because people in their 50s and early 60s have lower participation rates than those in their 30s or 40s.

Furthermore, it is commonly assumed that average labour productivity declines with age above some threshold age usually located somewhere between 40 and 50. This productivity decline is thought in part to be a consequence of age-related limitation in the physical and mental powers of older workers, and partly as an inevitable result of the increasing technological redundancy of older workers whose skills and training eventually become out-of-date. If this suggestion is true, it implies that an ageing of the population which increases the average age of the workforce will itself diminish the productive capacity of the labour force, even if participation rates are identical for workers of different ages. In practice, however, it is far from obvious that productivity does decline with age, that the skills of older workers are less useful than the skills of the young, or that older workers withdraw from the labour force through choice. Empirical investigation has shown that the relationship between individual age and labour force participation, productivity, income and job promotion is by no means straightforward, and so predictions about the impact of societal ageing on work and productivity covers a broad spectrum of optimism and pessimism. Chapter Four reviews this literature on ageing and the labour market and Chapter Six examines the link between ageing and productivity.

The fourth area in which economists have explicitly considered the consequences of population ageing is in the long-term implications for social security systems. This has been an important issue in applied economics since the mid-1970s and the research has produced a number of new insights into the economics of population ageing (Aaron et al., 1989; Cutler et al., 1990). The broad-ranging nature of social security means that questions of growth, distribution and labour supply are also often considered by economists who have as their starting point the way in which social security systems interact with demographic change. One important element in most social security schemes is an old-age or retirement pension. The payment of this pension is commonly considered to be a direct inducement to withdraw from the labour force because it provides a guaranteed income in exchange for no work. But this tendency to reduce labour supply may be countered by an opposite effect. The guaranteed pension income may induce older workers to take up different, more flexible and lower-paid work at a wage they would not previously have accepted. Workers below pension age who are unemployed because they cannot find work with acceptable pay (their reservation wage) may be tempted back into employment once they qualify for a pension income. The net effect of old age pensions on labour supply will therefore depend upon the mix of individual and labour market characteristics and pension scheme regulations, all of which will vary between places and over time.

Pensions also have a very important influence on distribution. In most modern economies social security pensions account for a substantial part of the income received by older people so they necessarily have a strong impact on the distribution of resources within the elderly population. These pensions tend to reduce income inequality and raise the income of the poorest elderly people to some minimum threshold. In so far as workers pay contributions to the state pension scheme when they are in employment and draw a pension in retirement, this system appears to the individual to be a system of life cycle redistribution of resources, and it has been claimed that this perception of a social security pension scheme can have a damaging impact on a country's long-term growth (Feldstein, 1974). Expectation of a state pension in old age may reduce an individual's attempts to accumulate private savings for old age. A reduction in private savings in an economy will drive up the interest rate, thus making investment less profitable, but reduced investment will lead to a lower growth rate in the future. Whether in practice people respond to state pension entitlements in this way, and whether population ageing has exacerbated this effect will be looked at in Chapter Five.

However, as pointed out already, at the societal level pension schemes can be thought of as systems for the redistribution of current output from younger to older generations, and this can cause problems if the successive generations are of very different sizes. If a large generation of retirees is succeeded by a small generation of workers, the contributions that need to be exacted from these workers to maintain the relative living standards of the pensioners have to rise. Whether the rise is large or small depends both on the specific regulations governing each social security scheme and on the scale and pace of population ageing in each country. In those places where contributions are projected to rise sharply in future decades, there has been talk of intergenerational conflict, of a direct clash of interests between the old and the young which could undermine the consensual basis of social security (Johnson et al., 1989). The plausibility of such predictions will also be evaluated in Chapter Five.

In summary it may be said that population ageing has a toehold on the ladder of current economic issues but that it is there more as an interesting curiosity than as a matter of pressing concern (for a comprehensive but somewhat dated survey of the US literature, see Clark and Spengler, 1980). Population ageing is seldom more than a peripheral element in writing on growth theory, distribution, labour markets or social security systems, perhaps because it is seen as too long-run an issue to be worth immediate attention. However, as the demographic data in Chapter Two reveal, the magnitude of future demographic changes in developed countries will require detailed and careful economic analysis. And the need for that analysis is already pressing, even if the effects of demographic change do not become fully apparent for two or three decades, since population age structures cannot be changed quickly, people near retirement cannot easily remake their retirement savings plans, and retired people cannot quickly be recruited back into the labour force. If the predictions of some economists are correct that pension systems will need to be drastically reformed, retirement ages raised, and savings rates increased in order to pay for population ageing, then these changes need to be inaugurated now so they can be implemented in an incremental way over the next thirty years. But if the arguments of others who say that marginal changes in existing market relationships will easily accommodate population ageing are correct, it is equally important that they be taken into account now in order to prevent costly, inefficient and unnecessary policy intervention.

Ageing and Sociology

Economists are not alone among social scientists in treating population ageing as a curiosity that occasionally touches but generally lies outside the mainstream of the discipline. It is perhaps particularly surprising that sociologists, whose declared aim is to study the way in which society functions and changes over time, have devoted relatively little attention to those demographic processes which are an important element of social change. Over the course of the twentieth century the basic shape of western society has undergone a profound rearrangement as birth and death rates have fallen. Around 1900 about 1 person in 20 in Britain was aged over 65 (the corresponding ratio in the United States was 1:25, in France 1:12, in Japan 1:18); today the ratios in these countries range from 1:9 in Japan to 1:6.6 in Britain. By the year 2025 it is projected that all these countries will have more than 1 in 6 of their populations aged over 65 (United Nations, 1985). How has this continuing shift in the balance between young and old been viewed?

One positive aspect of population ageing that was clearly identified in the 1950s was the reduction in the child-rearing burden for women (Titmuss, 1958). Since populations age primarily owing to a reduction in fertility, a concomitant of population ageing is a reduction in average family size and a fall in the average number of years women spend caring for dependent children. However, these past benefits of ageing may not be continued in the future. As the proportionate size of the elderly population increases, and as the share of the very old (85 plus) among this elderly population also rises, so the demand for care services will increase, because the incidence of physical and mental incapacity rises with age. It is probable that women will be the major providers of this care both because of custom and because women have a greater average life expectancy than men and so elderly women are more likely to provide care for their male partners than are elderly men for their female partners.

In Chapter Three we provide some estimates of how the public cost of care for the elderly is likely to rise with anticipated demographic change. It should, of course, be remembered that most care is provided neither by the public sector nor through the market place but instead by family members. The value of informal care in Britain in 1987 has been estimated at somewhere between £15.6 and £24 billion, compared with less than £4 billion spent by the public sector (FPSC, 1989). Informal intra-familial exchanges of services (or money) do not feature in most macroeconomic assessments of well-being because only monetized transactions can be adequately measured and included in GNP estimates. A more comprehensive measure of the social product would include all the output of goods and services by non-waged workers in the household sector; this would show both that older persons *receive* more services than those measured in the public accounts, and also that they *provide* many services to other household members. Sociologists have quite rightly noted that reliance on information in the public accounts produces an unduly negative view of older people and of old age, since these data emphasize the consumption of public services rather than the contribution by older people (and especially older women) to the social product (Thane, 1989; Arber and Ginn, 1991b). Recognition of the concept of a social product does not, however, have any impact on the financing of public services. Since the social product cannot be adequately identified, it cannot be taxed, so the financial costs of public services must necessarily be an imposition on the measured and taxable part of economic activity. Greater recognition of the amount of care provided by unwaged women workers in the household may change attitudes towards eligibility for or the level of pensions and care allowances, but it cannot reduce the tax implication of these transfer payments.

Aside from this discussion of the way in which the life course and caring responsibilities of women have been altered by the fall in fertility, sociology has had relatively little to say about the *process* of population ageing, and instead has confined itself to a discussion of the condition of old age and the position of elderly people in society (Fennell et al., 1988). This work is fragmentary, so much so that a recent literature review has suggested that 'sociology almost entirely neglects later life' (Arber and Ginn, 1991a: 260), though this is perhaps overly severe. In the 1950s and 1960s sociologists considered the social position of older people within the functionalist framework dominant within sociology at that time, and they developed an interpretation best summarized (and to some extent caricatured) in terms of the 'golden age' argument. On the basis of a casual acquaintance with a limited amount of historical and anthropological evidence, the argument was advanced that at some (undefined) point in the past old people had been revered and respected; in such 'traditional' societies old age was a golden age. Because literacy was exceptional, old people were repositories of knowledge, wisdom, law and custom by virtue of their long memories. And because property was vested in the patriarch who controlled the workings of the family farm, the elderly head of a household could exercise effective economic power and sanction over younger family members.

The modernization of society – the development of towns, the establishment of wage labour and a market economy, the extension of literacy and the formalization of education – all served to undermine the economic and cultural power of elderly people. Years of acquired skill could be replaced by a few months of formal training, and the power of property ownership disappeared when urban wages rose far above the productive capacity of family farms. Modernization, it was claimed, removed from elderly people their elite status, and put them on an equal footing with all other adults in a competitive market-oriented society. Unfortunately for these older people they could not really cope with the cut and thrust of untrammelled competition. They were neither as strong nor as quick nor as well educated as the young. In recognition of their inability to function adequately in competition with the young, older people increasingly chose to 'disengage' from competitive society and willingly retreat into a social and economic backwater labelled 'retirement'(Cumming and Henry, 1961). As the pace of technical change has accelerated over the course of this century the age of functional redundancy has declined, and so retirement rates, even at ages as low as 50 or 55, have increased. This very neat functionalist theory of the decline of 'the golden age of old age' is attractive but bogus.

Historical inquiries conducted over the last two decades have shown that in pre-industrial times older family members were tolerated rather than revered, and frequently they were not even tolerated, being cast to the mercy of charitable or Poor Law support rather than cared for by their families (Laslett, 1977:174–213; Quadagno, 1982). And many studies of older people conducted since the mid-1950s have shown that older workers often enter retirement not because they voluntarily disengage from the labour force through incapacity, but because they are forced out by a mixture of inducements, regulations and threats. Some of the economic approaches to the study of retirement considered in Chapter Four implicitly accept the disengagement theory by looking only for individualistic explanations of the retirement process. In practice, however, it can be shown that retirement depends upon much more than the choice of each individual worker in a freely functioning labour market.

A second approach to the position of the elderly in modern society has emerged from a liberal collectivist strand of sociological analysis. This emphasizes the role of progressive twentieth-century welfare legislation in redistributing to older people a larger share of the national product, thereby increasing their living standards and enabling them to participate in society as fully entitled citizens rather than having to withdraw into a semi-moribund and dependent retirement. This is almost an inversion of the 'golden age' model, and suggests that elderly people have never had it so good. However, the persistence of severe hardship for many older people must call into question the general applicability of this view. Furthermore, neither this optimistic view of twentieth-century progress, nor the pessimistic 'golden age' view, contributes much to a sociological evaluation of the process of population ageing, since they both concentrate on a static assessment of the position of older people in modern industrial society.

A different sociological interpretation of ageing has been developed by a number of radical scholars which goes some way towards incorporating the process of population ageing within a dynamic model of social change. This approach also starts from an assessment of the position of older people in modern society, and argues that the social and economic dependency of older people is not the natural outcome of inevitable deterioration in their mental and physical capacities, but is instead socially constructed through a complex network of welfare policies, retirement rules, legal restrictions and cultural norms (Townsend, 1981; Walker, 1981; Phillip-son, 1982). This conception of 'structured dependency' sees modern welfare policies more as a mechanism for controlling the elderly population than as a means of increasing their social freedoms. In the dynamic context of an ageing population in the late-capitalist societies of Western Europe and North America, the structuring of dependency in old age (particularly through compulsory retirement) provides an opportunity for the capitalist system to avoid crises of over-production by reducing the size of the labour force. Population ageing, in combination with increased retirement rates, therefore becomes a safety valve for the entire economic system; the old are called upon to bear the costs of an over-abundance of labour.

Structured dependency theory, like functionalist modernization theory, is elegant but not always accurate in its description of historical evolution (Smith, 1984). It is certainly true that the rise in retirement rates for older people in developed countries has coincided with a general expansion of welfare provision, but it is less obvious that this is directly related to recurrent crises of over-production. As the data on retirement and early retirement presented in Chapter Four show, although there may be some cyclical movement in retirement rates, the secular trend of increasing retirement is apparent whether unemployment and growth rates are high or low. Furthermore, it is difficult to demonstrate that the majority of state and corporate policy decisions affecting older workers have been taken with a deliberate intention of creating a reserve army of unemployed older workers. Historical studies of employer pension schemes, for instance, indicate that employers seldom had a coherent grasp of the way the schemes would work or of their impact on the labour market (Hannah, 1986).

None of the sociological theories of ageing is immediately acceptable on empirical grounds, and none of them emphasizes the *process* of population ageing rather than the *position* of older people in society as the primary focus of study. Expecting recent trends in population dynamics to be fully incorporated into broader theories of social change is, of course, asking for a great deal; so far sociologists have been unable to make a fully convincing response.

Ageing and Social Policy

It is more realistic, perhaps, to expect the details of population ageing to be addressed in the empirically grounded field of social policy rather than in broad and theoretical sociological models. In fact, social policy analysts have been among the pioneers in analysing the implications of the ageing of the industrialized nations (for instance Townsend and Wedderburn, 1965; Shanas et al., 1968) and this is for an obvious reason. Older people constitute a major client group for a wide range of social services, and so a rise in the proportion of older people in society is likely to affect both the scale and the nature of social service provision. Some of the analysis by social policy experts directly overlaps with and complements that carried out by economists on the cost of state pension schemes, but pensions are only one of the many issues relevant to social policy. Elderly people are major consumers of health care and nursing services, of care provided in residential homes, and of assistance provided by friends, neighbours and family. People over retirement age are, of course, also major providers of care and assistance to their spouses, other family members and friends.

This demographic impetus to the demand for and supply of social services can be estimated within fairly narrow bounds (though there is continuing dispute about the relative social service costs of the young and the old), but social policy analysts have demonstrated that there are many other determinants of social service provision, two of which merit particular attention. First is the extent to which definitions of ill health and disability are conditioned by social and cultural norms as much as by objective physiological criteria. Although research findings in medical gerontology are not without contention (for a critical review see Rogers et al., 1990), many people believe that the objective health status of people at age 60 or 70 (if not at age 80 or 90) has on average improved over the course of the twentieth century. But illness and disability are in part a function of individual, medical and social expectations. The pain and restricted mobility caused by arthritis that was once considered to be a natural consequence of old age is now viewed as a treatable medical condition. Septuagenarians now expect and are expected to be active and mobile members of society in a way quite different to that expected fifty years ago. To some extent these expectations have changed because the population is ageing, with the result that most people can reasonably anticipate living beyond 70, and older people constitute a growing and therefore very important client group for medical and welfare services.

The second important social determinant of demand for social services is the nature of the kinship links of elderly people. The decline in fertility that has produced an ageing of the population has also inevitably reduced the number of children, grandchildren, cousins, nieces and nephews available to call on for assistance in old age. The high rates of childlessness that have emerged over the last two decades in many countries will exacerbate this trend towards kinship isolation. Since family members are significant providers of services to aged relatives, changes in the extent of kinship links will have a direct impact on the demand for public social services. The changing scope of expectations and the shrinking of kinship networks both demonstrate that it is inappropriate to make projections of future demand for medical and social services on the basis of population estimates alone. In the next two chapters we will see how the inclusion of data on kinship or on disability can significantly alter the inferences to be drawn from demographic projections. But as most social policy studies make clear, future costs depend also on political decisions about where to spend and where to retrench, and these decisions will themselves be affected by the politics of population ageing.

Ageing and Politics

Political science has paid very little attention to ageing as a social process or to old age as a political identifier. The established political cleavages of class and race (and more recently of gender and of sexuality) appear to leave little room for political division on the grounds of age, and in most countries political issues are not perceived to have an age dimension to them. But this may be changing. Pensioner groups are becoming more vocal in the articulation of their political demands for a better standard of living, inspired perhaps by the pioneering campaign of the Gray Panthers in the United States. Meanwhile, also in the United States, there has been a political response from the pressure group Americans for Generational Equity (AGE) which argues that the old are receiving too large a share of the nation's resources at the expense of the young (Callahan, 1987; Longman, 1987).

These arguments and counter-arguments might be dismissed as peripheral to mainstream politics but for two reasons. First, political scientists have identified a process of class and party dealignment in many of the western democracies, as long-established political orientations appear to be dissolving, to be reformed along new, often single-issue lines such as environmentalism (Dalton et al., 1984). This suggests that the absence of old-age politics in the past should not be taken as a sign that it will not emerge in the future. Second, the demographic imperative of population ageing means that the electoral weight of people aged over 50 is rising. By 2025 the over-50s will make up over half the electorate in France, Germany, the United Kingdom and Japan, and over 46 per cent of the electorate in the United States (United Nations, 1985). If age-based politics does develop in the future, then the ageing of the population will turn the upward shift in age structure into a powerful political resource which the old could exercise in their own interests and against the interests of the young. If this were to happen, then the demographic time bomb might go off not when the mechanism of population growth stops ticking, but when the electorate votes to explode it.

Interpretations of Ageing

The diversity and the partiality of approaches to ageing taken within the social sciences has made it difficult for scholars in the new subdiscipline of social gerontology to develop a comprehensive and critical view of the social science of population ageing. A pioneering attempt to pull together the threads, the *Handbook on Aging and the Social Sciences* (first published in 1976, with a third edition in 1990), illustrates both the achievements and the problems. Essays in the most recent edition are more critical, cover a broader range of issues, and survey a literature that is far more extensive in 1990 than it was fourteen years earlier. But although interdisciplinary links are beginning to be drawn, there is still a tremendous distance between the approaches taken by different social scientists. A brief look through the chapters in the 1990 edition (Binstock and George, 1990) of the *Handbook* shows almost no overlap between the literature referred to in the chapters dealing with the economics of ageing and in those dealing with sociological interpretations. Furthermore, there is little point of contact between those authors who focus on the process of population ageing and those who analyse the social and economic circumstances of elderly people, despite the obvious impact of the former on the latter.

Our aim in this book is to outline some of the connections between the economics and the sociology of ageing, and between the welfare of elderly individuals and the economic impact of population ageing on society in general. We draw on economic, social and demographic data from a broad range of developed countries, and particularly from Britain, but we have tried to limit the intrusion of jargon from demography, sociology and economics, and to write in a non-technical manner that is accessible to readers from a wide variety of social science backgrounds. Chapters Two to Six present a critical review of the demography of ageing, of the distributional and welfare consequences of ageing for older people, and of the economic consequences for the labour market, the social security system, and for macroeconomic performance. The concluding chapter discusses possible policy responses to current or projected population pressures, and stresses that the inevitability of population ageing in the developed countries does not mean that the welfare or efficiency outcomes have already been determined. How our societies adjust to these novel demographic conditions will depend to a large extent on how well we understand and manage the complex process of population ageing.

2

The Demography of Ageing

The present social and economic policy debates about ageing have their roots in the growing concern over the perceived increase in dependency on the state of large numbers of elderly persons who are expected to impose rising burdens in terms of pensions, health and other services, on a relatively diminishing working population. Before addressing such issues it is instructive to look at the changing age structure of the population and the mechanics of that change. The demography of ageing can be seen as a dichotomy encapsulating both the dynamic process of population ageing and the static demographic characteristics of the current aged population.

This chapter is therefore concerned to first examine the change in absolute number, and proportionate size and composition of the elderly population within Britain since 1900, to make comparisons with other developed societies which have also experienced population ageing, and to look at the demographic forces which have brought about this growth in the relative size of the elderly population and the ageing of this subgroup of the population; secondly, survey changes in the demographic and quasi-demographic characteristics of the elderly population, such as their marital status, household composition and geographic location, and their relationship to dependency through the 1980s and 1990s; thirdly to consider population projections, and fourthly, assess the impact of population ageing on demographically determined support ratios, both social and economic, and examine critically the policy relevance of such measures.

Population Ageing

Before going any further it is necessary to distinguish between the concepts of individual and population ageing. Individual ageing is a continuous process, and a person ages inexorably from their time of birth through to the moment of death. Populations, however, can become older or younger depending on changes in the proportion of people in different age groups. The 'age' of a population is normally measured in one of three ways: by the proportion of elderly people in the population, generally taken in Britain as those over the state

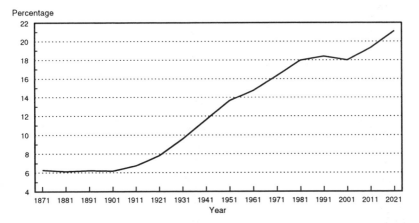

Percentage

Sources: Census Volumes 1871–1981; OPCS Population Projection 1987–2027
series PP2, no. 16
Note: women aged 60 and over, men aged 65 and over

Figure 2.1   *Proportion of the population aged 60/65 or over,
Great Britain 1871–2021*

pension ages of 60 for women and 65 for men; by the proportion of
children in the population, usually taken as those under age 16; and
by the median age of the population. By any of these measurements
Britain can now be said to have an aged population.

As we can see from Figure 2.1 the proportion of the population
who are aged 60/65 or over has increased dramatically over the last
century. In 1900 the proportion of the population of Great Britain
aged over what is now the statutory pension age (the retirement rule
was abolished in 1989's budget) was 6 per cent, and by 1991 this
share was estimated to have risen to 18 per cent (OPCS, 1991).

Figure 2.2 shows the absolute growth in the British population
and the changing age structure of that population over time. As well
as increasing in size in relative terms, the size of the elderly
population has risen in absolute terms by nearly 400 per cent this
century; from 2.2 million in 1901 to approximately 10.5 million in
1991. At the same time the proportion of children (i.e. persons aged
less than 16) in the population of Great Britain has fallen from 35
per cent to 20 per cent.

Looking at the median age as a measure of the 'age' of the
population of England and Wales confirms this ageing trend. In
1901 it was 24 years, by 1931 it had risen to 30.3 and in 1981 was
estimated to be 34.7 years. The median age is projected to increase
to 37.6 years by the end of the century and it could be as high as 40

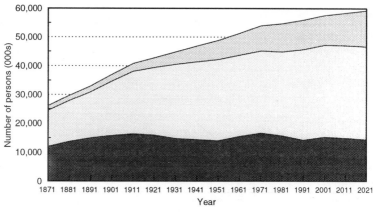

Figure 2.2 *Age structure of the population, Great Britain, 1871–2021*

by the end of the first decade of next century. This means that 50 per cent of the population would be aged 40 or more and 50 per cent aged less than 40 which is a dramatic shift in population structure in just under a century. The mean age of the population shows a similar dramatic rise; from 27.4 years in 1901, to 32.7 in 1931, and 37.3 in 1981.

Britain is not the only developed nation to have experienced such remarkable shifts in the age composition of its population. From Table 2.1 we can see that for practically all other developed nations the proportion of the population aged 65 or over has increased dramatically since the beginning of this century; in all but four of the countries examined the percentage has more than doubled and in two of the countries, New Zealand and Britain, levels are now more than three times those of 1900.

The United Nations suggests that any population with more than 7 per cent aged over 65 years is an 'aged population'. As can be seen from above all these countries exceed this level and so can be classified as 'aged nations'. How did this change in the age structure of the population come about? For an explanation we must look at the theory of population dynamics.

Population dynamics
The age structure in any one period is the result of a complex interaction between fertility, mortality and migration over time.

Table 2.1 *Trends in the relative size of the 65 and over age group in 14 advanced countries*

	Year	%	Year	%	Year	%	Year	%
Australia	1911	4.3	1933	6.5	1947	8.0	1985	10.2
Austria	1900	5.0	1927	6.8	1951	10.6	1985	14.3
Belgium	1900	6.2	1930	7.6	1947	10.7	1985	13.8
Canada	1901	5.1	1931	5.6	1951	7.8	1985	10.4
Denmark	1901	6.7	1935	7.5	1945	8.4	1985	15.1
France	1901	8.2	1931	9.4	1950	11.8	1985	13.0
Germany	1900	4.9	1933	7.4	1951	9.3	1985	14.8
Great Britain	1901	4.7	1931	7.4	1950	10.8	1985	15.1
Netherlands	1899	6.0	1930	6.2	1950	7.7	1985	12.1
New Zealand	1901	2.1	1936	6.6	1951	9.6	1985	10.2
Norway	1900	7.9	1930	8.3	1950	9.6	1985	15.7
Sweden	1900	8.4	1930	9.2	1950	10.3	1985	17.2
Switzerland	1900	5.8	1930	6.9	1950	9.6	1985	13.9
USA	1900	4.1	1930	5.4	1950	8.1	1985	11.9

Source: Scott and Johnson (1988: Table 1.3, p. 5)

Measures used frequently to reflect fertility and mortality levels are the general fertility rate, that is the annual number of births per 1000 women in the reproductive ages, and expectation of life at birth. The age structure at any time (t) is affected by the age structure of the previous period ($t - 1$) as peaks and troughs in the age distribution at a particular moment move forward in time. Thus changes in any, or all, of the vital rates in the past will influence the present age distribution. In a closed population (with no immigration/emigration) the age structure of a population is determined solely by fertility behaviour and mortality.

The fact that fertility is more important than mortality in the ageing of a population is one that is probably counter-intuitive to many readers. One might expect that the increasing number of elderly persons is due to falls in mortality levels and the consequent longer expectation of life. However, the level of fertility (along with the level of infant mortality) determines the number of persons feeding into the population pyramid at its base. This cohort moves up through the pyramid with time, the size of the cohorts thus influencing the total age structure. Unless mortality levels are very unstable, they will affect each cohort in turn in a similar fashion, shaving off the sides of the pyramid but leaving the underlying age structure relatively unchanged. Thus the most important factor determining the proportion of elderly people in the population has been not the improvement in the capacity to survive to pension age but rather the changes in the sizes of generations available to survive (Benjamin et al., 1985: 4).

That is not to say that mortality is unimportant. Improvements in mortality at older ages can contribute significantly to the ageing of the elderly population itself. The recent increase in the numbers of very old people, i.e. those aged 85 and over, has been larger than expected because of unanticipated falls in mortality among the elderly, particularly the very old (Preston, 1984). It has been estimated that about two-thirds of the increase in the mean age of the population of the United States between 1980 and 1985 can be attributed to mortality decline alone (Preston et al., 1988). It is now recognized that changes in mortality at older ages may influence both the size and the structure of the elderly population. Bourgeois-Pichat (1979) has suggested that, if fertility is at or below replacement level, mortality changes can cause population ageing from the apex rather than the base of the population pyramid.

To place these changes in context it is helpful briefly to examine the so-called demographic transition which characterizes the main developments that most western countries have experienced. There are four distinct stages of the transition:

1   An initial stage with high levels of fertility and mortality and low population growth rates. The population has a 'youthful' age profile with a high proportion of young people and relatively few older persons.
2   Mortality rates begin to fall in the second stage while fertility levels remain at a high level. Thus, the natural rate of population growth rises and so too does the size of the population. If the improvement in mortality is concentrated at younger ages the population structure may become younger at this stage.
3   Now fertility rates also begin to decline. The rate of population growth starts to tail off and the proportion of the population who are elderly begins to increase.
4   Fertility and mortality reach equilibrium. Population growth is again low, and could be approaching zero. The age structure of the population stabilizes with a relatively high proportion of elderly people.

As reductions in mortality alone are not able to bring about the ageing of the population from the base, demographic ageing thus begins only after mortality has fallen, rapid population growth has been established and the subsequent fertility decline is already under way. Therefore the 'age transition' which most developed countries have been undergoing during the last century follows the 'demographic transition', with the main engine of ageing being changes in fertility.

Table 2.2 *Expectation of life at birth for generations born 1841–1991, United Kingdom*

Year of birth	Males	Females	Year of birth	Males	Females
1841	39	42	1921	61	68
1851	40	43	1931	66	72
1861	42	45	1941	69.6	75.4
1871	44	49	1951	72.7	78.3
1881	47	52	1961	73.6	79.1
1891	48	54	1971	74.6	79.7
1901	51	58	1981	75.5	80.4
1911	56	63	1991	76.0	80.8

Source: OPCS (1991: Table 2, p. 5)

This pattern can be demonstrated using the British case. As we have seen from Figure 2.1, the percentage of elderly persons in the population, defined here as those of current pensionable age was remarkably stable from 1840 to 1900 at around 6 per cent. It began to increase rapidly from 1911, and its growth rate has only recently begun to slow, the proportion of elderly persons in the population reaching a temporary plateau at 18 per cent during the 1990s. How does this trend tie in with shifts in vital demographic rates?

The expectation of life at birth is a convenient measure of the level of mortality rates experienced by a particular birth cohort. It is a summary measure of the mortality rates prevailing in any particular year. Table 2.2 shows how mortality has fallen over the last 150 years. Mortality levels in fact began to decline in the latter part of the eighteenth century and continued to fall throughout the 1800s. As sanitation, cleaner water and better nutrition became more widespread as a result of economic growth, expectation of life increased. Over the period 1841 to 1901 an extra twelve years of life were added. People born in 1991 can now expect to live a further twenty years compared to those born in 1911. Most of this improvement is due to falls in mortality at younger ages. Average life expectation in the past was greatly reduced by the very large proportions of infants who died within a short period after birth. For example, for a male child born in 1841 his expectation of life was around 39 years, but if he survived to age 1 then his expectation was 47 years, and if he reached age 60 the expectation was 73 years. This compares with an expectation of life of about 79 years for men aged 60 now. Thus, although life expectancy at birth has increased dramatically, increases in expectation of life at older ages have been more modest.

Figure 2.3 shows the trends in birth and death rates per 1000

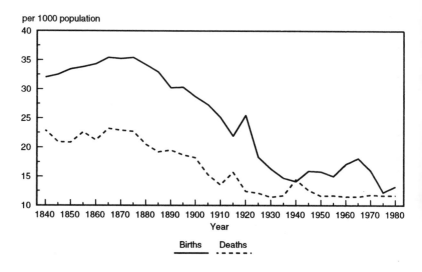

Source: Mitchell, 1988

Figure 2.3   *Crude birth and death rates, England and Wales, 1840–1980*

population. The mortality decline, as we have seen, was already under way by the 1840s and fertility rates began to decline from the late 1870s. The number of elderly people began to rise at a modest rate in the late nineteenth century, but the elderly population's growth rate did not exceed that of the population in general, leaving the proportion of the elderly in the population unchanged. It was not until 1911 that the number of persons aged over 60/65 grew at a rate exceeding that of the rest of the population; the peak birth cohorts of mid-Victorian Britain began to move into these older age groups and forty years of fertility decline reduced the numbers in the younger age groups. The rate of increase of the elderly population has fallen off in the last decade, due to the small birth cohorts of the First World War and (excepting the post-war baby boom of 1920–1) the inter-war years and the proportion of the population aged 65 and over will remain fairly static until the beginning of the next century. However, the ageing of the popula-tion is continuing with the ageing of the elderly population itself. This affects the median age of the population and also has important policy implications and so we will explore this phenomenon in a little more detail.

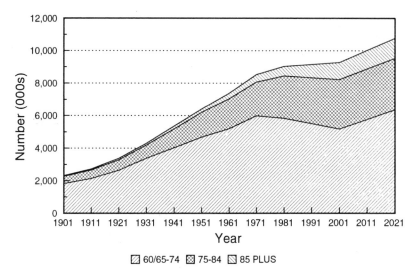

Source: Census data and population projections

Figure 2.4 *Age structure of the population of pensionable age, Great Britain, 1901–2021*

The Ageing Elderly Population

The elderly population forms a broad age group which itself is changing in composition over time. The effective age range of individuals in statutory retirement is approximately thirty-five to forty years. Because of the wide age span of the elderly population it is useful to divide them into two subgroups, with the 'young-elderly' consisting of those persons aged 60/65 to 74 and the 'old-elderly' of those aged 75 and above. This convention is now widely recognized, reflecting the importance of distinguishing the separate needs and characteristics of the young-elderly and old-elderly due to the heterogeneity of this group as a whole (Taylor and Ford, 1983; Evandrou and Victor, 1989).

As with the rest of the population the composition of the elderly group is influenced by demographic trends in the past. The current age structure of the elderly is the result of changes in the birth rate over a long period sixty to eighty years earlier; and, to a lesser extent, rises in life expectancy due to reductions in subsequent mortality rates at various ages. Figure 2.4 shows the changing age structure of the elderly population 1901–2021. From this it is apparent that Britain is currently experiencing a decrease in the number of young-elderly, a trend which will continue in the near future. Between 1981 and 1991 the number of people between ages 60/65 and 74 fell by 5 per cent. This is a consequence of both the falling number of births throughout the 1920s and 1930s, and the impact of the Second World War and the consequent casualties inflicted upon these and earlier birth cohorts. Post-war emigration, largely to the 'Old Commonwealth' countries of Canada and the Antipodes, also served to deplete the numbers in age groups now entering their 60s. The full effect of this 'age trough' is more evident in the projected age distribution of 2001. This trend is not reversed until the survivors of the post-Second World War baby-boom start to reach their 60s in the 2010s.

In contrast, up until 1905 the number of births was rising fairly steadily. Additionally, with the progressive fall in deaths due to improvements in public health and nutrition in the late nineteenth century, the number of survivors of successive cohorts reaching old age was increasing over time. Those born at the turn of the century are the survivors of the first generation to benefit from the fall in adolescent death rates in the first half of the century. The birth cohort of 1891–1901, which now accounts for the majority of the very old, that is those aged 85 and over, was the first in which over half lived to beyond age 65 (Grundy, 1991). Thus the number of those aged 75–84 and 85 plus increased throughout the 1970s and will continue to do so until the survivors of the trough in births during the First World War (partially offset by a peak in 1920) and those of the smaller birth cohorts of the 1920s and 1930s reach these ages.

Accordingly, the rate of increase of the group aged 75–84 will remain appreciable through the 1990s. At present 38.1 per cent of the elderly population are aged over 75 and 8.5 per cent are aged 85 years or more. Official population projections by the Government Actuary Department (OPCS, 1991) suggest that by the beginning of the next century (2001) these proportions will have increased to 41.4 per cent and 11.0 per cent respectively. The numbers aged 85 plus are expected to rise for the next thirty-five years (apart from a temporary decline in fifteen to twenty years time due to the trough of the First World War) to account for 13 per cent of all retired persons. The downward trend of births of the inter-war years will not lead to a downward trend in the population aged 85 and over until after 2030.

This ageing of the aged population itself has important policy implications for present and future levels of both social and especially economic dependency. The different age groups that comprise the elderly population exert differential demands on the health and social services, with the 85 plus group being the most

Table 2.3 *Ratio of females to males
in the elderly population 1881–1981,
Great Britain*

	f/m (60/65+)	f/m (85+)
1881	1.97	1.64
1901	2.05	1.74
1921	2.04	2.07
1941	2.03	2.20
1961	2.26	2.32
1981	2.02	3.26

Source: Selected Census volumes, 1881–1981

expensive per capita and over half of hospital beds now being occupied by those aged over 75. These age related differences in demand must be borne in mind, and this is a point to which we will return later in Chapter Three.

An important demographic derivative of the ageing population in Great Britain has been the increase in the proportion of females to males in the elderly population and this again has important implications for policy. Women in 1981 made up two-thirds of the population of pensionable age. This is partly because women aged 60–64 are regarded as 'elderly' whereas men are not classified as such until they are aged 65. However, this fact alone is not sufficient to explain the preponderance of women in the elderly population, as women continue to outnumber men in every elderly age group. From Table 2.3 it can be seen that in 1981 there were 3.3 women aged 85 or over for every man of the same age. Projections of the population structure (see Table 2.7 below) indicate that gender differentials among those aged over 60 are expected to decline with time, but women will continue to outnumber men especially in the older age ranges.

This progressive advantage in favour of women is primarily due to the (increasingly) lower mortality rates of women at middle-to-late ages compared with men. The fall in overall mortality has been accompanied by differential changes in sex-specific mortality rates. Between 1951 and 1981 the life expectancy of a man aged 65 increased by only 1.4 years from 11.7 years to 13.1 years; whereas for a woman of the same age the increase was nearly three years, from 14.3 years to 17.1 years (Grundy, 1991). The reasons for this differential decline are not yet fully understood. However post-war advances in medicine have been comparatively unsuccessful in combating some of the illnesses that are major causes of death for men over 45 – heart attacks, lung cancer, strokes, and other circulatory diseases. These factors are also major causes of death for women in the older age ranges, but they do not become as important until later in the age curve. Thus they differentially affect the sexes within the same age cohort, and contribute to the increasing ratio of women to men. The female/male discrepancy in life expectancy is expected to continue, although an increase in smoking by women in the past few decades may modify this somewhat in the course of time. Mortality levels at middle ages for women are currently deteriorating due to increasing death rates from lung cancer and ischaemic heart diseases, both of which are smoking related illnesses. The extent to which this trend will continue is as yet unknown.

Historical factors have also had an enduring impact on the sex ratio of certain cohorts as they aged. This is most markedly the case for the birth cohorts 1895–1905 that now make up the majority of the 'very-old', now aged 85 plus. The number of males in these cohorts was dramatically reduced by the heavy rates of mortality experienced among young males during the First World War. Their ranks were further depleted by post-First World War emigration which again predominantly consisted of young single men. The effect of these factors is clearly reflected in Table 2.3 with the female/male ratio for the entire group 60/65 plus peaking at about 2.3 in 1961 and that for the age group 85 plus rising to nearly 3.3 in 1981. However, considering the exceptional circumstances to which those cohorts born around the turn of the century have been exposed during the course of their lives, the rise in the ratio for the 60/65 plus group over time was lower than that which may have been expected. The excess of females over males is not a new phenomenon nor one thrown up by the unprecedented excess male mortality of war. Throughout this century there have been consistently more females than males and this trend looks set to continue in the next century.

The high sex ratios, differential mortality and the exceptional circumstances that the present elderly population has experienced are all interrelated and all have implications for the marital status and household composition of elderly people. Figure 2.5 shows that in 1985 there was a marked difference between the marital status composition of men and women aged over 65: 74 per cent of all elderly males were still married compared to 37 per cent for females, while conversely only 17 per cent of men were widowed compared to 50 per cent of women (OPCS, 1987). Of those elderly persons aged 85 and over some 42 per cent of men were still married but for women of the same age the proportion was only 9 per cent. Looking within the elderly as a group, in 1981 widows outnumbered married women by age 72, while widowers did not outnumber

74%

10%

37%

3%

3%

6%

17%

50%

Men

Women

[::] Married [ ] Single [ ] Widowed [■] Divorced/Separated

Source: 1985 General Household Survey

Figure 2.5   *Marital status of the population aged 65 and over
by gender, 1985*

married men until age 85 (Wall, 1984). This tendency for women to outlive their partners is due to the greater life expectancy of women, and is exacerbated by the tendency for women to marry men older than themselves.

Differential gender changes in mortality over time are reflected in the trends in marital status of the sexes since 1901 as shown by Figure 2.6. As mortality has declined the proportion of the elderly population currently married has increased while the proportion widowed has fallen. This change in composition has been more marked for males than females but at all stages a higher proportion of elderly men are currently married than women.

Perhaps of more interest is the proportion of the elderly population that has remained never-married. For men this proportion has remained steady at around 3 per cent throughout this century. For elderly women the proportion never-married has always been higher than that for men and has varied over time, reaching a peak in 1951 of 16.3 per cent. This peak reflects the sex ratio of available spouses, and the depletion of cohorts of young men in the early part of the century. The proportion of elderly women never-married had fallen to 10 per cent in 1985. This, however, masks differentials between age groups, with those women aged 75 and over being less likely to have ever been married than the younger elderly.

The large number of elderly women never-married or widowed (i.e. of single status) has been the cause of increased concern over the living arrangements of the elderly in recent years. As we shall

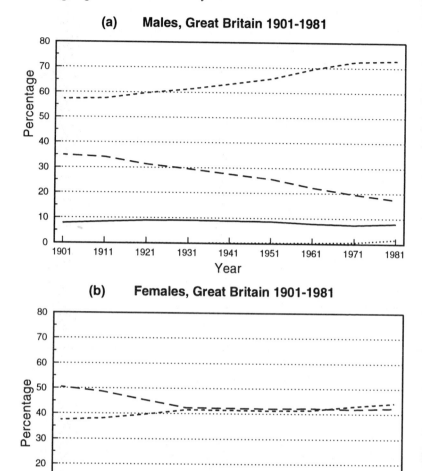

Figure 2.6   *Marital status of persons of pensionable age, Great Britain, 1901–81: (a) males; (b) females*

see below, in the last few decades there has been an increase in the proportion of the elderly living alone. Alarm over the cost of providing resources for the care of a growing number of elderly persons has prompted a re-evaluation of the role of the state in that provision. There has been a call for a 'return' to individual responsibility, self-help and a withdrawal of the collectivity. As Thomson notes 'the experiences of the Victorian era . . . have been cited on many occasions in support of a drive to make individuals more responsible for the welfare of themselves and their relatives' (Thomson, 1986a: 355). Indeed the White Paper *Caring for People* (DoH, 1989) was the latest in a series of government policy documents stressing the primary importance of informal care for the elderly and the personal ties of kinship. Chapter Three will further examine the scope for the elderly paying for care. Below, we examine the appropriateness of calls for a re-emphasis on the family by looking at the changing household composition of the elderly population.

Changing Household Composition and Spatial Distribution

Co-resident kin have been identified as an important source of assistance to elderly relatives in present times (Evandrou et al., 1985, 1986). Consideration of co-residence in the past as a means of support, and the extent to which household composition patterns have changed over time, may suggest the limits to which such a source of support may be relied upon in the future. When examining changes in the household composition of the elderly and its relationship to levels of dependency it is necessary to distinguish between those living in private households and those in public or private institutions.

Institutional Housing Sector
Over the past century the majority of older people have remained in the private sector, largely independent of publicly funded housing support. The institutional population has remained at a consistently low level throughout the last hundred years. In 1901 about 6 per cent of all elderly persons were resident in institutions, and this figure fell to around 3 per cent in 1981 – the majority now residing in communal homes. The proportion of the elderly population living in institutions has varied with age, the old-elderly finding independence harder to sustain due to increasing physical incapacity. In 1901 5.5 per cent of men aged 65–74 and 8.3 per cent of those over age 75 were resident in some form of institution, including poor law workhouses, hospitals and psychiatric institutions; by 1971 these proportions had fallen to 2.3 per cent and 7 per cent respectively. For women aged 65–74 in 1901 3.5 per cent were institutionalized compared with 2.3 per cent in 1971; on the other hand among women aged over 75 the percentage was 5.5 per cent in 1901 rising

to 10.2 per cent in 1971 (Thomson, 1983: 49). The unusually high number of never-married women in this cohort, as discussed earlier, may help to explain this relatively high value in 1971. If this is the case then it is probably a temporary phenomenon and rates of institutionalization for women will fall to comparable levels with men in the future. In 1981 19 per cent of those aged 85 and over lived in residential accommodation while only 1 per cent of those under 75 lived outside private households (OPCS, 1984). This age differential in residential accommodation may be of increasing importance in the next two decades as the ageing of the elderly population continues.

One point that emerges from these figures is that, contrary to popular belief, many of the elderly population remain independent and families are not neglecting their elderly members, increasingly consigning them to institutions. In the face of this widespread myth of increasing familial neglect it is perhaps the non-use, rather than the use, of institutional care for the elderly that is more worthy of remark. To examine the effect of household composition on dependency we must look at change within the private sector rather than any change between the sectors.

Non-institutional Sector
The following tables (2.4 and 2.5) give an indication of the long run co-residential experience of elderly persons. They demonstrate the extent to which elderly people have lived with others and in households headed by others. That is, they give an indication of the availability of proximate assistance, and of the independence of the elderly population. Headship rates, for instance, provide a measure 'of the extent to which the elderly retain the various responsibilities usually associated with the running of a distinct residential and consumption unit' (Wall, 1989: 125), or alternatively the extent to which the elderly do not have these responsibilities.

Table 2.4 shows increasing headship rates among the elderly over the last thirty years, following a period of relative stability. Wall's analyses of a sample from the 1891–1921 Censuses show a remarkable similarity in headship rates across four decades. Those rates are also very similar to those calculated for a collection of communities in 'pre-industrial' England by Laslett (Wall et. al, 1988; Laslett, 1977).

The proportion of elderly persons living alone has grown significantly over time. Table 2.5 shows that the higher rates of 'solitariness' experienced by women has been a consistent feature of all studies of household composition. However, again the onset of rapid change did not occur until post-Second World War. The levels

Table 2.4 *Proportion of elderly men and women reported as head of household, 1599–1985 (percentages)*

	Males	Females	All
1599–1796*	88	39	62
	(262)	(300)	(562)
1891	84	39	60
	(784)	(918)	(1702)
1901	84	37	58
	(753)	(925)	(1678)
1911	83	36	58
	(899)	(1065)	(1964)
1921	84	40	60
	(1130)	(1361)	(2491)
1951*	84	37	57
	(3.2m)	(4.5m)	(7.7m)
1980*	95	48	68
	(2635)	(3615)	(6250)
1985	96	56	72
	(1683)	(2473)	(4156)

* refers to those over 60 years of age
Sources: Falkingham and Gordon (1990: Table 12.2, p. 155) and 1985 General Household Survey datafiles

Table 2.5 *Proportion of elderly men and women reported as living alone, 1684–1985 (percentages)*

	Males	Females	All
1684–1769	6	14	10
1891	10	16	13
1901	7	13	10
1911	8	9	9
1921	10	18	14
1951	8	16	13
1962*	11	30	22
1980*	14	38	28
1985	20	47	36

* refers to those over 60 years of age
   N.B. Cell counts as in Table 2.4
Sources: Falkingham and Gordon (1990: Table 12.4, p. 157) and 1985 General Household Survey datafiles

reported in the 1951 Census seem more akin to those for some nineteenth-century communities than those for the last two decades. However, the number of elderly persons living alone appears to have increased dramatically over the last four decades, rising to 36.4 per cent in 1985.

Conversely the decline in the proportion of households with relatives (a proxy for the proportion of intergenerational households) between 1851 and 1951 from 20.2 per cent to 15.0 per cent is relatively modest; compared with the fall to 12.8 per cent one decade later, followed by an even sharper decline to 7.7 per cent in 1971 (Wall, 1982). Some of this decline in the proportion of households containing relatives may be spurious due to the overall increase in the number of households over time, but in absolute terms the frequency of the extended household has halved and the fall appears to be real rather than a statistical artefact.

Various demographic reasons can be proposed to explain these post-war changes in older persons' living arrangements. Changes in fertility, marriage and mortality rates have given rise to changes in the life cycle of individuals and these changes may in turn have contributed to the decline of intergenerational households and the rise of one person households. A falling age of marriage and lowered average age at which the last child is born, combined with closer spacing of surviving children as a result of lower infant mortality rates, have all led to a shortening of the duration of the nuclear family. With increasing life expectancy this has led to a lengthening of the 'empty–nest' phase of the life cycle, where the couple lives alone (Grundy, 1991: 142–4). Although there is now an increased likelihood of the existence during a person's old age of a member of the subsequent generation, data does not show that adult children are living with their parents in old age. Thus the temporal expansion of the family of direct descent is followed by fission into a larger number of more scattered households, and there has been a fall in the number of intergenerational households.

The reasons for the increase in the number of elderly single person households are not so clear. Traditionally this increase has been attributed to an increase in the number of persons never-married, especially among women, due to the special circumstances surrounding the cohorts born in the late 1800s and early 1900s. The casualties of the First World War, coupled with male dominated emigration led to a shortage of 'eligible men' in these cohorts. This accounts for the present high proportion of never-married women among the very-old; in 1981 15 per cent of women aged 85 plus were never-married as were 13 per cent of those aged 75–84.

Furthermore, elderly women are, at present, found to be characterized by a high rate of childlessness. A survey by Abrams (1978) found that a third of those women aged over 75 had no children, a fact which may contribute to the tendency for elderly (widowed) women to live alone. However, looking at the trend over time from Figure 2.6 it can be seen that the proportion of elderly women never-married has decreased in recent decades rather than increased as has the proportion of women who are widowed. Therefore, childlessness and single status alone are not adequate explanations for the change in household composition and the increase in the number of one person households among the elderly. In fact the increase in the propensity to marry and bear children after 1940, together with declining mortality at all ages, means that the proportion of older women that are married and that have surviving children is likely to increase until the second decade of the next century (Timaeus, 1986). The increase in the incidence of divorce and separation (equally) is not sufficient to offset the reduction in the proportion of the population that is widowed, or remains unmarried, nor to account for the rise in one-person households.

The rise may reflect the ageing of the elderly population itself, with an increasing proportion widowed in the older age groups. Wall (1984) has shown that household headship rates for widow/ers increased substantially between 1961 and 1981. Of the third of elderly people currently living alone 80 per cent of them are women, reflecting the sex differentials in mortality discussed above, and 44 per cent are men and women over age 75 reflecting the steep age gradient in mortality.

More important in the change in household composition may be *supply* factors influencing the establishment of separate households. The change in housing stock over the last two decades, with an increase in the overall number of dwellings, may have increased the opportunity to exercise choice over living arrangements. Between 1961 and 1981 the housing stock in Great Britain rose by 25 per cent from 16.2 million to 20.3 million separate dwelling units. The increase in the number of one-person households accounted for a large proportion of these additional housing units (*New Society*, 1986).

Various other explanations for the trend to separate living have been suggested. Ermisch (1984) points to rising real income among the elderly facilitating the establishment and maintenance of separate households, with housing seen as a choice element, demand depending on the income of the choosers. Warnes (1982) suggests that cultural and social changes have widened the differences between generations and as a result have decreased their mutual understanding and ability to cohabit. Both these explanations are plausible but they lack substantive supporting evidence. The rates of intergenerational social and occupational mobility may have increased such that children perceive living with their parents as a hindrance to their own social/occupational advancement but this case is not easy to demonstrate. The 'real income' hypothesis is also difficult to substantiate because of the problems involved in determining what threshold levels are necessary for the maintenance of a separate household, and what the mechanisms are whereby increased real income leads to particular housing choices.

Thus it remains unclear whether more of the elderly are living alone through choice, that choice facilitated by increased real income over time and a rise in the available housing stock, or because children are now more individualist and less willing to share their homes with the elderly. It seems likely, however, that older people *choose* to maintain independent households where possible. Thompson and West (1984), in their survey of residential preferences among the elderly, found moving in with relatives nearly as unpopular as entering an institution.

Whatever the reasons, the changing structure of household composition within the elderly population has important implications for the present and future levels of social expenditure and the 'financing burden' of an ageing population. Policy-makers have been concerned about the trend towards one-person households, especially in regard to care for the elderly. In 1985 over half of all elderly aged over 80 lived alone. Evandrou (1987) shows that the bulk of domiciliary services is directed at the lone elderly and so this trend would imply increasing levels of expenditure; given of course that the level of service provision grows in line with this and not that existing services are just spread more thinly. However, this is not to say that it is only elderly persons living alone who are dependent or require state support. Equally residential isolation does not necessarily imply increasing social isolation or familial neglect. The majority of personal care services required by the elderly continue to be provided by their relatives whether they are or are not members of the same household (Evandrou et al., 1986). Nevertheless, it is important that, within a climate of increasing emphasis on support from co-residential kin, policy-makers take into account that many elderly – particularly the very elderly – simply do not have, nor have they had co-residents; and over time they have had them less often. Residence in a younger relative's household was a rare phenomenon in the past, though marginally more frequent than at present (Falkingham and Gordon, 1990). Almost universally elderly persons have headed their own household or they have been married to the person who did.

Spatial Distribution of the Elderly Population
The geographical residential patterns of the elderly, in terms of the changing social and spatial distances which may separate an aged

person from relatives or friends, are related to their ability to maintain independent living arrangements, and therefore are a potentially important influence on their degree of economic dependence on society. Furthermore, the changing spatial patterns and the resultant skewed distribution of the elderly have created distinctive local age structures which have an impact on local old age dependency ratios, and has an important bearing on the range of support services provided by a particular local authority: 'The practical consequences of growing old age dependency are magnified by the population's rising expectations, the elderly's increasingly independent living arrangements, and their increasingly uneven geographical distribution' (Warnes, 1982: 18). Any survey of the elderly population, particularly for local policy or planning purposes, therefore has to take into account the fact that the elderly are not evenly distributed across the country.

In 1981 the elderly population of Britain was disproportionately concentrated in coastal areas, with ten south coast districts having over 30 per cent of their population over statutory retirement age compared with the national average of 18 per cent while the 'new town' areas of rapid planned growth, such as Milton Keynes, experienced a concentration of half the national average (see Table 2.6). This configuration contrasts with the spatial age distribution of the population in the 1920s where the elderly were present in disproportionate numbers in a central rural belt stretching across England from Norfolk in the east to Cornwall and Central Wales in the west (OPCS, 1984).

The majority of this change in the distribution of the elderly over time is due to increased retirement migration to specific areas. Although elderly people form a small proportion of the total cross local authority migration stream in any given period, their migration patterns are of influence as a relatively large number of migrants are attracted to a relatively small number of destinations. Prior to the 1930s, migration of older people was not the major force in bringing about large proportional gains in the elderly population. Of more importance were the migration flows of the rest of the population, in particular from areas experiencing population decline with the out-migration of the younger generation of working ages. This helps to account for the relatively high proportion of elderly persons in rural areas early this century. However, during the 1930s and 1940s substantial growth of retirement zones in coastal areas occurred, particularly those areas close to London and the major conurbations. Spatially the general pattern of migration has been one of movement from cities and conurbations to coastal towns and resorts. The largest flows have been to the nearest coastal areas, for

Table 2.6   *Local authorities with the highest
and lowest fractions of their population
aged over pensionable age*

	% population of pensionable age
Rother, E. Sussex	35.3
Worthing, E. Sussex	34.9
Eastbourne, E. Sussex	33.5
Christchurch, Dorset	32.3
Arun, W. Sussex	32.0
Hove, E. Sussex	31.0
East Devon	30.7
West Somerset	30.2
Tendring, Essex	30.2
Bournemouth, Dorset	30.1
Surrey Heath, Surrey	11.2
Stevenage, Herts	11.2
Hart, Hants	11.2
Bracknell, Bucks	11.0
Chiltern, Bucks	10.8
E. Kilbride	10.7
Redditch	10.6
Harlow, Essex	10.0
Tamworth, Staffs	9.8
Cumbernauld	9.2

Source: Warnes and Law (1984: Table 3)

example from London to the south coast and East Anglia, from Liverpool and Manchester to the Lancashire coast and Wales, and from the Midlands to Wales and the South West Region.

The retirement centres of the South East began to develop first. As early as 1921 some counties, notably Sussex and the Isle of Wight, were already marked as areas of retirement concentrations, with Bexhill, Bognor Regis and Worthing as the focal destination points. This was followed in the 1950s by expansion in the coastal areas of Wales and the North West Region. East Anglia and the South West Region are the most recent growth areas.

The development of areas attractive to retired people in the first half of the century was closely linked to the location of second homes and places of 'known recreational potential' (Allon-Smith, 1982). Initial retirement migration was fairly small and largely confined to the upper classes and the wealthier sections of the population, but over time flows have increased in magnitude and there is evidence that the practice is moving down the social scale with migration movements including more lower-middle class and working class elderly people especially since the 1960s. Allon-Smith

(1982) has suggested that changes in retirement practices with compulsory retirement at ages 60/65, coupled with increased wealth due to improved pension schemes and more extensive property ownership, have contributed to both greater geographical and social mobility among the elderly. This trend of migration at older ages to traditional holiday areas is not confined to Britain. The post-war period has seen the creation of distinctive retirement enclaves in Florida and Arizona in the United States, along the Gold coast in Australia and the Mediterranean coast in France and other European countries (Vergoossen and Warnes, 1989).

It must be noted that despite regional imbalances in the proportion of the population of pensionable age the majority of elderly persons do not migrate but age 'in situ'. Only around 10 per cent of the total population move in any one year, and over half of these moves involve relocating within 4 kilometres of origin. It is the heavily area-specific destination of those that do migrate that gives rise to the uneven national distribution of elderly persons, with important consequences for planners in those areas. Migration flows have slackened in the last decade. Areas that are old established retirement areas are now faced with the prospect that not only do they have above average proportions of elderly people but they are also likely to have within the elderly population an above average proportion of the very elderly. One extreme example is Worthing which has four times the national average proportion of the very-old (85 plus) (OPCS, 1984) with all the problems inherent with such an aged age structure. This has important implications for local old-age dependency rates and policy planning. In retirement areas there is, at present, a chronic shortage of facilities, particularly within the NHS for 'non-vital' age related operations such as hip replacements. This can give rise to further increases in demand for other state funded services such as personal social services due to increased incapacity.

The future spatial distribution of the elderly depends on future migration patterns which are even more difficult to predict than fertility or mortality trends. However, it is unlikely that past rates of retirement migration will be sustained, especially with the present fall in the numbers reaching retirement age. Should future generations choose to remain and age in situ the regional and local pictures may be very different in the next century when the 'young' population of Milton Keynes becomes 'old'! Before going on to assess how these demographic changes have been dealt with by policy-makers, it is important to look in more detail at future projections of the composition of Britain's population.

Population Projections

Since the population structure in the near future will consist very largely of people already born it is possible to make population projections up to the year 2001 with a fair degree of accuracy. To project beyond that point however it is necessary to make a number of assumptions regarding fertility rates, longevity, and migration. Fertility rates are influenced by a complex interaction of social factors such as attitudes towards marriage, contraception, the desirability of having children and trends in what is thought to be the ideal family size. Given the high degree of uncertainty in predicting how these factors will change over time it is extremely difficult to forecast future trends in fertility. Migration rates are also difficult to predict. For most of the last 200 years Britain has experienced a net loss of population from migration. The early 1960s saw an excess of immigrants over emigrants, but this immigration has been stemmed by the introduction of new legislation, limiting the categories of legal immigrants. The late 1960s again saw a net outflow of population and over the last twenty years the overall trend has been erratic, making future predictions uncertain. Mortality, in contrast, has displayed a more stable relationship over time in the absence of 'shocks' such as wars or epidemics. Its future pattern is largely dependent on advances in medical knowledge, particularly in areas such as the treatment or prevention of malignant neoplasms and heart disease. It is prudent to bear all these 'influencing' factors in mind when drawing policy inferences from population projections.

Table 2.7 shows the projected changes in the composition of the UK population aged 60 or more up to 2031, using the Government Actuary's principal projection based on 1989 (OPCS, 1991). These projections take into account general improvements in mortality rates, but some speculative adjustments have been made for future increases in the number of deaths occurring from AIDS. As it is not clear to what extent deaths from this source will continue to rise, the current projections may over estimate future mortality declines. Additionally, and perhaps more pertinent when using population projections for our purposes, the migration assumptions employed here explicitly take no account of any future migration that may occur in response to the changing age structure of the population. The Government Actuary recognizes that a steady growth in the number of persons of pensionable age, combined with a constant number of persons in the working age groups, could result in immigration to meet the increased demand for labour. However, the short-term assumption of zero net migration is not varied, with

Table 2.7   *Selected statistics for the UK population aged 60 or above, 1991–2031 (middle series projections; numbers in thousands)*

	1991	2001	2011	2021	2031
Population 60 plus	11907	12064	13471	14762	16555
Percentage of total population	20.7	20.4	22.4	24.3	27.1
Ages (number)					
60–64	2876	2838	3706	3732	3939
65–69	2760	2531	2944	3107	3866
70–74	2268	2280	2291	3014	3061
75–79	1850	1926	1821	2152	2287
80–84	1261	1319	1372	1406	1864
85–89	631	776	862	842	1014
90 plus	261	394	475	509	524
Ages (%)					
60–64	24.2	23.5	27.5	25.3	23.8
65–69	23.2	21.0	21.9	21.0	23.4
70–74	19.0	18.9	17.0	20.4	18.5
75–79	15.5	16.0	13.5	14.6	13.8
80–84	10.6	10.9	10.2	9.5	11.3
85–89	5.3	6.4	6.3	5.7	6.1
90 plus	2.2	3.3	3.5	3.4	3.2
Sex ratios					
60–64	107.5	104.6	105.4	104.7	102.9
65–69	116.0	109.7	107.0	109.2	108.0
70–74	131.4	121.4	116.3	116.7	115.3
75–79	156.9	141.1	130.2	127.0	127.3
80–84	199.8	177.1	157.8	148.8	150.4
85–89	269.0	240.4	203.5	182.5	176.3
90 plus	392.5	342.7	276.9	230.5	210.1
Total	137.7	131.3	124.2	121.5	120.3

Source: National Population Projections 1989 based Series PP2 no. 17, OPCS (1991)

the Government Actuary stating 'it is not considered that the proposed longer-term assumption of a balance of inward and outward migration needs to be modified on account of these expected demographic changes' (OPCS, 1991: 8). Rather the official view is to prefer a scenario of greater productivity among the indigenous workforce than an addition to that workforce by immigration. If indeed the latter scenario is correct then the following estimates regarding the proportion of the population who are retired may be over estimates. Nevertheless, despite the provisos surrounding population projections, it is useful to look into the twenty-first century.

From Table 2.7 it can be seen that the proportion of the UK population aged 60 or over will remain stable up to the beginning of the next century, and then will increase dramatically to comprise over a quarter of the total population by 2031. By this time, nearly 10 per cent of those aged over 60 will be aged 85 or more, and over a third will be above age 75. This translates into 1.5 million persons aged over 85 and 5.7 million over age 75 compared to 0.9 million and 4 million respectively in 1991. Interestingly the sex ratio of all age groups within the elderly population falls over time. Women continue to outnumber men, but to a much smaller extent than has been the case this century.

These demographic trends discussed have given rise over the last decade to fears of a demographic time bomb, with an increasing proportion of the population dependent on a diminishing working population. In 1991 the proportion of the UK population aged 16–59/64 was 61 per cent, but by 2031 the same group will only constitute 56 per cent of the total. The ratio of pensioners to workers will thus increase by nearly 50 per cent, from 0.33 pensioners per worker in 1991 to 0.48 in 2031. Below we look at how policy-makers and others have used such ratios in the past and assess critically to what extent they are useful measures for estimating the 'burden of dependency' upon the working population.

Population Ageing and Policy – Demographic Determinism?

Negative attitudes to population ageing by politicians and policy-makers are fairly recent. There was some recognition of the problem of population ageing prior to the Second World War. However, it was the effect of falling fertility and the decline in the rate of population growth, rather than the effect of the changing age structure, which dominated the debate. In the 1940s attention was drawn to the dangers of an ageing population with the publication of the report of the Royal Commission on Population (1949). This increasing concern coincided with development and expansion of public pensions and the social security system and is perhaps not unconnected.

The ageing of the population has again emerged to the forefront of the political arena, not least because of the perceived increased dependency on the state of large numbers of elderly people. This growing dependency is seen as imposing a rising welfare burden, both in terms of increased pension entitlements, and in the higher demand for health and other social services, on a relatively diminishing working population; and so has generated concern over future levels of social expenditure. A central theme of the social security reforms in the mid-1980s was the government's assessment of the levels of expenditure on pensions which would be necessary to maintain an ageing population (DHSS, 1985a, 1985b). Given the problems in estimating future changes in the costs of welfare benefits, much of the debate has centred around demographically determined changes in economic dependency ratios. Ratios of national insurance contributors to pensioners were presented to support the argument that the cost of the State Earnings Related Pension Scheme (SERPS) would be prohibitive, and in the event the SERPS scheme was substantially modified by the Social Security Act of 1986 (see Chapter Five). However, if we look at the factors affecting changes in welfare expenditure in the past, we can see that *economic* trends as well as *demographic* trends have been of importance in determining dependency ratios. An increase in the average age of the population alone need not necessarily engender any economic problems.

Re-examining Dependency Ratios
Historically, both economists and demographers have used the dependency ratio of a population to measure the 'burden' on the economy. The dependency ratio is a measure of how many 'dependent' people there are in an economy per non-dependent person, i.e. worker. It is calculated as the number in the non-economically active population divided by the size of the economically active population. At the most simplistic level, and indeed the most widely used level, the dependency ratio can be calculated as those aged 0–19 (or 0–15) and 60/65 plus divided by the population aged 20–59/ 64. In this instance age alone defines whether or not a person is to be treated as dependent.

Given this definition, an increase in the gerontic (old age) dependency ratio, which is calculated as the number of people of pensionable age (comprising the 'non-economically active' population) divided by the population aged 20–59/64 (comprising the economically active population), is a simple demographic consequence of population ageing. As the relative number of aged persons in the population increases so too must the gerontic ratio.

From Figure 2.7 it can be seen that the gerontic ratio has increased steadily throughout this century, reflecting the continuous ageing of the British population over this period. Looking at successive Censuses, the old age dependency ratio has increased from 12 old persons per 100 in the working age ranges in 1901 to 34

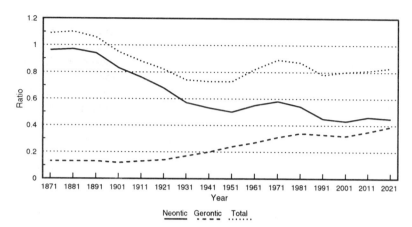

Sources: Census Volumes 1871–1981; OPCS Population Projection 1987–2027
series PP2, no. 16

Note: women aged 60 and over, men aged 65 and over

Figure 2.7   *Dependency ratios, Great Britain, 1871–2021*

in 1981 and this figure is projected to rise yet higher to reach 39 by
2021. It is these figures, among others, that have given rise to the
current pessimism surrounding the ageing of the population.

However, demographic factors taken in isolation do *not* determine the ratio of workers and non-workers. Given the change in the
structure of the labour market and shifts in labour force participation rates that have taken place over the past two or three decades it
is necessary to rethink age based dependency ratios. With changing
trends in the employment of women and the rise of the spectre of
unemployment the validity of distinguishing between 'worker' and
'dependent' on the grounds of gender and age are increasingly
questionable. Furthermore, as Chapter Four discusses in more
detail, there is nothing sacrosanct about the age 60 or 65 to make it
the dividing line between the productive and unproductive phases of
the life cycle.

Dependency levels have been generally under-estimated when
calculated solely on an age basis. If economic activity, including
unemployment, is taken into account, although some people previously defined as dependent on age criteria, such as people over
age 65 still in employment, now fall into the non-dependent
category, this is far outweighed by transfers in the reverse direction
(Falkingham, 1987). Is it appropriate then to attribute rising
dependency ratios to the phenomenon of the ageing population,
and to treat ageing as an 'economic bad' which increases depend-

ency independently of other economic forces? The changing level of labour force participation of different groups of the population and the rate of unemployment also affect dependency over time. Falkingham (1987, 1989) redefined dependency ratios using economic activity status rather than age to define dependency and attempted to quantify the importance of labour market changes versus age structural effects on dependency levels over the time period 1951–81.

To disaggregate the trend over time of the 'employment participation weighted' dependency ratio into that part due to change in age structure of the population, and that due to changes in the labour market, it is necessary to standardize the ratio in order to net out the other effects in turn. The dependency ratio can be written as

$$Dep = \frac{Px - Px.Ex}{Px.Ex}$$

where Px is the size of the population in age group, x, and Ex is the real economic activity rate (taking into account sickness and unemployment) of the population age group x. By keeping either of the component parts constant over time it is possible to see the effect on the ratio of the change in the component allowed to vary.

It was found that changes in the labour market were more important in influencing dependency than demographic trends. This finding in itself was not surprising in view of the changes in aggregate economic activity, particularly increases in female labour force participation and rising unemployment, that occurred over the period. However, it serves to remind us of the importance of economic movements, and the sensitivity of the dependency ratio to them, which some official forecasts have ignored. Simple dependency ratios, taking no account of the complex shifting patterns of labour force participation tell us almost nothing about economic dependency. Furthermore, dependency ratios in the future may not be comparable with those of today as technological advances continue to decrease the number of workers needed to produce goods and services.

But how meaningful is even a refined dependency ratio? If the dependency ratio is constructed with the aim of examining the problem of financing state transfer payments then worker versus non-worker ceases to be the measure we are interested in. It has been argued that the numerator should include only those who are eligible beneficiaries of government schemes (Creedy and Disney, 1988). Furthermore, the denominator often includes all workers, whether part-time or full-time. This is particularly important for women where 28 per cent of women aged 16–59 were working part-time in 1988 (OPCS, 1990). Thus it may be preferable to produce a measure of 'full-time equivalent' persons.

However, non-participation in paid employment need not imply social dependency or inactivity, even though it may involve economic transfers from the working population. Many elderly persons are active in the informal labour market and in voluntary work as well as making important contributions within the family and the wider community and this needs to be taken into account. Future estimates of dependency are complicated by the fact that increasing formal labour market participation, particularly by women, may be accompanied by a fall in the 'home production' of child care and care of elderly relatives, making the net gains in the overall social product ambiguous.

Much work takes the gerontic ratio as given and views levels of pensioner dependency in isolation from the rest of the economy. However, it is only a fraction of dependency. Even if we briefly return to simple-age based measures, Figure 2.7 demonstrates that the rise in the number of elderly persons has been accompanied by a fall in the number of young non-workers. If both 'dependent' age groups are combined the overall dependency ratio has been remarkably stable throughout this century.

But this treats all 'dependent' persons equally. For a more realistic prediction of the future public costs of an ageing population it is necessary to weight the total 'dependent' population by their public expenditure requirements. The composition of that population has changed over time, with a shift to higher numbers of elderly persons and a reduction in the number of children. Studies of social welfare expenditure in the United States have shown that the per capita cost of government programmes for elderly persons is considerably greater than that of per capita costs for children, and thus the overall level of dependency is increasing. According to UK Government Expenditure Plans (HM Treasury, 1989a), per capita health and personal social service expenditure for those aged 75 and over was £1,570 in 1986/7 compared with £615 for those aged 65–74 and £360 for the population as a whole. Changes in composition *within* the elderly population and an increase in the number of very-old will thus exacerbate this upward trend. Furthermore, there is also the added dimension that expenditure on children is often seen as an investment in future human capital while expenditure on the aged is not.

Many commentators have concentrated on the division between elderly persons and children (Thomson, 1986b; Johnson and Falkingham, 1988) but if we are to weight the social costs of a dependent school child as different from those of a pensioner so too must we include those of an unemployed person. This further complicates the picture and makes accurate predictions all the more unlikely. Changes in the age structure may affect the rate of unemployment. With skill and labour shortages already being predicted for the future unemployment may decline, reducing this area of social expenditure and offsetting (to some unknown extent) rises in expenditure on the elderly population.

Thus the alarmist views on population ageing may prove unfounded, and the true picture certainly more complex. As Blaikie and Macnicol (1989) pointed out the 1954 Phillips Committee accurately predicted that Britain would have 9.5 million pensioners by 1979, but the declaration that drastic measures, including raising the age of retirement, would be essential proved unnecessary. Experts have exaggerated the problem before and in future we should be wary of simplistic demographic determinism.

One final point to bear in mind when talking of the problems inherent in population ageing in developed countries is that the first world is not alone in undergoing a fundamental restructuring of its population age structure. In countries where economic development and concomitant falls in mortality and fertility have been recent and rapid, the shift to an older population structure is occurring at an accelerated pace. In France, it took 115 years to move from a position of having 7 per cent of the population aged over 65 to having 14 per cent. The same change took 75 years in the USA and 85 years in Sweden. In comparison it is predicted that Japan will take only 26 years to undergo the same restructuring, and

Table 2.8 *Number of persons aged 60 or over (millions)*

	1950	1975	2000	2025
China	42.5	73.3	134.5	284.1
India	31.9	29.7	65.6	146.2
USSR	16.2	33.9	54.3	71.3
USA	18.5	31.6	40.1	67.3
Japan	6.4	13.0	26.4	33.1
Brazil	2.1	6.2	13.9	31.8
Indonesia	3.8	6.8	14.9	31.2
Pakistan	3.3	3.6	6.9	18.1
Mexico	1.3	3.1	6.6	17.5
Bangladesh	2.6	3.3	6.5	16.8
Nigeria	1.3	2.6	6.3	16.0

Source: Table from plenary session 'Ageing and Developing Countries: A New Challenge' Alex Kalache, British Society of Gerontology Conference 20–22 September 1991

in China, with her one-child policy, the transition period is expected to be even shorter (Thane 1989: 59–60). Table 2.8 shows the change in the numbers of the population aged 60 and over for those countries that will have more than 16 million persons aged over 60 in the year 2025. In the 75 years 1950–2025 many developing countries will undergo radical shifts in the composition of their population. By 2025 nearly 300 million persons aged over 60 will be living in China, a seven-fold increase. For Brazil the corresponding increase will be a staggering sixteen-fold at a time when the population as a whole is predicted to have only quadrupled in size. By placing the British experience into a global framework, worries about the increasing numbers of elderly people in Welwyn Garden City or Worthing may yet seem parochial.

3

Income, Wealth and Health in Later Life

The financial costs of an ageing population referred to in the previous chapter can be seen as having two main dimensions: the costs involved in providing income support in terms of pensions and other benefits to the elderly population; and the cost of social support and health care provision. This chapter will examine both these issues. Rather than focusing purely on the societal level in terms of the aggregate amount of resources necessary to maintain an ageing population, it will employ a more disaggregated approach using the individual as the level of analysis in order to assess the current, and future, demand for such state funded support within the elderly population.

Running parallel to the debate concerning the rising burden imposed on a diminishing working population by a growing retired population with increasing pension demands is the contention that the elderly now have 'never had it so good'. The 1985 Green Paper on Social Security Reform which first proposed the abolition of SERPS as a result of fears of its rising cost due to the ageing of the population (see Chapter Two) also concluded that 'many pensioners are now as well off as workers with families' (DHSS, 1985a: 11). Such claims challenged the conventional wisdom of later life being synonymous with low income and deprivation and led the then Minister of State for Social Services to remark at the 1989 Help the Aged Sheltered Housing Conference: 'It is simply no longer true that being a pensioner tends to mean being badly off. . . . For most it is a time to look forward to with confidence. The modern pensioner has a great deal to contribute and a great deal to be envied' (Moore, 1989: 3). These pronouncements reflect a new image of later life which stresses the affluence of those over retirement age. People, it is argued, are retiring with higher incomes, larger occupational pensions and more than ever before are likely to own assets in the form of their own home. The growth in services aimed specifically at older people such as package holidays, financial services and private sheltered housing developments are taken as indicative of the greater purchasing power and, therefore, affluence of older people.

In the United States evidence of growing affluence among the elderly population has fuelled debate over the issue of whether the welfare state has become over-generous to the retired population at the expense of families with children (Johnson and Falkingham, 1988) (see also Chapter Five). Although official UK government publications have hinted at such phenomena, for example: 'By the 1950s and 1960s pensioners were the major cause for concern [regarding poverty]. Now the position has changed and in 1985 it is families with children who face the most difficult problems' (DHSS 1985a: 2, para 1.12), overt intergenerational conflicts have not emerged in Britain. However, a clear policy insinuation of the new perspective upon the financial circumstances of pensioners is that government spending on the old can be restricted, as an increasing proportion are now so affluent that they no longer need to be reliant upon state support. This is an attractive policy option as retirement pensions are the largest single item in the social security budget at a cost of £21,000 million in 1989–90 (HM Treasury, 1990).

The perceived existence of affluence among the retired population has been used as justification for recent discussions about means-testing for certain benefits and services directed at the elderly population. The increase in the average level of material comfort was cited as a reason for not automatically exempting pensioners from liability to pay the new National Health Service (NHS) charges for eye tests and dental checks (Martin, 1990). In the course of defending government proposals to remove housing benefit from anyone with £6,000 worth or more of assets (later revised to £8,000), Edwina Currie, then junior minister at the Department of Health and Social Security (DHSS) declared in April 1988 that we are in the 'era of the Woopie' ('well off older person'). Proposals for social services included in the White Paper *Caring for People* (DoH, 1989) suggested that clients will be expected to meet the 'economic cost' of services, if they can afford to do so. The ideology of the Woopie thus gives credence to the idea of targeting of pensions and other benefits to the elderly population, and the increasing privatization of care. 'Ability to pay' has already become the catch-phrase of the 1990s.

However, many commentators have appeared unconvinced that the income position of the elderly has in fact improved in recent years. In the same month that John Moore expressed optimism concerning pensioners' financial well-being, Norman Willis, General Secretary of the Trades Union Congress (TUC) felt able to make the comment that 'the majority of pensioners were acutely aware that the current state pension was not enough to allow a person to live even a frugal life' (TUC, 1989: 10).

Are the elderly population as a whole better off, or is it that certain sectors of that population are more prosperous while the majority of the elderly still live in, or on the margins of, poverty? Is there a growing group of Woopies, increasingly able to live without dependence on the State, or are they just more visible; a product of the flurry of activity within the marketing and advertising world? If such a group are to be used to justify policy changes it will be important to know about the characteristics of such affluent pensioners and whether it is prudent to expect the number of this group to increase over time. It will be equally important to know how many persons remain in poverty, dependent on the state for income support. This chapter will explore these issues, looking both at the absolute and relative income position of the elderly population as a whole, and the distribution of income within that subpopulation, as well as examining the health and disability status of the elderly and the distribution of marketed and non-marketed services along with the ability to pay for those services.

A 'Golden Age for Oldies'?

The last decade has seen a shift in the traditional view of old age as a time of impoverishment and need. It is possible to identify a series of official UK government publications which have laid emphasis upon the affluence rather than the poverty of older age groups. This view was first expressed in 1984 when it was asserted in a background paper to the 1985 Social Security reforms that 'During [the last thirty years] we have seen a major improvement in the position of pensioners' (DHSS, 1984). Subsequent statements in other 'Reform of Social Security' Green Papers confirmed this view: 'about half of all pensioners are now owner-occupiers and have a self-sufficiency and independence denied to their predecessors' (DHSS, 1985a: 11, para. 4.3); and 'a great deal has been achieved in raising pensioners' living standards over the past forty years' (DHSS, 1985b: 3, para. 1.26). And in October 1989 the then Secretary of State for Social Services declared: 'By 1986, pensioners' net average incomes from all sources had grown by 23 per cent more that prices since 1979 – twice as fast as the income of the population as a whole.'

This position was substantiated by Guy Fiegehen in his essay on 'Income after Retirement' in the 1986 edition of the government statistical service flagship publication *Social Trends* (CSO, 1986). In it he demonstrated that pensioners' share of total personal disposable income had risen from 7 per cent in 1951 to 15 per cent in 1984/ 5; while the retired population had increased from 13.5 per cent to 18 per cent of the total population over the same period. This improvement was due, he argued, to a rise in the real value of the state pension; with a single person's pension increasing from about a fifth of average net male manual earnings in 1951 to around a third in 1981/2, and a married couple's pension rising from 30 per cent to 50 per cent of net male manual earnings in the same time span. Thus, as well as an *absolute* increase in value, there has also been a *relative* improvement in the position of the elderly, with pensioners' disposable income per head standing at about 70 per cent of non-pensioners in 1985/6 compared to about 40 per cent in 1951.

These claims were reiterated by other government officials. Members of the Economic Advisers' office at the DHSS, writing in the following year, stated that 'the average incomes of single and married pensioners grew by more than a third in real terms between 1970 and 1985' (Dawson and Evans, 1987: 243).

Sanguine statements as to the real value of pensioners' income are not confined to government commentators. Recent work by academics has tended to confirm this view. Barr and Coulter (1990), found that real spending on social security for the elderly rose from £13.7 billion in 1973/4 to £23.1 billion in 1987/8. Although the number of recipients increased from 7.7 million to 9.9 million, at the same time the real value of pensions increased. This rise was due to two factors. First, the level of the basic pension increased from £35.90 (1987 prices) in July 1974 to £39.50 in July 1987; and secondly SERPS became payable during this time period. As a result they estimate that average benefit in 1987 prices, including both the state retirement pension and supplementary pensions, per recipient rose from £32.00 per week in 1973/4 to £44.80 per week in 1987/8. Although it is clear from Barr and Coulter's work that the real level of state benefits directed towards pensioners have risen over time, many commentators have been at pains to stress that this rise in income has occurred from a very low base (e.g. Walker, 1988: 54). Highlighting this is the claim that in 1987 an estimated 2,330,000 pensioners still lived on the margins of poverty, defined as below 50 per cent average income (Oppenheim, 1990).

Furthermore, optimistic statements regarding the *relative*, as opposed to the absolute, position of the elderly are not necessarily supported by other official statistics. Mark Abrams, in an essay also published in *Social Trends* (CSO, 1984), concluded that 'between 1959 and 1981 the real expenditure per capita in the average household where the head was aged 65 or over rose substantially – by at least 40 per cent, but even so, it almost certainly failed to match the gains enjoyed by the rest of the population'. The discrepancy between the conclusions of Fiegehen (1986) and Abrams is all the more surprising given that Abrams's calculations were based upon 'special pensioner households' which derive at least 75 per cent of their income from state benefits and which therefore should have benefited most from the rise in the value of the national insurance pension which Fiegehen stressed as so important to the overall trend. A more detailed criticism of Fiegehen's optimistic view has been provided by David Thomson (1987) who concluded that Britain in the 1950s appeared to offer its dependent elderly a higher standard of living, relative to that of the rest of the population, than it did by the 1980s.

In previous work we examined the reasons for the divergent views of what has happened to pensioners' incomes over the last three decades (Johnson and Falkingham, 1988). There we pointed to the unit of analysis chosen by different commentators. Fiegehen, along with Dawson and Evans, takes individuals as the basis of his analysis while Abrams and Thomson work at the level of the household. Because of divergent demographic and economic developments between pensioner and other households since the 1950s, a household analysis presents a much more pessimistic picture for the elderly population (Johnson and Falkingham, 1988: 139). The rise in female participation in the labour market, from 35 per cent in 1951 to 49 per cent in 1986, has resulted in an increase in two-earner (and hence richer) non-pensioner households. At the same time, average non-pensioner household size has fallen from 3.57 to 2.67 persons, which has further increased the per capita resources of people in non-pensioner households. In contrast, there has been a decline in employment for persons aged over 65, with a consequent reduction in earned income. The average size of pensioner households has also fallen, but whereas a decline in household size has been beneficial for the living standards of people in non-pensioner households this is not the case for pensioner households. The bulk of pensioner income is derived from the state (see Table 3.2 below) and is therefore *directly* determined by the number of people over pensionable age in the household, while the bulk of non-pensioner household income comes from employment, and wage levels are unrelated to household size.

The above discussion suggests that income data alone are unable to provide an unequivocal answer to the question of whether pensioners have experienced an economic improvement relative to other sectors of the population. The choice of individual or household analysis profoundly affects the calculations and other economic and demographic developments further complicate the picture. However, other sources of information are subject to the same qualifications. Statistics regarding the composition of supplementary benefit recipients are often cited as supporting evidence for

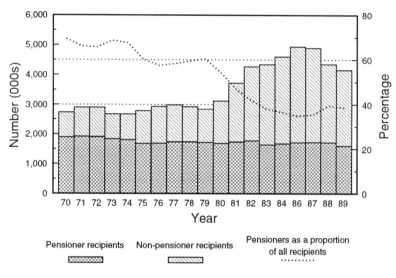

Figure 3.1 *Supplementary benefit (and income support) recipients, 1970–89*

the view that the economic status of the elderly population has improved relative to the rest of the population. Figure 3.1 shows pensioner households as a proportion of supplementary benefit claimants over the last two decades. Note that income support replaced supplementary benefit from 11 April 1988.

In 1970 almost two-thirds (64 per cent) of those claiming supplementary benefit were pensioners compared with just under two-fifths (39 per cent) in 1989. At first sight it appears that this is strong evidence that the elderly population has improved its relative income position within society. However, if one looks at the absolute size, rather than the proportion, the number of pensioner claimants has been remarkably stable, the higher number in 1970 being due to those older pensioners who had insufficient contributions for entitlement to a full national insurance pension. The absolute number of elderly persons in receipt of supplementary benefit fell during the 1980s, from 1,739,000 in 1979 to 1,607,000 in 1989, which may indicate a small but positive change in overall economic circumstances. However, the fall is not a startling one. The decline in pensioners as a proportion of all claimants is not due to increasing affluence among the elderly, but rather to the increase in the number of non-elderly low income families, particularly those of the long-term unemployed, who after twelve months are no longer eligible for unemployment benefit. Once again we must be

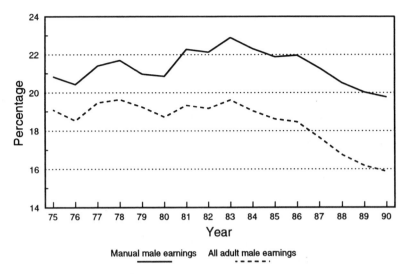

Figure 3.2   *Standard rate of pension as a proportion of average male weekly earnings, 1975–90*

aware of other economic changes when drawing conclusions from the data.

An alternative approach is to look at the relative value of the standard rate of pension as a proportion of average male weekly earnings. This approach has been criticized by Thomson (1986b, 1987) as too aggregated an approach, not representing a realistic proxy for income levels for the majority of pensioners. Most retired people have extra income from sources other than state benefits, and of those that do not the majority receive payments additional to, or instead of, the basic pension. Notwithstanding these criticisms, many studies have compared the level of state pension with average wage rates to illustrate the relative position of the retired vis-à-vis the 'average earner'. It can be argued that the relative value of the basic pension is a crude estimate of the replacement rate for pensioners, demonstrating to what extent the pension acts to replace wage income.

Figure 3.2 uses data from the *Social Security Statistics* (DSS 1988, 1990a), the *New Earnings Survey* (DE, 1990) and the DSS *Abstract of Statistics* (DSS, 1990b). It shows that the relative value of the pension kept pace with average gross male earnings throughout the 1970s and in fact pensioners improved their position in comparison with manual workers, receiving an amount equivalent to almost 23 per cent of weekly manual earnings compared with only 21 per cent

Table 3.1   *Ratio of public pensions to average wages in manufacturing*

	1969	1975	1980
Canada	24	33	34
France	41	60	66
West Germany	55	51	49
Italy	62	61	69
Japan	26	37	54
UK	27	31	31
USA	30	38	44

Source: derived from Aldrich (1982)

in 1975. However, the relative position of the standard pension vis-á-vis gross earnings has been constantly eroded throughout the 1980s. This is due to the indexing of pensions uprating to prices during this latter period rather than to whichever was the highest – the rate of growth in prices or wages. The rationale for linking pensions to earnings was succinctly put by Hockerts – 'workers should participate in economic growth not only during their working life (by way of wages) but in retirement (by way of pensions) as well' (1981: 239). This link has been broken in the United Kingdom with the effect that the relative value of the basic pension compared to earnings has fallen and will continue to do so.

Table 3.1 shows how the relative size of the state pension in Britain fares in relation to other advanced economies. Out of the seven OECD (Organization for Economic Cooperation and Development) countries listed, the United Kingdom had the fifth highest replacement ratio in 1969. By 1980, however, the United Kingdom recorded the lowest level of pensions relative to average earnings. Although the UK replacement rate had actually risen by 3 percentage points, the relative position of pensions in all other countries had improved at a much faster rate. This was especially the case in Japan. West Germany was the only country to experience a fall in the replacement level over time. Germany has traditionally had high levels of public pensions under the state insurance scheme originating from Bismarck's welfare legislation. There, public policy concerns over the long-term costs of such high pensions prompted reductions in benefits and provided for a temporary suspension of indexation in 1979–81 (Bosanquet et al., 1990). It appears that in the international league table the United Kingdom's treatment of older people has been less generous than elsewhere.

From the various data presented above, it appears that any statement regarding improvement in the relative income position of the retired population should be viewed with circumspection. An

alternative method by which to establish the trend in the relative
position of the elderly population may be to examine the share of
government expenditure directed towards the elderly in comparison
with other groups within the population. This approach may also
shed light on intergenerational questions such as whether the
elderly population is improving its relative position at the expense
of the young.

In Johnson and Falkingham (1988) we examined the value of the
retirement pension, supplementary benefit and child benefit over
the period 1948 to 1987. The real value of the state pension
increased, but it was far from clear that this increase was at the
expense of benefits specifically targeted at families with children.
Child benefit and supplementary benefit to families also rose in real
terms over the period, and at very similar rates. We also endeav-
oured to calculate differential rates for expenditure on health and
personal social services by age group. Again it was found that there
had been no obvious shift from the mid-1970s to mid-1980s in the
relative generosity of expenditure on these services between age
groups. There is no evidence to show that welfare trade-offs
between client groups work in this simplistic manner.

Our previous analysis was limited to cash benefits only. Government funded welfare transfers also include numerous benefits in
kind. Among the largest of these in social expenditure terms are
benefits from education, health, personal social services and housing. Figure 3.3 shows the distribution of the value of selected
benefits in kind by age group. The monetary value of these benefits
was derived by applying cost data to utilization rates obtained from
analysis of the 1987 General Household Survey (GHS) (see Evandrou et al., 1992, for fuller details of calculations). Unfortunately
the 1987 GHS contains no information on use of personal social
services. Unsuprisingly, benefits in kind from state funded education are received primarily, but not exclusively, by the younger
members of the population. Benefits in kind from housing are fairly
evenly distributed across all age ranges although the older subgroups of the population do tend to receive slightly higher subsidies.
Receipt of health care benefits is greater among the older population and women in middle age. If benefits from personal social
services had also been included this would have served to increase
the value of benefits received by the elderly population as a
disproportionate share of these services is consumed by that client
group. Taken together it is clear that the distribution of benefits in
kind is U-shaped with age, with people receiving higher levels of
benefit at the beginning and end of their life cycles.

This picture is only of one point in time and provides no evidence

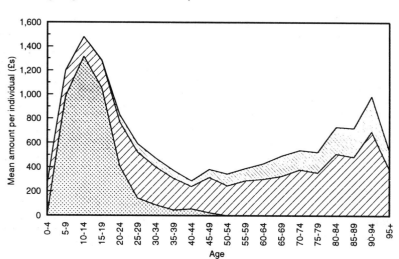

Source: 1987 General Household Survey

Figure 3.3   *Benefits in kind to five-year age groups, 1987*

as to whether the shape or amplitude of the curve has changed over time. However, from examining other data on service expenditure it is possible to hazard the conclusion that if changes in the distribution of benefits in kind by age have occurred over time, those changes are towards the young rather than to the old. Education spending per capita on nursery education rose by 81 per cent in real terms over the period 1973/4 to 1988/9. Per capita spending on primary and secondary education also rose by 36 per cent and 24 per cent respectively over the same period (Glennerster and Low, 1990: 82). However, health service expenditure on geriatric inpatient and outpatient care increased by 17 per cent from 1976/7 to 1986/7. This was over a time period where the client group had grown in size by over 6 per cent, so increases in per capita expenditure would be lower still (Le Grand et al., 1990: 113).

It is clear from the foregoing discussion, that although it may be true that the absolute position of the elderly as a group has improved over time, it is not possible to conclude that the elderly as a whole have become a relatively more affluent group. Nor would it be fair to say that the elderly population has been benefiting at the expense of other, younger, members of society. There is no evidence in Britain of a transfer of public resources away from children towards the elderly population, either cash benefits or benefits in kind. Thus, any discussion of intergenerational conflict for welfare resources establishes a false dichotomy as economic inequality *within* age groups is greater than that *between* age groups. As much recent work has pointed out it is a fallacy to treat the elderly population as a homogeneous group and there is considerable inequality among pensioners. To make any forecasts as to whether it would be rational to expect the demands of the retired population to reduce over time as that section of society becomes less dependent on state support, and to predict the magnitude of any such reduction it is necessary to look within the elderly population itself. We begin by looking at the components of pensioners' incomes and how this composition has changed over time. We then look at the shape of the current income distribution, and go on to examine the contribution of different sources of income across the pensioners' household income distribution.

Income Distribution and Sources of Income in Later Life

There are four main sources of income available to persons in later life: income from the state, occupational pensions, earnings, and income from savings and investment. Furthermore, as will be discussed below, it is becoming increasingly possible to generate additional income from releasing home equity.

Table 3.2 shows the contribution of these different sources to pensioners' gross total incomes in the United Kingdom and how the composition of total income has changed over time, while Table 3.3 gives the same information for selected OECD countries. The most notable trend across all countries is the decline in the relative importance of income from employment, reflecting decreasing labour force participation among older workers (see also Chapter Four). In the United Kingdom and Japan the reduction in employ-

Table 3.2 *Sources of pensioners' gross incomes, Great Britain (percentages)*

	1951	1961	1974	1979	1986
All social security benefits	42	48	55	61	59
Occupational pensions	15	16	15	16	20
Savings and investments	15	15	13	11	14
Employment	27	22	17	12	7

Source: derived from Table A.3, p. 15, CSO (1986) and written answer col. 222 *Hansard* 17 May 1989

Table 3.3   *Sources of pensioner households' gross incomes, Canada, Japan, USA (percentages)*
a) Canada

	1965	1971	1975	1982
State pension schemes	28	33	37	37
Private pensions	8	11	11	11
Savings and investments	14	18	17	25
Employment	44	35	30	21
Other	6	3	5	6

b) Japan

	1975	1979	1981	1984
All social security benefits	26	41	45	54
Property income	10	11	8	9
Employment	56	44	44	35
Other	8	4	3	3

c) USA*

	1962	1967	1976	1980	1984
Social security and public assistance	37	38	42	41	39
Private pensions (inc. govt. employees)	9	12	13	14	13
Savings and investments	16	15	18	22	28
Employment	29	29	23	19	16
Other	9	6	4	4	4

* Individuals not households
Source: derived from Tables 3, 5 and 7 pp. 837–9 Holtzmann (1989)

ment income has been almost completely offset by increased income from social security benefits, whereas in Canada and the United States transfer income has increased but the share of asset income has risen even more.

In the United Kingdom, the share of occupational pensions and asset income remained relatively constant from 1951 to 1979. However during the last decade occupational pensions have increased their share of pensioners' total gross income from 16 per cent in 1979 to 18 per cent in 1983 to 20 per cent in 1986. This is not surprising given the increase in coverage of occupational pension schemes that has occurred since the Second World War. In 1953, 6.2 million employees were in occupational pension schemes. By 1963 membership had risen to 11.1 million, and coverage peaked in numerical terms at 12.2 million in 1967 (see Table 4.4). Payment of occupational pensions has lagged behind membership rates. In 1953 only 0.9 million pensions were in payment. This figure rose to 2.9

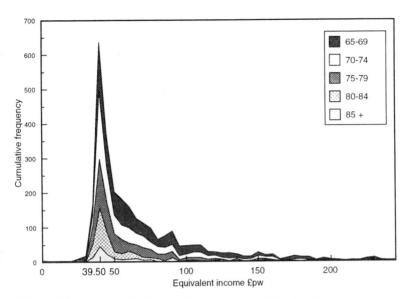

Figure 3.4 *Income distribution for persons aged 65 plus, 1987*

million by 1971, and reached 3.7 million in 1979. Throughout the 1980s the number of persons in receipt of occupational pensions had grown rapidly as schemes became more mature and the large birth cohorts of the early 1920s retired. In 1987 the number of pensions in payment from occupational pension schemes is estimated to have been about 6 million. Of these, 3.3 million pensions were paid to former male employees compared to 1.4 million paid to female employees. An additional 1.3 million pensions were paid to surviving dependents of ex-employees, primarily widows (Government Actuary, 1991). Despite this increase in the coverage and receipt of occupational pensions, state benefits have consolidated their influence as the dominant source of pensioners' incomes. The heavy reliance of pensioners upon state benefit for their income illustrates that the level at which these benefits are paid remains crucial to the living standard of the majority of older people.

Figure 3.4 shows the shape, and age structure, of the pensioner income distribution in 1987 (from analysis of the GHS) while Figure 3.5 presents the cumulative income distribution of the pensioner population compared with that of the total population. The income data used is that from the 1987 General Household Survey. Family income has been adjusted using an equivalent income scale to take into account different family sizes and compositions. The equivalence scale used was that of the Royal Commission on the Distribu-

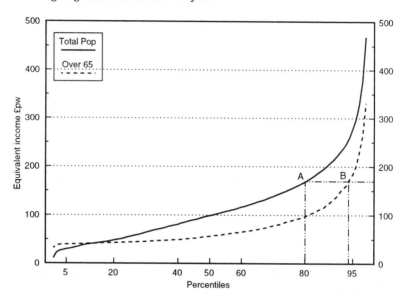

Figure 3.5   *Cumulative income distributions, 1987*

tion of Income and Wealth (1978). Each individual is taken to have
a living standard measured by the equivalent income of the family
they belong to, with the reference category being a single person
family. The results are therefore at the individual level and are
presented in terms of numbers of persons rather than families or
households. Thus, the distributions illustrated are those of equivalent family income of the individual.

It is clear from Figure 3.4 that the distribution of income among
persons aged 65 and over is highly skewed, with the peak being
around the level of the basic pension (£39.50 in April 1987). Over a
third of all persons in this age group have a weekly equivalent
income of around this level. Figure 3.5 shows that, except at the
very bottom of the income distribution, those aged 65 and over
experience a relatively lower level of income than the population in
general. For example, the top quintile of the income distribution
have an income of £168 or more per week, denoted by point A.
However, the top quintile of the population over 65 have incomes of
over £97 per week. Only those in the top 6 per cent of the elderly
population in 1987 were located in the top 20 per cent of the total
population (point B).

Within the elderly population, the majority of those having
incomes above the median (£56.30) were aged under 75. As can be
seen in Figure 3.4 the outer ends of the tail of the distribution are

Table 3.4 *Pensioners' incomes by source, 1987 (£ per week)*

	Quintile group				
	Bottom	2nd	3rd	4th	Top
All social security benefits	42.80	55.10	62.60	71.10	64.50
Occupational pensions	1.66	4.30	10.40	21.70	78.40
Savings and investment	2.70	3.80	6.10	13.10	78.60
Employment	0.20	0.50	1.40	3.90	33.30
Total gross income	47.50	62.30	80.50	109.80	254.80
Social security as a percentage of total gross income	90	87	78	65	25

Source: Written answer col. 307–10 *Hansard* 25 July 1990

almost exclusively aged under 75, while almost no individuals aged over 85 had incomes in excess of £80 per week. Thus to speak of the elderly population as a homogeneous group with regard to income, as with other characteristics, is quite clearly fallacious. The reasons for these differentials lie in the contribution that incomes from different sources make to total income across the distribution.

Table 3.4 highlights the heterogeneity of financial circumstances among pensioner households. The most notable differences are in the contribution social security benefits and occupational pensions make to total gross income. For the bottom 60 per cent of the pensioner income distribution social security payments comprise well over three-quarters of their income, whereas for the top 20 per cent state benefits contribute only one-quarter. This is despite the fact that the absolute amount of benefit received by the more affluent group is higher than that received by the lowest 60 per cent. Generally the amount of state benefit received varies little across income quintiles.

In contrast, receipt of income from occupational pensions increases as one travels up the income distribution, and the weekly amount received rises sharply for those situated in the top quintile to comprise around a third of their total gross income. Incomes from savings and investments follow the same pattern, as does income from employment. This is in part due to the fact that the proportion of households in receipt of income from occupational pensions varies across quintile groups, with only 23 per cent of the bottom quintile receiving an income from this source, compared to 53 per cent of households located in the middle quintile and 81 per cent of those in the top. However, among households in *receipt*

Table 3.5 *Selected characteristics of the Woopies and all persons aged over 65*

Percent	Woopies	All 65 plus
Male	53	41
Under 75	76	60
Married	68	51
More than two adults in the household	4	8
Non-manual social class	90	41
Owner-occupiers	90	48
Own outright	79	44
Employed	14	4
Occupational pension	60	38
Asset income	92	55
Good health	62	40
Central heating	87	64
Car	83	38
Video	16	7
Dishwasher	17	2

Source: Authors' calculations from 1985 General Household Survey datafile

there remain marked differences in the amount of income received. In 1987, those households in the top quintile group received on average 13.6 times more (£96.80 in 1989 prices) than those in the bottom (£7.10) and over twice as much as the average across all groups (£44.80) (*Hansard*, 1990). Thus previous labour market experience, and the ability to accrue occupational pension contributions as well as the accumulation of savings and investment assets, appear to be the key determinants of a higher income stream in later life.

If any group are to be in a position to be independent from state support it would be those located at the very top of income distribution of the elderly population. Falkingham and Victor (1991) carried out an analysis of this group using data from the 1985 GHS, and some selected results are shown below. Well off older persons (Woopies) were defined as those elderly persons whose incomes placed them in the top quintile of the total individual equivalent income distribution of Great Britain. From Table 3.5 it can be seen that 'Woopies' are characterized by high rates of home ownership (in particular outright ownership), higher than average access to consumer durables, and high levels of car and video ownership. In terms of sociodemographic features they are disproportionately male, aged under 75, and come from non-manual occupation groups. They are also more likely to be married and live in one or two person households. Only 4 per cent of Woopies resided in a household with more than one other adult. They are more likely than on average to be in good health and also are much more likely to live in a household with central heating.

Although a substantially higher proportion of those defined as Woopies were in paid employment in the week before being interviewed than on average for the elderly population, the vast majority, 86 per cent, were not. Therefore, for the majority, current employment income was not a contributory factor in their higher income. However, 92 per cent of Woopies were in receipt of asset income, that is income from a bank account, building society or from dividends. Furthermore, 60 per cent were in receipt of an occupational pension compared with only 38 per cent of the over 65 population in general. This confirms the earlier finding of the role played by occupational pensions in determining income in later life.

This bivariate approach does not allow for interactions between these characteristics, but rather provides an indication of what factors may be of importance. Constellations of social and economic variables may interact to influence the relative chances of an older person experiencing poverty or becoming a Woopie. Falkingham and Victor (1991) therefore also carried out a probit analysis to calculate the probability of being defined as a 'Woopie' given various characteristics. Their analysis included an indicator of past occupation, that is social class as defined by the Registrar General, as well as receipt of an occupational pension, investment income and owner occupation. The analysis showed that the 'Woopies' are likely to be younger, male, have been employed in non-manual jobs and have access to non-state sources of income. These characteristics are the reverse of the well known risk factors associated with poverty in later life.

To conclude this section, it is clear that differentials in later life with regard to income are strongly correlated with factors acquired during working life. Payments of premiums for private pensions are clearly related to the income and employment history of the individual. Unemployment, part-time work and early retirement may well preclude the building up of non-state pension contributions for certain groups, especially women. Thus, it is likely that the continued emphasis on private rather than public provision will result in increasing inequality in income within the older age groups. Although the growth of occupational pensions may lead to the emergence of a highly visible minority of wealthy elderly, this group should not be unduly focused upon, obscuring the reality of later life as experienced by the poorer majority of pensioners. It is likely that as we go into the next century, the 'two nations in old age' first identified by Titmuss in the 1950s – those in receipt of an occupational pension and those without – will continue to endure.

From the evidence presented above, few elderly outside of the group we have characterized as Woopies have incomes of sufficient size to be able to survive without state benefits or to make a significant contribution to the cost of any substantial form of care. Below we go on to examine elderly persons' wealth, and the ability, if any, to generate income from that wealth. The main form of wealth among the elderly population, as indeed among the population as a whole, is home ownership.

Housing Tenure and Housing Equity as Income

Housing tenure has attracted considerable attention in recent years. Murphy and Sullivan (1983, 1985) have proposed that it acts as a discriminatory variable and is an alternative, and more powerful, indicator of the socioeconomic status of individuals and households than traditional measures like occupation. Housing tenure, and the corresponding availability of various amenities, is of importance as a measure of the 'quality of life' of older people. It has also recently assumed significance in that certain types of housing are seen as a form of equity that can be released to provide an additional source of income in later life. There are a growing number of equity release schemes where an elderly owner-occupier can obtain a capital sum or income stream by either using the property as security for a repayable loan or by exchanging all or a part of the equity. Thus, elderly owner-occupiers can be seen as possessing an asset which can be used to purchase goods and services.

One option for releasing equity has always existed, that is 'trading down'. By selling a more expensive house and replacing it with a cheaper one home owners can unlock some of the equity, causing capital 'leakage' from the housing market. Aside from 'trading down', and excluding loans involving the repayment of capital as well as interest, there are three main ways in which elderly owner-occupiers can raise money from their house and not have to move. These include maturity loans, home income plans and home reversion plans. The mechanics of these schemes do not concern us here but rather which, and to what extent, elderly people will be in a position to exploit such equity release schemes. For a discussion of the operation of these schemes see Gibbs (1991: 386–8).

We begin by examining the housing tenure distribution among the elderly population. Home ownership has been increasingly seen as the preferred tenure type. In 1971, 22 per cent of households owned outright and a further 27 per cent owned with a mortgage. By 1988 these figure had risen to 24 per cent and 40 per cent respectively (OPCS, 1990). Comparing 'elderly only' households with 'all' households shows that elderly people are less likely than others to be owner-occupiers and more likely to live in local authority accommodation or in privately rented unfurnished rooms. From the 1988 GHS, 64 per cent of all households were owner-occupied and 30 per cent were rented from local authorities or housing associations while the percentages for 'elderly only' households were 52 per cent and 39 per cent respectively. The most striking feature in tenure distribution is that elderly people are twice as likely to live in privately rented unfurnished accommodation than the general population with 11 per cent of the population aged over 75 and 6 per cent of those aged 65–74 in this sector. This is largely a cohort effect, and as the older elderly move out of this sector, through death or entry into an institution, it is anticipated that this anomaly will disappear over time.

However, although fewer elderly people are owner-occupiers than the population in general, a significant majority are home owners and of those that own their own homes, the vast majority own them outright. In 1988, only 5 per cent of all 65–74 year olds and 3 per cent of those aged 75 and over had a mortgage, compared with 49 per cent and 47 per cent respectively, who were outright owners.

What is the relationship of tenure with income? Is it the case that the rich 'own' and the poor 'rent'? Murie (1983), using data from the 1975 GHS found a significantly larger fraction of poorer households located in the local authority sector than in the owner-occupier. Evandrou and Victor have used the 1980 GHS to investigate the links between income, resources, social class and tenure. They stressed the relationship between labour market histories and subsequent incomes in old age and conclude 'those who had been employed in professional occupations had higher incomes, and were therefore less likely to experience poverty, than those from manual groups' (Victor and Evandrou, 1987: 265). They also found that there was a strong correlation between occupational class and tenure, 'home ownership was the preserve of the professional classes and renting the province of those from manual backgrounds' (Evandrou and Victor, 1989: 118). Thus prior analyses suggest that there is a relationship between income and wealth in the form of home ownership.

Figure 3.6 shows the tenure distribution for persons aged 65 and over by quintile group of the equivalent family income of the individual (as defined previously), from the 1974 and 1985 General

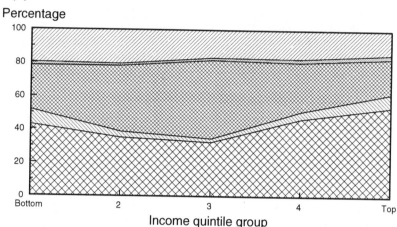

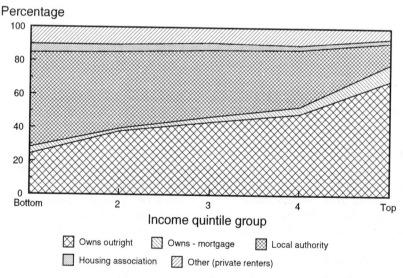

Source: Authors' own analysis of General Household Survey datafile, 1974, 1985

Figure 3.6   *Tenure by equivalent income quintile group:*
(a) 1974; (b) 1985

Household Surveys. The most notable changes over time are the reduction in the size of the privately rented sector and the expansion in the proportion of elderly persons who are owner-occupiers. In 1974, the relationship between income and owner-occupation was U-shaped, although significantly more persons located in the top quintile of the income distribution owned than persons in the bottom quintile. By 1985 the relationship between income and tenure had become linear, with the proportion owning their own homes rising between each quintile group: 65 per cent of those in the top income quintile owned their home outright and a further 11 per cent owned with a mortgage. In contrast, only 24 per cent of those in the bottom quintile owned outright, 5 per cent owned with a mortgage and 61 per cent lived in accommodation rented from a local authority or housing association. Nevertheless, despite the strong relationship between income and tenure what is most striking is that home ownership is not confined just to those in the top income quintile, and that most older owner-occupiers, regardless of relative income, own their houses outright. Thus, it may be reasonable to infer that many older persons possess considerable wealth in the form of home equity.

However, there is some evidence that elderly owner-occupiers' property tends to be less valuable than that of younger households. The 1981 and 1986 *English House Condition Surveys* (DoE, 1983, 1988) found that elderly owner-occupiers were more likely to own properties deemed to be in poor condition, lacking basic amenities or requiring major repairs. The value of 'unfit' dwellings in the 1986 survey was found to be, on average, 37 per cent lower than that of 'fit' ones. Similarly houses lacking basic amenities had an average value 30 per cent lower than those having all amenities. This confirms a more general trend that amenities for all 'elderly only' households, regardless of tenure, are generally worse than average and a significant minority of elderly persons are living in inadequate or inappropriate housing conditions (Henwood and Wicks, 1985). Private households which at the time of the 1981 Census were composed of elderly persons only were more likely than those with no elderly persons to lack some basic amenities, for example 5 per cent of 'elderly only' households lacked a toilet and 4.1 per cent a bath compared with 2.7 per cent and 1.9 per cent respectively for all households (OPCS, 1984).

The fact that elderly people tend to own property that contains fewer amenities, is less well maintained, and hence less valuable draws into question the proposition that elderly owner-occupiers have a substantial holding of wealth. Equally, it is not necessarily the case that those who are 'income poor' are 'housing rich'. Rather

Table 3.6   *Equity by income for households with head over retirement age, England 1986*

Income per annum	Amount of equity			
	Under £25,000	£25,000– £49,999	£50,000– or more	All older households
Under £3,000	70	49	44	52
£3,000–£5,999	21	41	46	38
£6,000 or more	9	10	10	10
No. of households	601	1125	822	2548

Source: Mackintosh et al. (1990: Table 18, p. 38)

those elderly persons with higher incomes are also those most likely to own the houses worth the greatest amount of equity. Table 3.6 illustrates this.

Thus there is a group of elderly owner-occupier households who are income poor and not particularly house rich. Although they do have an asset that is not available to tenants, as Mackintosh et al. (1990: 38) point out, they may carry added problems of disrepair with it. From this, one can hazard the conclusion that the present elderly population are not necessarily as wealthy as would be supposed from an initial glance at the data. Bosanquet et al. (1990) predict that rates of owner-occupation will continue to increase within the elderly population as rates of home ownership are higher among the new cohorts entering retirement. They estimate that the housing assets of older people will rise from £218 billion (1989 prices) in 1990, to £279 billion in 2000. However, they warn that pensioners will be affected by future changes in levels of house prices and that these are unlikely to reach the heights of those prevailing in the 1980s, which stimulated the then embryonic sheltered housing market. They conclude that 'the dawning of the age of the affluent elderly will not come until the baby-boom generation retires in the second decade of the twenty-first century' (Bosanquet et al., 1990: 38).

Even if there is a sizeable constituency of older persons with substantial wealth holdings in the form of housing equity, this does not mean that these people will be willing to take advantage of equity release schemes to withdraw wealth from housing. Venti and Wise (1990), using longitudinal data from the Retirement History Survey in the United States, concluded that the majority of elderly persons have no desire to reduce housing equity. This may be because the present schemes offer very poor rates of return (for a detailed analysis of the merits and disadvantages of such schemes see Leather (1990) and Hinton (1990)) or because elderly persons wish to preserve their assets in order to leave them to their heirs – 'the bequest motive'.

Demand for Care in Later Life

Most of the work on economic dependency has focused on the anticipated rise in the cost of income maintenance for an ageing population. However, the other side of the 'cost of ageing coin' is assuming an increasingly important role. As we have seen the growth rate of the proportion of 'very elderly' persons is projected to be rising and the costs of social support and medical care for this group will necessarily accelerate into the next century.

The pensions debate has become caught up in a number of other debates, specifically that of the idea of individual versus collective provision. The belief in the rising affluence of elderly persons is increasingly being used to justify reductions in, or introduction of charging for, services mainly used by the elderly population. The last decade has seen a major extension in the personalization of private care costs, along with the rapid growth of sheltered accommodation and the proliferation of private residential and nursing homes.

First, this section will examine the prevalence of disability among the elderly population in an attempt to assess the current demand for care. It will then venture to provide a range of estimates of the future number of disabled elderly people into the next century. Finally, it will survey briefly the changing balance in the mixed economy of care provision over the 1980s and go on to consider whether increasing personalization of financing care is a viable option. Are those who can afford to pay for care those that need it?

Arber and Ginn (1991b and forthcoming) examined the level of functional disability within the population aged 65 and over living in private households in 1985. By using the responses to six different questions concerning the ability to carry out everyday tasks such as shopping, washing unaided and cutting their toenails, they constructed a disability scale. Figure 3.7 shows that elderly women are more likely to be substantially disabled than elderly men, with twice as many experiencing a severe level of disability. This level of disability is likely to require some provision of domestic and/or personal care on a regular basis. Table 3.7 reveals how levels of functional disability vary with age and gender within the elderly population. Not surprisingly levels increase with age, and within every age group women experience higher average levels of incapacity than their male counterparts.

To what extent the number of elderly disabled people will rise

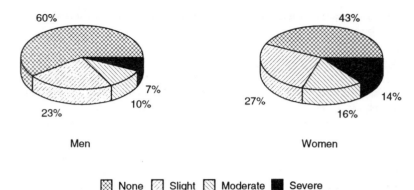

Men   Women

☒ None ▨ Slight ▨ Moderate ■ Severe

Source: Arber and Ginn, 1991b

Figure 3.7   *Disability level of elderly men and women, 1985*

Table 3.7   *Disability level of elderly men and women by age group (percentages)*

	Age group									
	65–69		70–74		75–79		80–84		85 plus	
	M	F	M	F	M	F	M	F	M	F
None	72	63	63	49	54	35	37	24	14	11
Slight (1–2)	17	23	24	29	26	32	20	26	34	19
Moderate (3–5)	6	9	8	14	10	17	22	25	29	27
Severe (6+)	5	6	4	7	11	15	11	24	24	45
N =	522	588	437	615	324	493	135	269	59	188

Source: Arber and Ginn (forthcoming: Table 5.1)

over the next four decades largely depends on the changing morbidity levels of the elderly. There is no way of accurately forecasting the health status of those who will be elderly in 2021. Fries (1980, 1989) predicts that improvements in life expectancy at later ages would slow and that reductions in age-specific incidence rates for chronic illness would exceed reductions in age-specific mortality rates. Thus he argues that the 'average period of diminished physical vigour will decrease, that chronic disease will occupy a smaller proportion of the lifespan, and that the need for medical care in later life will decrease' (1980: 130). He hypothesizes that as preventive health care evolves we will see a 'compression of morbidity' and a decrease in the level of disability at older ages. If this projected reduction in the duration of chronic illness is forthcoming there would result an implied per capita reduction in health care costs. Thus Fries's thesis provides grounds to predict an offset to the expansion in health expenditure expected from an increasing number of elderly people.

However, this optimistic view regarding the 'compression of morbidity' is the subject of much debate (Manton, 1982; Schneider and Brody, 1983; Grundy, 1984; Brody, 1985). It largely hinges on the idea that mortality remains constant at older ages, that is people in the future will on average live for a similar timespan as is the case presently, but will do so in a more healthy state. This assumes that maximum average life expectancies have already been attained. Olshansky (1988) has challenged the notion that the US population has indeed reached an 'upper bound' to longevity. If mortality rates at older ages do continue to fall into the next century then although the onset of chronic disease may occur chronologically later, older people may spend as many, or more, years in a morbid state as now. Furthermore there is the question of whether or not the onset of chronic disease can be postponed. This must remain a matter for speculation given the present dearth of knowledge about the epidemiology and aetiology of some of the major disorders, such as dementia, that affect the very old (Grundy, 1991).

The evidence in Britain points to falling mortality rates at the upper end of the lifespan. The proportion of people living to over 90 is projected to continue to increase. So too is the absolute number of 'very-old' (i.e. aged 85 or over), people. Those people who will be elderly in the next century will have lived in a different environment to those who are currently retired. The particular characteristics of today's elderly will not be replicated in future cohorts. They may be more healthy but this will not obviate need for social and medical services. Grundy (1991) estimates there will be an additional 300,000 elderly persons with chronic disease and 100,000 with moderate or severe functional disability within the next decade.

Using population projections (see Table 2.7) and the age–gender specific disability rates presented in Table 3.7 it is possible to produce estimates of the number of elderly persons experiencing moderate or severe disability by the year 2031, assuming a steady state level of morbidity. Given that Arber and Ginn's data are based on a survey of private households these figures will produce an under-estimate of the true prevalence of elderly persons in the population being disabled, since it is likely that incidence of disability will be higher among the institutional population. Nevertheless, Figure 3.8 suggests that the number of elderly persons experiencing a moderate level of disability will rise from 1.25

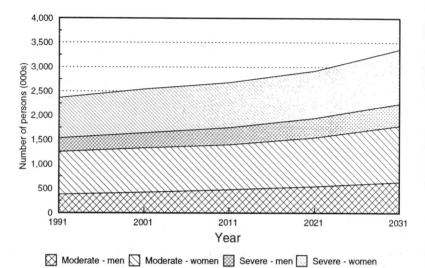

Figure 3.8   *Projection of the number of moderately and severely disabled elderly men and women, 1991–2031*

million in 1991 to 1.78 million in 2031. The numbers suffering from severe disability will increase by 470,000 over the same period from 1.11 million to 1.58 million. Thus, in the space of forty years there will be an estimated additional 1,001,000 moderately or severely disabled persons aged over 65.

Of course, the steady state assumption may be unrealistic. Evandrou et al. (1985) produced a similar table to that of Arber and Ginn, using the same disability scale but based upon the 1980 GHS. Although the categories used do not match exactly, it is possible to compare the change in the proportion of men and women classified as moderately or severely disabled between the two surveys in 1980 and 1985. Within every group, except men aged 65–69, the proportion who were disabled declined over time. However, due to low cell counts this decline can only be taken as indicative of a trend towards improved health at later ages. In the absence of any concrete evidence, and given the fact that the projection probably under-estimates levels due to the exclusion of the institutional population in the calculation of the disability rates, the steady state assumption is perhaps as good as any that can be applied.

Paying for Care?

With an extra million elderly persons in need of some form of care support the type of provision, and resultant cost, of that care should be the subject of as much discussion as has been the case for public provision of pensions. It is important to distinguish between provision and financing of care. The debate concerning provision of care, and the changing balance of that provision between state, private and informal sectors, has been ongoing for much of the last two decades. This has been adequately reviewed by numerous government policy documents, academics and other commentators and is not the primary focus of the discussion here (see DoH, 1989; Evandrou et al., 1990). On the other hand, the debate concerning the balance between state and personal funding of social care in the 1990s has not been given such a public airing. It could be argued that there has been a process of stealth with the National Health Service and Social Services Departments increasingly abdicating responsibility and shifting it into the private arena, with an increased personalization of care costs. The goal posts have shifted and social care increasingly has a price on it (Oldman, 1991).

Before going on to examine the feasibility of shifting the balance of funding for *marketed* care services between the state and individuals it is important to note that *non-market* informal care continues to constitute the major source of support to frail elderly individuals. Recent government data indicates that there are 6 million adults in Britain who provide consistent care for disabled elderly people and other incapacitated adults and children (Green, 1988). The estimated value of total informal care provided in 1986 was £24 billion (FPSC, 1989). In contrast, statutory personal social services support was £3.4 billion in 1987/8. It is clear from recent government policy documents (DHSS, 1988; DoH, 1989) that policy planning explicitly relies upon the continued provision of care and support from informal carers. Implicit in this reliance is an element of cost control, as the majority of such care provision does not entail social expenditure. Only 2 per cent of carers presently receive invalid care allowance (DSS, 1990a). Therefore any shift in the balance of provision between marketed and non-marketed services may be seen as a 'privatization' of care costs in terms of the opportunity cost of time spent caring, travel, resources etc. and in that it reduces what otherwise would have needed to be spent on state services.

However, although it has been a cornerstone of current government policy it is arguable that it will not be a viable option to continue to rely on the informal sector as a means of providing care which has little cost in terms of social expenditure. It is likely that the increasing number of disabled elderly persons will not be matched by a proportional increase in the potential pool of carers. As we have seen in Chapter Two there has been an increase in the number of frail elderly living alone, and a decline in co-residence in a younger relative's household. Demographic trends will be compounded by factors such as the increasing participation of women in paid employment (Henwood and Wicks, 1984). David Eversely calculated that the typical couple married in 1920 and still alive in the mid-1980s had forty-two living female relatives of whom fourteen were not employed outside the home. The typical couple married in 1950 are however likely when they reach 80 to have only eleven living female relatives of whom only three will not be in paid jobs (Leat and Gay, 1987: 4). Since Eversely did his calculations women's employment rates have continued to rise, as have rates of family dissolution. Furthermore, even if there will be a 'sufficient' supply of informal carers it is questionable how long they will, and should, continue as *unpaid* care providers. The 'carers lobby' is becoming increasingly vocal as academics and others continue to quantify the financial implications of having caring responsibilities, for example in terms of broken career paths, part-time work and increased expenditure (see Glendinning, 1989; Evandrou, 1992). How long governments will be able to ignore calls for an adequate carers' benefit to offset for such costs is debatable, but implicit central government reliance on unpaid family care as a means of controlling public expenditure may, and should be, short lived.

Looking at the formal, marketed, sector the main source of non-institutional care in old age is that provided by local authorities. The 1980s have seen the introduction, and extension, of charges for domiciliary care by many social services departments. By 1985, ninety metropolitan authorities and county councils charged for the provision of home helps. As Clarke (1984: 76) argues, charging is a 'method of introducing the privatization of social services by rationing public services, thus forcing the elderly to turn to the private sector'. With the gradual withdrawal of the state there has been an 'increased personalization in the costs of care'. To what extent is an extension of this trend possible, bearing in mind the discussion above regarding the income position of the elderly?

It is not necessarily the case that those who can afford to pay for care are those that need it. Table 3.8 pursues the relationship between income and health status by considering the proportion of each quintile group of the elderly population who report ill health, and those who are unable to perform certain everyday tasks unaided. If income and health were unrelated the proportions in each quintile group would be the same. The top quintile group are least likely to be unable to do these, with only 17 per cent being incapable of doing their own shopping compared with around 29 per cent of the poorest 40 per cent. Thus, those most in need of

Table 3.8   *Elderly persons unable to perform certain tasks at all or without help*

| | Quintile group | | | | |
	Bottom	2	3	4	Top
Shopping	27.4	30.6	21.3	24.6	16.6
Stairs	9.2	11.2	8.9	8.3	3.7
Walk	12.3	15.2	11.6	11.1	5.2

Source: Authors' analysis of 1985 General Household Survey datafiles

Table 3.9   *Use of services by the Woopies*

	Woopies	All aged 65 plus
District nurse	1.1	5.0
Home help	4.0	9.5
If yes, more than one day a week	0.0	47.2
Meals on wheels	0.6	2.5
Lunch club	1.1	1.9
Day centre	0.6	5.6
Private chiropody at a surgery	10.3	4.3

Source: Authors' analysis of 1985 General Household Survey datafile

assistance with everyday tasks are also least likely to be able to afford paid domiciliary help. This is confirmed by the analysis of Victor and Evandrou (1987). They examined the relationship between disability and social class. They found persons from lower social classes experienced a higher likelihood of being disabled in later life. As we discussed earlier, persons categorized as being members of lower occupational groups are less likely to have built up occupational pension rights, and experience a lower level of income.

Looking at publicly supplied domiciliary and health service use within the group classified as being Woopies compared with that of the population aged over 65 as a whole, it can be seen from Table 3.9 that the scope for introducing or increasing charges in the current system would again result in little reduction in overall public expenditure. Those defined as Woopies, and consequently those most able to pay for care, use personal social services much less than the elderly population per se. This, presumably, is because they are younger than the total 65 plus population. Where the 'affluent' elderly do make use of them, they use these services much less intensively. For example, although 4 per cent of Woopies are visited by a home help, none of them are visited more than once a week compared with 47 per cent of clients in general. This suggests that the personal social services are already 'targeted' at the lower income groups and the scope for increasing charges to users may be severely limited. This is confirmed by analysis of service receipt and income in Evandrou et al. (1990). Unfortunately the 1985 GHS does not include many indicators of the use of private services. But it is clear that those classified as Woopies do make more use of private services than the elderly population in general, with 10.3 per cent using a private chiropody clinic.

Although private sector provision of residential care has grown rapidly throughout the 1980s, to comprise over 50 per cent of the total residential and nursing home places, the majority of clients are still state funded. Out of an estimated total of 444,000 residential clients (all sectors) only 22 per cent (98,000) were private paying clients whereas income support funded clients accounted for nearly a third (141,000) (Laing, 1991: Table 1). In fact between 1979 and 1989 income support funding of private and voluntary care homes increased from £10 million to over £1000 million (DoH, 1989). Given that those on income support are among the least well off elderly people the scope for moving the burden of finance from the collective to the individual appears very limited. Even if the government can overcome the political obstacles involving expectations and stigma that lie in the way of introducing means-testing, it is still questionable how much the government would save by the targeting of such benefits. Much depends on the definition of needy, or alternatively the criteria necessary for graduating to Woopie status.

For the purposes of preliminary estimation with regard to means-testing it seems reasonable to take the number of pensioners with incomes over the age allowance range to be 'rich pensioners' since the age allowance is specifically designed to help pensioners. (The age allowance is a higher personal tax allowance allowed in full up to an income of £12,300 per annum (1990/1) and then tapered away at a rate of 1/2 until the allowance reaches the standard married or single allowance as appropriate.) Using TAXMOD (Atkinson and Sutherland, 1988) at the LSE it was found that means-tested benefits, were they to be introduced at the current threshold employed for the top of the age allowance taper, would result in approximately 230,000 pensioner families (3.25 per cent of the total) being excluded. A further 100,000 pensioner families currently lie in the taper. Thus even if means-testing was introduced at the bottom of the taper this extra 1.5 per cent would hardly make up a massive constituency.

A more likely source of saving would be the reduction in take-up of benefit that means-testing implies. Universal benefits have an almost 100 per cent take up rate. But elderly people are among those least likely to apply for benefits where there is a means-test (DSS, 1989). Of those pensioners living on low incomes in 1987 1.9 million received income support. However, a further 0.9 million were estimated to be eligible but failed to claim it (Johnson and Webb, 1990: 11) – and these are the least well off in the population. A take-up rate of less than this estimated 67 per cent could therefore be expected for additional benefits if income testing were introduced. Far from targeting state benefits and provision away from the affluent members of the retired population, who number very few in any case, benefits would be removed from the most vulnerable groups and targeting could actually result in the poor being made even worse off.

The above discussion has focused on the potential for an increasing proportion of currently publicly funded provision to be met by individuals by means of an extension of means-testing or informal care. A final point that deserves consideration within this section is the impact of the growth of the *formal* private sector in funding provision. The UK financial sector now believes that privately funded long-term care (LTC) insurance has the potential to be a viable method of funding social care. It is worth examining in brief a number of new and innovative products that emerged in the first half of 1991.

In February, Cannon Lincoln launched its 'Oasis Plus' plan which provides an add-on to its personal pension plan (PPP). By opting to take a 10 per cent cut in pension the policy holder is assured a pension of between double and triple in size should they become disabled. The disability premium is triggered by a qualifying level of functional disability. In March Eagle Star entered the market with a different product – the 'care fees payment plan'. A one-off payment out of capital from, for example, the sale of a house, buys a policy which then pays at regular intervals acting like a series of endowments. This is not really insurance but is more like a pure financial product. A third variation was introduced by the Commercial Union in June. Their initiative, entitled the 'Third Age' included two separate products: 'well being insurance' and 'life plus insurance'. These were aimed at the 45 plus age group and a monthly payment gives policy holders entitlement to insurance cover for future disability. Payments are made direct to the care providers and can be to residential home operators or to carers. Thus the scheme encompasses care in the policy holder's own home as well as institutional care.

The expansion of such schemes, while providing a means for people to plan for their health care needs in later life, may serve to increase inequality within the elderly population. Just as receipt of an occupational pension is dependent on previous labour market experience so too will be these new financial market products. Some of them assume that the client already has a personal pension plan, with the long-term care insurance being an addition to that pension. Others require the availability of a substantial capital sum out of which a policy can be bought. As we have seen both home ownership and private pensions are related to labour market experience. Thus access to these products will clearly be limited to those at the upper end of the income distribution, and we may see the emergence of a *new* two nations in old age, the cleavage being one of access to quality care in old age. To avoid this, the link between access to health care and income in later life should be weakened not strengthened.

Conclusion

The ageing of the population has given rise to a number of debates. The most widely publicized is that the ageing of the population will increase the burden of pension financing at a time when the size of the work force will be diminishing. However, the pensions debate has become caught up in a number of other debates, specifically that of the idea of individual versus collective provision. The belief in the rising affluence of elderly persons has increasingly been used to justify reductions in, or introduction of charging for, services mainly used by the elderly population. The discussion in this chapter has focused on five main questions:

1   Whether the elderly population as a whole is relatively better off today than has been the case in the past.
2   Has there been the emergence of an affluent group of elderly within the elderly population and what characteristics are identified with such a group?
3   Is it realistic to anticipate that the elderly population, and specifically the group identified as affluent, will be able to pay for care?; what is the potential of housing equity to increase the number of elderly people able to do so?
4   What is the current state of the demand for care, outside of institutional care and how is this likely to increase over time?
5   Are those that need care also those that can pay for care; what scope is there for reducing the future financial burden of the ageing population by means testing health care and other benefits to the elderly?

Although there is clear and uncontroversial evidence that real incomes have increased among the retired population over the last thirty years, it is not possible to state conclusively that there has been an improvement in the relative income position of the retired population vis-à-vis the non-retired. The last twenty years have seen a restructuring of poverty, with pensioners making up a decreasing proportion of the total number living on or below the poverty line, however defined. However, the elderly population have not moved out of poverty at the expense of younger members of society and their families. Rather they have been joined by an increasing number of low income families, particularly those of the long-term unemployed. Furthermore, there is no evidence of a transfer of public resources away from children towards the elderly population. Discussion of intergenerational conflict for welfare resources therefore establishes a false dichotomy as economic inequality within age groups is greater than that between age groups.

This can be seen by examining the distribution of income within the elderly population. The income distribution is heavily skewed and the vast majority of elderly persons have equivalent incomes around the level of the basic pension. However, those elderly who accumulated occupational pension rights and investment assets during their working life experience a much higher level of income than those that did not. 'Woopies' are likely to be younger, male, have been employed in non-manual jobs and have access to non-state sources of income. These characteristics are the reverse of the well known risk factors associated with poverty in later life.

Payments of premiums for private pensions are clearly related to the income and employment history of the individual. Unemployment, part-time work and early retirement may well preclude the building up of non-state pension contributions. Thus the inequalities established before retirement will endure beyond participation in the labour force. In 1955 Richard Titmuss described Britain as having 'two nations in old age' – one group relatively fortunate benefiting from an occupational pension and being able to draw on savings, the other group receiving only the basic state pension and being dependent on means-tested assistance. Given the substantial increases in the number of persons long-term unemployed or in receipt of supplementary benefit/income support during the 1980s and the continued emphasis on private rather than public provision it is likely that Titmuss's two nations in old age will persist well into the next century.

Although home ownership has become increasingly widespread and is now the modal form of housing tenure the potential for viewing home equity as the source of an additional income stream in later life is severely limited. Among the recommendations of the Griffiths Report (DHSS, 1988) was the suggestion that there should be increased utilization of housing equity to pay for care costs. The private sector has responded and a number of home equity release schemes have been established. However, there is some evidence that elderly owner-occupiers' property tends to be less valuable than that of younger households, lacking basic amenities or requiring major repairs. The fact that elderly people tend to own property that contains fewer amenities, is less well maintained, and hence less valuable draws into question the proposition that elderly owner-occupiers have a substantial holding of wealth. Equally, it is not necessarily the case that those who are 'income poor' are 'housing rich'. Rather those elderly persons with higher incomes are also those most likely to own the houses worth the greatest amount of equity. Therefore, housing equity release may well not provide any significant addition to the number of elderly people able to live independently of the state and/or pay for care.

The number of elderly people experiencing a moderate or severe level of disability likely to require some provision of domestic and/or personal care on a regular basis is estimated to be approximately 2.4 million in 1991. This is predicted to rise by a further 1 million in the next forty years to 2031. The number of informal carers is likely to fall over the same time period. Therefore alternative methods of providing care to frail elderly people need to be addressed. The debate on provision of care is well developed. However, discussion as to the balance in the burden of financing care has not received such a public airing.

There is evidence of a movement away from collective finance towards an increased personalization of care costs. However the ability of most elderly people to meet such costs is severely limited. The financial sector has begun to develop new long-term care insurance products, but access to these is likely to be limited to the same group that has accumulated occupational pension rights during the working life. Thus care issues are becoming linked with income issues. Titmuss's two nation in old age regarding income may also become true as regards health and access to health and domiciliary care provision.

One policy option would appear to be to introduce means-testing for a number of services used by the elderly population, in an attempt to target public resources to those in most need. However this may well exacerbate inequalities while at the same time failing significantly to reduce public expenditure. The number of affluent elderly persons is relatively small and is likely to remain so into the next century. Relatively few claimants would be excluded by means-testing benefits, while administrative costs would escalate. Savings from means-testing would be minimal, while at the same time we might run the risk of removing benefits from those most in need.

4

Work and Retirement

Work and retirement inevitably loom large in any assessment of the economic impact of population ageing. As the preceding chapter has made clear, whether an older person is in work or retired, and whether extensive or minimal pension entitlements have been accumulated are key determinants of economic well-being. Any changes in employment and retirement patterns in the future will, therefore, have a direct impact on the welfare of future generations of older people. They will, however, also have a substantial impact on general macroeconomic performance – rising retirement rates imply a reduction in labour supply and an increase in the cost of pension finance. Whether the pension effect will, in the long run, be positive or negative for the economy as a whole depends upon a variety of institutional and conceptual issues that will be looked at in Chapter Five; here we will concentrate on the way retirement practices combine with population ageing to affect and be affected by the labour market. To motivate the discussion, the first part of the chapter will review data on past retirement behaviour in Britain and a number of other developed countries. The second part will then describe and evaluate the large number of alternative hypotheses that have been advanced to explain the observed trends. The final part of the chapter will then consider the overall plausibility of economic and other social science explanations of retirement and their relevance to future population and labour market projections.

Retirement Trends

Retirement is a complex phenomenon and a definitional problem. The word is commonly taken to mean the process of voluntary and permanent withdrawal from the labour force at some relatively advanced age, and the simultaneous receipt of a pension income. But this definition is very restrictive. Take the following six cases:

1   John M, aged 67, self-employed electrician, draws state retirement pension but still works 'now and again, for friends, like'.
2   Arthur B, aged 59, former miner, suffering from acute lung failure, in receipt of a disability pension.
3   William S, aged 58, accountant, took early retirement (and large

'golden handshake') from a multinational corporation when it was rationalizing its staff. He now works in a small accountancy partnership in a provincial town 'just to keep my mind alert; I don't need the money, but it's more interesting than golf'.

4 Frank G, aged 64, former steelworker, made redundant when his company went bankrupt earlier in the year, not able to find alternative employment, drawing unemployment benefit, and considered by the Department of Employment to be 'early retired'.

5 Daphne R, aged 62, housewife, mother and grandmother 'and proud of it', has not worked since the birth of her first child thirty-seven years ago and has 'no intention of starting now!'. Her civil servant husband has another 18 months to go before he retires.

6 Mary L, aged 61, used to do a lot of local cleaning jobs, 'all cash-in-hand stuff, of course', but has stopped now her husband has taken early retirement (at 64) from the local engineering factory.

None of these people fit the definition of having permanently and voluntarily withdrawn from the labour force and simultaneously started to receive a pension, yet they might all, under one definition or another, be counted as members of 'the retired population'. Both Daphne and Mary are over 60, the age at which women who have paid independent contributions into the British National Insurance system qualify for a retirement pension, but because they have no personal contribution record they will receive a state pension only when their husbands reach 65. Nevertheless, because they are over 60 they will typically be described as 'retired'. John is also over the state pension age (65 for men) and is drawing the pension, but he is still working from time to time. William is also working, despite the fact that he is drawing a very substantial occupational pension. Both William and John are, from the point of view of their respective pension schemes, retired workers. Arthur and Frank are effectively retired in so far as they are never likely to work again. They are also both in receipt of a state provided income in recognition of their inability to earn an income. In a survey of labour force activity they might both describe themselves as retired, even though neither withdrew from work voluntarily and neither receives a state retirement pension.

This definitional problem is compounded by the obvious fact that people change what they do over time. Two years from now Arthur may be dead (one less 'early retired' person), William may have given his brain a rest and taken up golf full-time (one more 'early retired'), Mary may have gone back to the cleaning jobs because

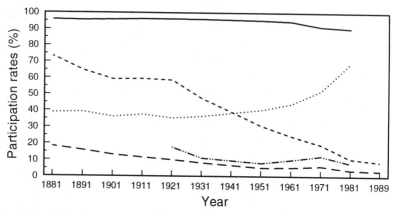

Sources: Censuses of England and Wales, 1881–1981; OECD, 1990

Figure 4.1   *Labour force participation rates for males and
females, England and Wales, 1881–1989*

they couldn't live on her husband's pension, but this is not recorded
in official statistics because her work is still all 'cash-in-hand stuff'.
Recent research on longitudinal data sets in the United States which
have traced the work patterns of individuals over a number of years,
shows that retirement is for many people a complex process
involving changes in labour market status and labour inputs over a
number of years (Grad, 1990; Quinn and Burkhauser, 1990: 318-20;
for similar conclusions for the United Kingdom see Laczko, 1988).

   No cross-sectional 'snapshot' view of labour force participation
can adequately represent this diversity of retirement trajectories.
We need to bear this in mind when analysing data on retirement
because most of the aggregate and long-run information is drawn
from Censuses or labour force surveys which allow for little or no
diversity in retirement behaviour. Frequently these surveys classify
people either as being in the labour force or as retired, and they
make little allowance for the fact that the experience of retirement
has changed over time and varies greatly between individuals.

   Despite this limitation of Census data, it is the best starting point
for an overall view of long-run changes in retirement patterns.
Figure 4.1 presents the total labour force participation rate for
working age (15–64) males and females in England and Wales for
each Census year between 1881 and 1981 together with OECD data
for 1989, and also the participation rate for older men and women.
The graph shows that the participation rate for working age males

barely changed between 1881 and 1951, but since then has declined, mainly because of the rising numbers of young adults in further and higher education. The rate for men over 65, however, has fallen fairly consistently; according to the Census, in 1881 almost three out of four men aged 65 plus were in employment; by 1981 the proportion had fallen to around one in ten, and is now even lower. In 1987 only 7.6 per cent of men aged 65 plus in Britain were in employment, and of this working group, only one-third was engaged in full-time work (Eurostat, 1989).

The pattern for women is strikingly different, with working age female labour force participation rising markedly after the Second World War, and with older women also to some extent following this upward trend, at least up to 1971. Because of a reduction in 1940 in Britain in the state pension qualifying age for women (from 65 to 60) employment rates are given both for all women aged 60 and above and for all women aged 65 and above; the trends for these two differently defined age groups are very similar. We should be aware, however, that the selection of any specific age threshold is a form of definitional ageism, a presumption that a particular age threshold has the same economic meaning in 1981 as in 1881 (Percheron and Remond, 1991: 143-50). In order to take account of this bias, we will go on to examine labour force participation over a range of age bands to see whether chronological age is related to labour force participation for age groups above and below 65. But for the moment it is worth seeing whether other countries have witnessed similar trends over time in the labour force participation of the over 65 population, or whether British labour market behaviour is unique.

Figures 4.2 and 4.3 show the twentieth-century labour force participation rates for men and for women over 65 for Britain, France, Germany and the United States. It is clear from Figure 4.2 that the downward trend in employment for men over 65 is common to all four countries. This is an important finding, because it suggests that there may be common causes for this pattern that will not necessarily be related to the specific conditions of any national pension scheme or employment structure. For older women (Figure 4.3) the picture is more complex; although France and Germany share with Britain a downward trend, the United States has a more erratic pattern, with participation rates lower than those of the other countries in the late nineteenth century but higher in the late twentieth century. This should caution us about leaping to general and monocausal explanations for changes in retirement behaviour over time, and about applying the same explanations to both male and female workers.

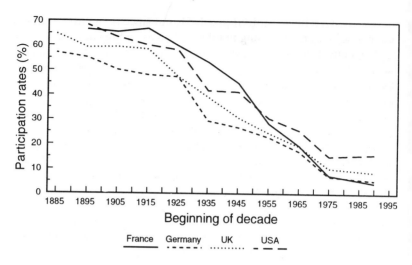

Sources: *Études et Conjoncture*, 1953; Conrad, 1990; Jacobs et al., 1991; as for Figure 4.1

Figure 4.2   *Labour force participation rates for men aged 65 plus, 1885–1989*

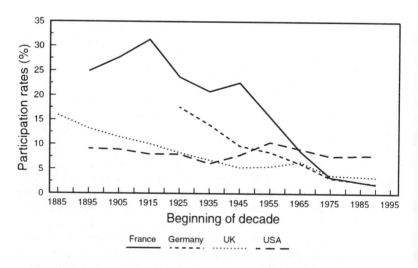

Sources: *Études et Conjoncture*, 1953; Conrad, 1990; Jacobs et al., 1991; as for Figure 4.1

Figure 4.3   *Labour force participation rates for women aged 65 plus, 1885–1989*

Although the data in Figures 4.2 and 4.3 can give a general sense of change over time, they are severely limited by the use of a fixed age threshold. Sixty-five is the most common minimum age for the receipt of a state pension in developed countries, but it is by no means universal; the United States, for instance, allows reduced-rate social security pensions to be paid to people from age 62, and Denmark sets its pension age at 67 (OECD, 1988c: 36). If the age of qualification for the state pension is a major determinant of retirement practice, then international comparisons of employment above age 65 will bias figures up for some countries (those with a higher pension age) and down for others. Furthermore, most of these pension ages were set forty or more years ago, and the relevance of the age threshold then in terms of the average fitness and competence of older workers may be very different from its relevance today, both because of changes in the nature of work and changes in work-related disability.

One indication that a fixed age threshold used in comparative studies may change its functional meaning over time comes from an analysis of the average actual age of retirement. Comparing 1960 with 1983/4, the average age at which American men withdrew from the labour force fell from 66.8 to 63.6 years, and for women from 65.2 to 63.3; for white-collar workers in Germany the comparable figures are from 65.2 to 62.0 for men and from 62.8 to 60.8 for women (OECD, 1988b: 78). It seems sensible, therefore, to refine the outline view of Figures 4.1 to 4.3 by examining changes in labour force participation for a number of different age bands, in order to see whether the trends for the 65 plus population are reflected at lower ages.

Table 4.1 shows the long-term development of labour force participation rates by five-year age bands for the population aged 50–69 for the same four countries that feature in Figures 4.2 and 4.3. Retirement for men over 65, which was exceptional at the beginning of the twentieth century, has now become the norm, with the transition from there being a majority to a minority of men over 65 in employment occuring in the period 1925–50. However, for men aged 60–64 participation rates remained fairly stable until 1970 (though with a gradual downward trend in France), but since then have fallen abruptly in all the countries. For men aged 55–59 there is also some evidence of a decline since 1970, though of much less severity than for men in their early 60s. It would appear from this data that retirement for men over 65 is not a natural part of the life course but instead a creation of the late nineteenth and early twentieth centuries, and that retirement for men aged 60–64 is a creation of the 1970s and 1980s.

Table 4.1   *Long-term development of labour force participation rates for older men and women in France, Germany, UK and USA*
a) *France*

	Men					Women				
	50–54	55–59	60–64	65–69	65+	50–54	55–59	60–64	65–69	65+
1896		—86.4—			66.6		—32.2—			24.9
1906	—91.8—		85.1	78.0		—50.4—		44.4	37.8	
1911	93.5	89.2	83.4		65.6	51.0	48.3	43.4		27.7
1921	95.1	91.7	85.7	78.6		54.0	51.6	47.0	41.0	
1926	94.2	89.2	82.4	73.8		47.8	44.8	39.9	33.5	
1936	91.0	83.2	74.0	65.4		46.1	42.2	36.4	29.0	
1946	93.1	85.4	76.3	66.5		50.2	46.1	40.1	31.3	
1954	94.0	82.0	69.9	49.3		46.8	42.0	33.5	20.2	
1962	93.0	83.5	67.9	36.5		45.3	41.5	31.9	16.9	
1970		82.9	68.0		19.5		46.0	34.3		8.6
1985		67.8	30.8		5.3		42.08	18.9		2.2
1989		68.1	24.1		4.4		44.7	17.7		1.9

b) *Germany*

	Men					Women				
	50–54	55–59	60–64	65–69	65+	50–54	55–59	60–64	65–69	65+
1882	—91.5—		—79.3—			—24.9—		—22.2—		
1907	—90.4—		—71.2—			—36.6—		—30.1—		
1925	—92.4—		79.7		47.4	—37.3—		31.9		17.6
1933	—86.9—		67.0		29.7	—34.8—		27.0		13.1
1939	—89.7—		71.4		29.5	—36.9—		28.0		14.0
1950	93.4	87.4	73.0		26.8	33.9	29.4	21.2		9.7
1961	93.9	88.9	73.0		22.9	37.8	32.5	21.1		8.4
1970		88.4	71.8		17.2		36.4	20.4		6.1
1985		75.3	31.8		5.1		34.5	9.7		2.1
1987		83.8	36.5		5.4		41.7	11.8		2.0

c) *UK*

	Men					Women				
	45–54	55–59	60–64	65–69	70+	45–54	55–59	60–64	65–69	70+
1911	—94.1—			—56.8—		—21.6—			—11.5—	
1921	96.8	—91.9—		79.8	41.2	20.7	—19.1—		15.1	6.5
1931	96.7	94.1	87.6	65.4	33.4	21.0	18.8	16.3	12.2	5.5
1951	97.9	95.4	87.8	48.7	20.9	34.0	27.7	14.4	9.0	3.2
1961	98.6	97.1	91.0	39.9	15.2	43.3	36.9	20.4	13.0	3.1
1970	97.5	95.3	86.7	—20.1—		59.4	50.1	27.9	—6.4—	
1985	92.1	81.8	54.5	—8.2—		69.1	51.6	18.6	—3.0—	
1989	89.4	77.4	53.5	—8.8—		70.0	52.3	22.3	—3.3—	

Table 4.1 *continued*

d) USA

	Men				Women			
	45–54	55–59	60–64	65+	45–54	55–59	60–64	65+
1890		—95.2—		73.8		—12.6—		8.3
1900	95.5	—90.0—		68.4	14.7	—13.2—		9.1
1910		—92.1—		63.5		—16.2—		8.9
1920		—93.8—		60.2		—17.1—		8.0
1930	96.5	—90.2—		58.3	20.4	—16.1—		8.0
1940	92.0	87.9	79.0	41.8	22.5	18.5	14.8	6.1
1950	92.0	86.7	79.4	41.4	32.9	25.9	20.6	7.8
1960	93.3	87.7	77.8	30.6	46.7	39.7	29.4	10.4
1970	93.2	88.3	71.7	25.7	54.2	48.8	34.8	9.0
1985	90.4	78.9	55.1	15.2	64.2	50.1	33.2	6.8
1989	90.3	78.7	53.8	15.9	70.2	54.5	35.3	7.8

Sources: derived from OECD (1990); Jacob et al. (1991)

For women, on the other hand, it seems that paid employment beyond the age of 65 has never been particularly common (the higher rates for France in the earlier years are a consequence of more extensive female participation in the large agricultural sector), although participation rates for women aged 55–59 have, if anything, risen over the period 1950–70. This reflects a general increase in the labour force participation of women (especially married women) since the Second World War, and appears to run counter to the employment trajectories of older men. However, data on the participation rates for different birth cohorts, which we will look at below, will qualify this conclusion.

We should be aware of possible biases in these numbers which can affect the overall interpretation. First, different definitions of labour force participation have been used in different countries and at different times. Secondly, formal retirement from economic activity is more likely to occur when work involves wage labour (as in most industries) than when it is performed for non-monetary returns (as on a family farm). Some of the apparent increase in retirement over time may, therefore, simply reflect a shift in economic structure over the past century from agriculture to industry, or a change in the way in which Census enumerators recorded labour force details. Recent recalculations of labour force participation in Britain, France, Germany and the United States which take account of these structural changes suggest that participation rates for men aged 60/65 plus in industry were fairly stable at the relatively low rate of around 60 per cent from the late nineteenth century to the 1930s, and only then began to fall

(Ransom and Sutch, 1986, 1988; Conrad, 1990; Johnson, 1991). Historical work on the Poor Law in Victorian Britain also shows that pension payments or doles to men over 65 were common even in agricultural areas, which is indicative of a general social and administrative acceptance of withdrawal from work at or around that age (Thomson, 1984). We therefore have to be circumspect in putting a date to the emergence of retirement as a widespread social phenomenon – the fact that existing data appear to trace the origins back to the late nineteenth century may do little more than reflect the fact that we have no reliable data for the period before 1880. We can, however, be confident in saying that the *normalization* of retirement after 65 as an expected element in the life course of men is a creation of the mid-twentieth century.

Another way of examining the timing of changes in retirement practices is by looking at the employment experiences of successive birth cohorts rather than age groups. In Table 4.1 the comparability of the data for any particular age group in different Census years is limited by the fact that they relate to different people (those aged 50–54 in 1970 are in the 65–69 age group by 1985) who may have had very different life cycle and labour force experiences. It is, however, possible to look at the age related employment patterns over time for groups of people born at different dates – this is done for British men and women in Figures 4.4 and 4.5. The participation rates for men between the ages of 20 and 60 were much the same for those born in 1837–41 as in 1937–41. At higher ages, however, it is apparent that participation rates have fallen over time and are lower for the more recently born cohorts. For women, on the other hand, age specific participation rates below age 60 have generally increased for successive cohorts, have fallen and then risen for the age group 60–64, but have declined for women aged 65 plus. As each birth cohort ages, however, the employment probabilities for its members decline after age 54. This shows that the increase since the Second World War in women's labour force participation between ages 50 and 64 is a consequence of higher rates of participation for later-born cohorts *at all ages* rather than simply an increase in employment probabilities at older ages.

A final way of examining labour force participation rates is to disaggregate the overall figures into separate industries or occupations to see whether all sectors of the economy exhibit similar patterns. Table 4.2 presents information on the occupational distribution of British men aged 65 and above and in employment between 1881 and 1971. Occupations for all Census years have been reclassified (as far as is possible) according to the 1971 standard industrial classification; this is a somewhat rough and ready pro-

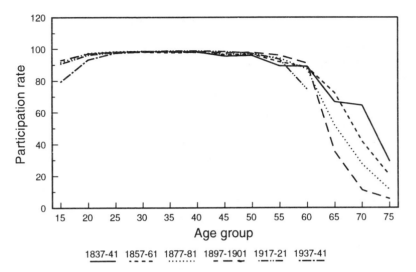

Source: Johnson, 1991

Figure 4.4   *Labour force participation rates by age for successive birth cohorts of English men*

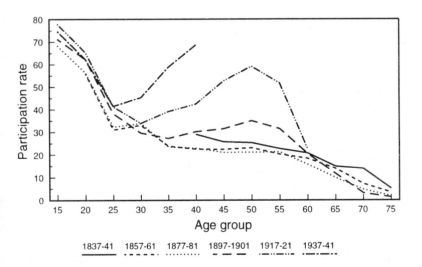

Source: Johnson, 1991

Figure 4.5   *Labour force participation rates by age for successive birth cohorts of English women*

Table 4.2   *Index of occupational concentration, males aged 65 and over England and Wales*

Occupational sectors	1881	1891	1901	1911	1921	1931	1951	1961	1971
1. Agriculture	1.84	2.10	2.46	2.25	1.96	2.46	1.91	2.15	2.74
2. Mining	0.47	0.51	0.54	0.55	0.58	0.61	0.72	0.09	0.12
3. Chemicals	0.83	0.71	0.71	0.89	0.79	0.89	0.35	1.22	0.71
4. Glass	0.57	0.59	0.63	0.73	0.66	0.83	0.54	0.49	0.45
5. Metals	0.65	0.62	0.53	0.70	0.96	0.73	0.97	0.69	0.51
6. Electrical	*	0.15	0.11	0.16	0.17	0.19	0.22	0.25	0.22
7. Engineering	0.61	0.70	0.70	0.77	0.60	0.69	0.54	0.51	0.38
8. Wood	1.23	1.04	1.07	1.20	1.39	1.43	1.12	0.77	0.67
9. Leather	0.97	0.98	0.99	1.27	1.42	1.86	1.77	1.71	1.76
10. Textiles	0.73	0.60	0.68	0.67	0.83	1.16	1.12	1.19	0.85
11. Clothing	1.56	1.51	1.42	1.35	1.45	1.79	1.61	1.93	1.78
12. Food	0.83	0.85	0.85	0.79	0.91	1.20	0.91	0.99	0.99
13. Print/paper	0.52	0.54	0.58	0.65	0.81	1.03	1.01	0.98	0.65
14. Rubber/plastics	1.21	1.19	0.91	0.79	1.00	1.09	0.68	0.55	0.53
15. Construction	0.90	1.02	0.96	1.27	1.51	1.38	1.01	0.83	1.00
16. Decorators	0.50	0.63	0.68	0.90	1.14	1.03	0.91	0.84	0.58
17. Machinery	0.42	0.53	0.60	0.76	0.78	0.97	0.97	0.63	0.44
18. Labourers	1.22	1.24	1.53	1.92	1.41	1.22	1.28	1.41	1.65
19. Transport	0.52	0.50	0.57	0.58	0.59	0.56	0.56	0.57	0.60
20. Stores/packing	0.53	0.49	0.55	0.90	0.81	0.89	1.17	1.35	1.43
21. Clerks	0.30	0.29	0.32	0.39	0.47	0.52	0.77	1.15	1.23
22. Sales	1.04	1.71	1.14	1.14	1.13	1.26	1.43	1.44	1.39
23. Service	0.94	0.96	1.19	1.12	1.83	1.21	1.90	2.25	2.83
24. Administration	0.91	0.74	0.51	0.48	0.43	0.51	1.34	1.10	0.74
25. Professional	1.13	1.31	1.33	1.26	1.26	1.72	0.96	0.83	0.71
26. Defence	0.92	0.42	0.49	0.04	0.02	0.06	0.01	0.02	0.02
27. Other	1.38	1.72	1.91	1.51	1.62	1.25	0.58	1.42	0.82

(* denotes no data available)
Note: The index of occupational concentration relates the percentage of the 65 plus workforce in any occupational sector to the percentage of the total workforce employed in that sector. For instance, if 8 per cent of the 65 plus workforce is employed in a sector, but only 6 per cent of the total workforce (i.e. the aged are relatively over-represented), the index would stand at 1.33. Any figure above 1.0 shows older workers to be over–represented in a sector and any figure below 1.0 shows them to be under–represented.
Source: derived from Censuses of England and Wales, 1881–1971.

cedure for the Censuses up to 1911, but one that has been attempted with some success by Lee (1979). Before 1881 retirees were listed under their previous main employment category, so it is not possible to extend the analysis back any further. In order to normalize for wide variations in size between industrial sectors, the number of men aged 65 plus working in each sector has been converted into a concentration index which relates the percentage of the aged workforce employed in any sector to the percentage of the total workforce employed in that sector. Any number above 1.0 shows older workers to be over-represented in a sector, and any number below 1.0 shows them to be under-represented.

Aged workers can be seen to be consistently over-represented in relatively low-paid, low-status occupations – agriculture (sector 1), clothing (11) and general labouring (18) – and consistently under-represented in certain high-wage sectors – engineering (7), transport (19), glass and ceramics (4). Some sectors show employment patterns that are affected by legislative or customary restrictions on older workers – mining (2) and the armed forces (26) are examples of this. In the new, high-wage sector of electrical engineering and electronics (6) older workers have consistently been greatly under-represented, whereas in clerical work (21), the elderly move from under- to over-representation during the course of this century.

These index numbers appear to show that although the proportion of men over 65 in employment has fallen markedly over time, the sectoral concentration of those who do work has remained fairly consistent, a finding true for most developed economies (van der Wijst, 1987). This in turn suggests that certain types of work have long been viewed as 'suitable' for older workers. But even this result is not unambiguous. While the workforce concentration index sets the age distribution in any sector in relation to the workforce as a whole, it does not place it in the context of relative changes in the size of each sector. It is possible, for instance, to have a consistent over-representation of older workers in a particular sector even though that sector experiences above average retirement rates simply because total employment in that sector is declining rapidly. This is an inevitable consequence and limitation of the Census data, which record not the positive act of retiring from employment, but rather the continued performance of paid work. In practice, most Censuses and surveys tell us nothing about the process of retirement; we simply have to make inferences about retirement from the age structure of the workforce.

In summary then, this brief survey of different ways of looking at twentieth-century retirement trends has shown:

1 Retirement rates for men aged 65 plus have increased sharply in all developed countries at least since the inter-war period. Since the 1950s most men over 65 have been retired.
2 Retirement rates for men in their early 60s have increased sharply since 1970.
3 Average retirement rates for older women have been affected by a general increase in female labour force participation since the

Second World War, but a cohort analysis shows that more recently born women have lower rates of participation above age 65 than do earlier birth cohorts.

4   There is considerable similarity in these trends between countries, particularly for men.

5   There is great variation within Britain between industrial sectors in the likelihood of older men being employed.

Explanations of Retirement

Having described the trends, and noted points of similarity or divergence between countries or industries and over time, we now need to explain why these changes in retirement practice have occurred. If, for example, it is shown that they are a consequence of a growing functional incapacity of older workers in developed economies, then future population ageing is likely to lead to a significant reduction in the available productive workforce. If, on the other hand, increased retirement is the result of a more doctrinaire ageism on the part of employers or a consequence of retirement conditions built into social security schemes, then policies to counter institutionalized ageism or to reform social security could increase the work opportunities of older people and the supply of productive workers despite population ageing. The explanations that have been advanced to explain these trends can be divided into push and pull factors – those which determine whether workers leave the workforce unwillingly (a fall in labour demand) or willingly (a reduction in labour supply). The push factors we will examine include health and disability, mandatory retirement rules and unemployment; the pull factors include savings and pensions and social security entitlements.

Health and Disability
Poor health and disability have been found consistently to be positively related to retirement, but it is not clear whether or how this relationship has changed over time. Surveys of retired men in Britain in 1977 (Parker, 1980) and of early retirement in Sheffield (Walker, 1985: 218) both found that ill health was an important factor in the retirement decision. These findings confirm the conclusion of a number of American interview and questionnaire surveys that ill health is the most important self-reported reason for retirement. However, doubt has been cast on the validity of these results, because interview and questionnaire surveys of retired people may encourage them to give socially acceptable reasons for

retirement such as ill health rather then self-interested ones such as leisure preference, and because the individual focus of the interview technique encourages respondents to advance personal rather than structural explanations for their behaviour (Campbell and Campbell, 1976: 373; Bound, 1991).

In an attempt to put some quantitative weight on the significance of health, Zabalza et al. (1980) developed a model of the labour supply decisions of older people, using individual data relating to a sample of 1417 British men aged 55–73 and 1178 women aged 50–73. This indicated that poor health was a significant positive influence on the retirement decision, though not the dominant influence suggested by some interview surveys. The reliance in this study on subjective personal assessments of health status may introduce the same bias for which the interview surveys have been criticized. One US study by Hurd and Boskin (1984) using longitudinal data from the Retirement History Survey attempts to minimize this bias by using self-definitions of health status in 1969 for a panel of workers aged 58–63 whose labour force participation was then followed over the next five years. Again health was found to be important, with workers who reported ill-health when aged 58–63 having significantly lower labour force participation rates at age 65 than workers who reported good health at younger ages.

Health status, therefore, appears to be an important influence on retirement, and in particular on early retirement, decisions, even when post hoc justification of retirement behaviour is avoided by using measures of pre-retirement health status. It is not clear, however, how the influence of health status on individual retirement decisions relates to long-run changes in the overall participation rate. As the demographic data in Chapter Two show, there has been an unequivocal improvement in the life chances of older men and women in all developed countries over the course of the twentieth century. Yet at the same time, there seems to have been an increase in recorded rates of age specific morbidity (illness) in both Britain and the United States, largely because of a rise in the incidence of circulatory disease (Verbrugge, 1984; Ford and Frischer, 1992). These findings run counter to the influential views of Fries, who argues that we are now experiencing a 'compression of morbidity' as disabling conditions are increasingly confined to the last years of the ever-expanding life-span (Fries, 1980). This disagreement about the nature of trends in morbidity lies partly in the difficulty of drawing inferences about changes over time from successive cross-sectional surveys, and partly from changing attitudes towards and conceptions of ill-health (Rogers et al., 1990). As both medical ability and access to medical services have increased over time, so has the likelihood that people will recognize their own ill-health and declare it in surveys of well-being.

Rather than grapple with the manifest problems of self-perceptions of health status, it may be better to look at a measure of functional incapacity such as work disability. Again in both Britain and America the recorded disability rates for men over 55 have increased significantly since 1970 (Feldman, 1983; Piachaud, 1986). However, measures of disability are not necessarily any more concrete than are self-reported indicators of health; disability may vary according to the subjective definitions of doctors, social security administrators, and workers themselves. Piachaud has shown that the considerable rise in recorded disability among men over 55 in Britain between 1971 and 1981 does not appear to have been caused by any rise in objectively defined disability. Instead he found that 'about half the increase in economic inactivity ascribed to disability is attributable to the worsening labour market; the other half may be due to the general increase in the relative value of social security benefits, changing individual, medical or administrative standards of disability, or quite other factors' (Piachaud, 1986: 159).

It may be argued, of course, that fixed measures of health status are inappropriate to any investigation of the link between health and retirement, because over time the mental and physical demands of work may alter in such a way as to render those formerly capable of work now unemployable, or vice versa. It is not valid to conclude, therefore, that because recorded morbidity and disability rise with age and because age specific morbidity and disability appear to have increased over the last twenty years, that older people have in consequence become less employable. Extensive studies in Britain by industrial sociologists and psychologists in the 1950s and early 1960s of the work capacity of older people found that they were quite able to compete with younger workers in jobs where they were able to exercise some control over the pace of their work (such as skilled manufacturing), but they found it increasingly difficult to sustain work, such as on a production line, which was conducted at an externally imposed pace (Clark and Dunne, 1955; Welford, 1958). The increased mechanization of manufacturing employment since the Second World War may therefore have increased work stress for older people and forced some out of the labour force, but the great expansion of service sector employment over the same period, in which the pace of work is more often controlled by the worker him- or herself, has probably increased the range and number of employment opportunities most suited to older people.

Furthermore, it should be pointed out that an increase in the average recorded disability of 55 or 60 year olds tells us nothing about the proportion of people affected unless we know something about the variance of disability. Recent research shows that individuals do not become less differentiated physically, behaviourally or socially over the life course (Maddox, 1992; Rabbit, 1992). Average figures conceal the fact that most 55 or 60 or 65 year olds are not disabled, and are quite capable of performing all the mental and physical tasks required of most workers.

In the studies that have been made of the relationship between health and retirement there is a consensus that health is an important influence on retirement decisions, and particularly on premature or early retirement. The 1977 survey of retirees in Britain showed that 47 per cent of men in the sample who retired below the age of 65 said that they did so because of illness, compared to only 1 per cent of men who retired at or above the state pension age (Parker, 1980). There is little evidence, however, to suggest that deteriorating health status is responsible for the enormous reductions in labour force participation of men aged 65 plus since the Second World War, or of men aged 60–64 since 1970. The fall in the number of older workers far outnumbers all measurable increase in illness and disability within the older population.

Mandatory Retirement

A second factor pushing older workers out of the labour market is the existence of mandatory retirement, usually linked to the regulations governing pension schemes. Hannah (1986) has shown that many early pension schemes established in the second half of the nineteenth century were extremely flexible about retirement age. They often specified a minimum pension age, but the expectation was that workers would continue to work until their failing physical powers forced them to retire. For example, of workers drawing pensions from the long-standing South Metropolitan Gas Company scheme in 1919, 20 per cent had retired between the ages of 55 and 59, 42 per cent between 60 and 65, 25 per cent between 65 and 70, and 9 per cent between 70 and 78 (Hannah, 1986:130). But over the course of the twentieth century it has become common to specify a 'normal' age of retirement.

A number of forces have worked together to produce this normalization, and of these the role of the state has been very important. In Britain taxation rules introduced in 1921 relating to pension funds typically required the stipulation of a 'normal' retirement age. Furthermore, the establishment of 65 as the pension qualifying age in 1928 (reduced to 60 for women in 1940) for those manual workers covered by the National Insurance system encouraged occupational pension schemes for manual workers to adopt the same retirement age. The incorporation of all workers, whatever their occupation or status, in the Beveridge National Insurance scheme in 1946, and the payment of a state pension to all insured men at 65 and women at 60, gave a strong incentive for all occupational pension schemes to follow suit.

Of course, a 'normal' pension age is not the same thing as mandatory retirement, but in practice there has been a convergence. A survey of British employers carried out in 1949 showed that 80 per cent of male and female workers in the banking, insurance, shipping, gas and electricity sectors worked in companies that had a fixed retirement age. This was true also of 50 per cent of workers in retailing and 19 per cent of manual and 28 per cent of clerical workers in manufacturing and construction (*Ministry of Labour Gazette*, April 1949: 121–2). The 1977 retirement survey which asked workers why they had retired found 53 per cent of men who retired at 65 said they did so because of mandatory retirement. Of those men who said they had been (or would be) forced at 65 to stop working, 65 per cent said this was because of the employer's policy, 3 per cent said it was a trade union policy, and 27 per cent reported that it was a result of a joint decision taken by employer and trade union (Parker, 1980).

There are several reasons why both employers and trade unions might favour mandatory retirement at a fixed age. For unions it is a way of protecting formal wage rates. If older workers are (or are believed to be) less productive than younger workers, then employers may want to pay them a lower wage. If the payment system is based on piece work this is straightforward – less work performed means a smaller wage packet. But if workers are paid on a time basis – per hour or per day – a reduction in the rate of pay for older workers may undermine union negotiated pay scales. Hourly pay or measured day work has been widely substituted for piece work in British manufacturing industry since the Second World War, and in consequence unions have increasingly advocated mandatory retirement in order to protect the economic interests of the majority of their members.

For employers, especially large employers, mandatory retirement is a bureaucratic convenience. For a completely flexible retirement system to work efficiently for the employer, it must involve the repeated and accurate measurement of the marginal productivity of each older worker – retirement (or a wage cut) would be imposed when the worker's marginal product fell below marginal cost (i.e.

the wage rate). Individual monitoring of such intensity is very costly and in practice this sort of fine calculation is impossible to perform when an individual's output is part of the collective product of a large team. It is therefore easier, and possibly more cost-effective, for personnel managers to operate mandatory retirement schemes on the rule-of-thumb that no worker above a certain age is worth employing.

A second reason employers impose mandatory retirement on their workers relates to the way in which they manage their internal labour markets (Lazear, 1979). In order both to establish a disciplinary hierarchy and to minimize the costs of staff turnover, large organizations frequently establish an age related remuneration structure in which pay rises with age and length of service. This typically means that younger workers are paid considerably less than their marginal product, but older workers are paid somewhat more than their real value to the company (for empirical support for this, see Kotlikoff, 1988). This can be thought of as a system of deferred payment, in which the loyal and long-serving worker is rewarded in later career for his or her contributions to company performance in earlier years. This remuneration structure makes for standardized career profiles and simple personnel management, but it also produces its own problem – how to get rid of older workers who are costing the company more than they are worth and who are blocking the promotion of younger workers. To demote them or cut their wage would undermine the age related hierarchy which is part of the overall employment strategy within the firm. To sack them would send signals to younger workers that in the end loyalty to the employer does not pay. But to require them to retire in exchange for a company pension is a publicly acceptable way of forcing them out of the workforce which does not undermine the working of the firm's internal labour market. In fact the pension can be seen as another part of the deferred payment system which stretches from the first day of employment to the final day of retirement.

The expanding role of large corporations in the labour market throughout most of the twentieth century (though perhaps not in the last few years of small business growth), and the increasing formalization and bureaucratization of the employment contract, suggests that mandatory retirement could be a key factor in the dramatic decline of labour force participation rates for men since 1900 (Hannah, 1986: 133–7). The paucity of available data for Britain makes it impossible to test this hypothesis directly, but some inferences can be drawn from research carried out in the United States. In 1978 an amendment to the Age Discrimination in Employment Act forbade US employers in all but a handful of special cases to impose retirement on workers below the age of 70, and a further amendment in 1986 effectively prohibited mandatory retirement at any age. Despite its apparently dramatic nature, the legislation has had little overall effect on retirement behaviour. This is possibly because the proportion of the US workforce that was forced to retire because of mandatory retirement rules seems to have been small (Fields and Mitchell, 1984). A study by Morrison (1988) shows that, other things being equal, the effect of the 1978 amendment was at most to encourage 200,000 older workers to stay in employment who otherwise would have left the labour force. While this legislative change may have been of great significance to individuals who were approaching 65 and who wished to stay at work, in macroeconomic terms it was trivial – an increase in total US labour supply of only 0.2 per cent.

In practice, however, other things have not been equal, and the prohibition of mandatory retirement in the United States has been accompanied by a fall rather than a rise in the average age of withdrawal from the labour force (for men, from 64.0 in 1975 to 63.9 in 1980 and 63.6 in 1983/4). If retirement rules were a dominant factor in explaining retirement trends then their widespread presence in Britain and their rarity and ultimate abolition in the United States should have produced divergent long-run trends in the labour force participation of older workers in the two countries; in fact, as Figure 4.2 shows, the trends are very similar. And in Japan, where 87 per cent of firms employing 30 or more workers have mandatory retirement rules, labour force participation among older workers should be minimal (Japan Institute of Labor, 1986). In reality, Japan has the highest rate of participation for older men of any developed country – in 1985 37 per cent of Japanese men aged 65 plus were in employment. Clearly mandatory retirement is not of itself an adequate explanation of twentieth-century retirement trends.

Unemployment
The third factor that may push older workers out of the labour force is unemployment. If older workers are viewed by employers as less desirable than younger workers (for whatever reason), then they are likely to be dismissed first and hired last as overall labour demand changes. Such age prejudice on the part of employers could have an effect on participation rates at older ages over both the long and the short run. A downturn in demand for the goods or services produced by any particular firm might induce employers to dismiss older workers for any or all of the following reasons:

1 The marginal productivity of older workers is lower than that of younger workers, and the wage rate is the same or higher.
2 Unions may acquiesce in the removal of older workers but would oppose the dismissal of younger workers.
3 Older workers are less adaptable and are resistant to changes in the production process.
4 Older workers are not worth retraining because the number of years of future productivity will not recompense the employer for the cost of training (i.e. the depreciation period is too short).

If some or all of these factors are at work, then we should be able to identify in the short run a positive relationship between changes in the unemployment rate and in retirement or early retirement rates. Over the course of the twentieth century, however, it is clear that this relationship has not existed – there is no rising secular trend in unemployment to match the fall in participation rates shown in Figure 4.2. It has been argued, however, that there has been a long-term structural change in the nature of capitalist employment relations which has disguised the overall fall in demand for workers by redefining the nature and scale of the normal working lifespan. (Phillipson, 1982; Shragge, 1984). In order to deal with an excess of labour, entry into the workforce has been postponed (more formal education), work inputs have been curtailed (more holidays and a shorter working week), and exit from work has been accelerated (a fall in the age of retirement). In this interpretation, rising retirement rates should be seen as a substitute for, rather than a correlate of, rising unemployment.

What evidence is there to support either the short-run or the long-run hypothesis? Figure 4.6 shows labour force participation rates for men aged 55–64 for a number of industrial countries; it is apparent that in both the United Kingdom and France the proportion of older men who were in work fell abruptly from 1981 when both these countries were experiencing a sharp recession. But although this casual observation of trends looks convincing for these two countries, it is not repeated for the other nations in the graph, even though the recession of the early 1980s affected both the United States and West Germany.

This relationship between unemployment and the labour force participation of older men can be examined more formally by looking at correlation coefficients. If an increase in recorded unemployment puts pressure on older workers in particular to leave the labour force, then there should be a large negative correlation between the year-on-year changes in unemployment and participation rates. It is possible that an increase in unemployment will take

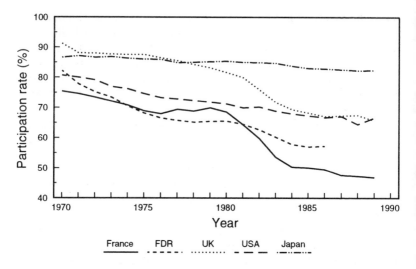

Source: OECD, 1990

Figure 4.6 *Labour force participation rates in selected OECD countries, males 55–64*

Table 4.3 *Correlation coefficients between changes in the unemployment rate and labour force participation rates of older men, 1970–89*

		ΔU	ΔU_{-1}
France	55–59	−.3457	−.2050
	60–64	−.3056	−.1531
	55–64	−.3159	−.1253
West Germany	55–59	−.1338	−.2082
	60–64	−.1214	−.5003
	55–64	−.4363	−.5268
Japan	55–59	−.0754	−.3320
	60–64	−.3996	+.1286
	55–64	−.3251	−.0024
UK	55–59	−.1118	−.3180
	60–64	−.4316	−.6181
	55–64	−.3727	−.5604
USA	55–59	+.0995	−.2557
	60–64	−.1377	−.3693
	55–64	−.0092	−.4108

Source: derived from OECD (1990)

some time to affect older workers, so in Table 4.3 correlation coefficients are presented both for simultaneous changes in participation and unemployment rates (ΔU) and for a one-year lag (ΔU_{-1}) which assumes that a change in unemployment last year leads to a change in participation rates this year. Annual data for the period 1970–89 has been used for France, West Germany, Japan, the United Kingdom and the United States, and participation rates for men aged 55–64 and for the subgroups 55–59 and 60–64 are examined. With two exceptions all the coefficients are negative, but they are generally low, suggesting that the inverse relationship between changes in the unemployment rate and the participation rate for older men is quite weak. The negative relationship is strongest for 60–64 year old men and lagged unemployment in Britain, but this same relationship is trivial for France and positive for Japan. When these results are compared across countries there is very little consistency in them.

Nevertheless, a number of studies have shown that labour market conditions in both the 1930s and the 1980s have had a significant impact on the likelihood of older men in Britain remaining in employment. In 1938 the unemployment rate for 60–64 year old men was twice that for men in their early 30s, a consequence in part of the greater duration of unemployment experienced by older men (Riddle, 1984). Individual data drawn from the Labour Force Survey and the General Household Survey over the last decade show similar patterns. However, these surveys also show that the number and complexity of routes out of the labour force has increased in this period to such an extent that previous conceptions of retirement or early retirement may no longer apply (Casey and Laczko, 1989). In particular, the Job Release Scheme introduced in 1977 allowed men aged 60–64 and women aged 59 in full-time employment to give up work and receive a bridging payment until normal pensionable age provided that their employer agreed to replace them with an unemployed person. Also in 1981 men aged over 60 who had been unemployed for over a year and who were eligible for the means-tested supplementary benefit (now income support) were allowed to claim the higher long-term rate of benefit and were no longer required to register as unemployed. Further changes in 1983 extended this entitlement and had the effect of removing some 200,000 men aged over 60 from the official number of people registered as unemployed. At the same time the proportion of 60–65 year olds in receipt of invalidity (sickness) benefit also rose sharply. The British government quite deliberately opened up new routes out of the labour force for older men, in order both to reduce the recorded number of unemployed workers and to try to minimize unemployment among younger workers (Laczko and Phillipson, 1991). Similar labour market policies were pursued by most European governments (Guillemard, 1989; Kohli, 1992; Rein and Jacobs, 1992).

The existence of more ways out of the labour market for workers below the state pension entitlement age does not necessarily mean that more workers were forced out. In practice it is difficult to determine who jumped and who was pushed. Government inducements for men aged under 65, together with generous early retirement or redundancy packages offered by employers to older workers, and developing social expectations that it is both normal and socially responsible to give up work before 65, combined to pressurize 'volunteers' into withdrawing from the labour force. As a consequence, ill health, which had been found to be the most important determinant of early retirement in Britain in the 1970s (Parker, 1980; Altmann, 1982), was claimed to be the reason for leaving the last job by only 3 per cent of men aged 60–64 who identified themselves as early retired in the 1983 General Household Survey (Laczko et al., 1988). But these detailed surveys also show considerable economic variance within the early retired population. Almost half of the men who said they had retired early from manual jobs lived in or on the margins of poverty (defined as 140 per cent of the supplementary benefit level), whereas less than one in five men from non-manual occupations had similarly low incomes. The most obvious difference between the two groups was that the 'non-poor' had very extensive occupational pension coverage – 87 per cent – compared with just 48 per cent for the 'poor' population (Laczko et al., 1988). This suggests that some older men have indeed been pushed out of work and into an impoverished 'early retirement', whereas others may well have chosen to exchange work for well-financed leisure.

It is, however, virtually impossible to draw clear conclusions from this type of individual questionnaire survey either about the quantitative significance of labour market conditions on early exit from the labour force or about changes over time in any such relationships. The surveys allow non-employed respondents below retirement age to describe themselves as unemployed, discouraged (i.e. those not looking for work because they believe no jobs to be available), long-term sick, retired or simply not wanting work. It seems unlikely that these categories will have the same meaning for all respondents; in fact it has been found that the same respondents may change their self-ascription of the reason for leaving employment between the first and the follow-up interview (Bytheway, 1987). It is also unlikely that the meaning ascribed to the alternative definitions of non-working status will be consistent across successive cohorts of respondents, since the social context of unemployment, redundancy and early retirement has itself changed quite rapidly in the 1980s. Moreover, it is difficult to draw a coherent picture of the underlying labour market reasons for early exit from individual responses, because individuals seldom have full information about the motivation lying behind any particular employer's hiring and firing strategy. What is needed for a balanced assessment of the reasons for retirement is detailed information from both individuals and employers, but this is seldom available.

Government policy in the 1980s was undoubtedly designed to make withdrawal from the labour force for men aged 60–64 easier and less costly than it had been hitherto, and the government's motivation was concern over the high recorded level of unemployment. Survey data indicate, but cannot prove, that a combination of government schemes and economic pressures on employers induced or forced more men in their late 50s or early 60s to withdraw from the labour force, and this is consistent with the apparent acceleration in early retirement rates for 55–64 year olds shown in Figure 4.6, and with the negative (though weak) correlation coefficients shown in Table 4.3. The early 1980s peak in unemployment does seem to have accelerated the fall in participation rates for older men, particularly in Britain, but unemployment does not seem to be an adequate explanation of the pronounced long-run downward trend in participation from the early 1970s.

Even longer-run interpretations of retirement and early retirement that locate the trends within an over-arching critique of capitalist development are yet more difficult either to support or to counter with quantitative evidence (Phillipson, 1982; Macnicol, 1990a). According to advocates of structured dependency theory, changes in the nature and meaning of retirement over the course of the twentieth century are a central element of the way in which labour markets increasingly have been structured in the interests of capitalist employers, and it is therefore impossible to draw clear inferences from data relating to retirement. Official statistics of retirement are essentially derived from labour force participation and pension system data, and have little or nothing to say about the retirement process or the motivation of people who withdraw from the workforce. Survey and questionnaire data may reveal something about an individual's motivations and aspirations, but it is likely that a really effective structuring of work opportunities for older people will also produce a similar structuring of social and cultural attitudes. Older people may indeed choose retirement, even if this is not objectively in their best interests, because they have been encouraged or indoctrinated to believe that retirement is a desirable goal.

A strength of this line of interpretation is that it locates changes in observed retirement practices within a broad framework of social and economic evolution, and in this respect is quite different from most economic interpretations of retirement behaviour which emphasize individual choice. A weakness is that the role of false consciousness (people being persuaded to believe retirement is desirable when in fact it does them harm) is not demonstrable in any unambiguous way, and so remains very much an article of political faith. We will return in the final section of this chapter to the question of how or whether alternative explanations of changing retirement patterns can be reconciled. For the moment we will simply review some of the more important criticisms of structured dependency theory.

If the rise of retirement as a socioeconomic phenomenon in the twentieth century is in fact a consequence of the way in which older workers have been siphoned off by the capitalist system into a reserve army of the unemployed, then we should be able to find evidence of older people having enjoyed more favourable social and economic treatment in pre-capitalist societies. In fact, as was mentioned in Chapter One, few historians believe in a pre-capitalist 'golden age of old age' (Smith, 1984). And in more recent times it is far from obvious that work has always been preferable to retirement or that withdrawal from the workforce necessarily and inevitably has increased the dependency of the individual retiree. In practice many jobs are tedious and many people look forward to giving up work (though not the social contacts of the workplace). In our increasingly consumerist society where social status is measured as much by ownership and purchasing power as by employment, work is of diminishing significance in the establishment or maintenance of social worth; retirement no longer defines a state of socioeconomic dependency. In some respects it never has done – to define a 65 year old recently-retired millionaire as in some sense more economically or socially dependent than a 64 year old unskilled labourer is to ascribe to formal labour market status a unique determining power which it clearly does not possess (Johnson, 1989a).

Structured dependency theory also under-emphasizes the choices facing individual workers and over-emphasizes the extent to which the process of capitalist development has been deliberately directed. It tends to view older people as a subject group to be acted upon by social and economic policies and imperatives rather than as the object of their own wishes, either willingly and genuinely choosing retirement or actively resisting retirement policies imposed by others. At the same time it pays little attention to the mechanisms by which the interests of capitalist development are articulated and co-ordinated by the many and diffuse companies, individuals and government agencies which have a bearing on the work and retirement opportunities of older people. There is a rather unsatisfying touch of conspiracy theory in structured dependency writings which is ultimately unconvincing. Some retirement behaviour must be explained not by the forces pushing people out of work but by the forces attracting them to leisure; not structured dependency but financial independence.

Savings and Pensions

Retirement, whether voluntary or forced, whether planned or unanticipated, necessarily involves the cessation or the reduction of employment income (retirement does not always lead to the *cessation* of employment income because many people continue to work informally, occasionally or part-time after they have retired from their primary career job). An abrupt fall in income would appear to be a strong disincentive to withdraw from the labour force for most people unless this income, or a substantial part of it, can be replaced from another source. Private savings or occupational pensions can provide just such a replacement income, and may therefore be a major factor in persuading people to substitute leisure for work, and investment or pension income for employment income. Whether in practice this is a primary cause of retirement, and whether increasing personal wealth and expanding pension entitlements can explain the normalization of retirement in the twentieth century are questions for empirical investigation. But before looking at the data, we will briefly review the theoretical model within which savings, pensions and retirement decisions are usually analysed.

The model generally used by economists to relate these events or patterns of behaviour to each other is known as the life cycle hypothesis. The model is an elegant and logically consistent heuristic device which allows us to think about the way individuals (or households) plan the inflows and outflows of economic resources over their life cycle. At its simplest, the model is based on income and consumption profiles of the type shown in Figure 4.7. The consumption expenditure for the individual or household is viewed as being relatively constant over time, though with some increase in mid-life when luxury expenditures may be high, and with a tailing-off in old age as frailty reduces the scope for participation in a number of social activities. Income, however, is seen as much more hump-shaped, typically being below consumption expenditure at low and high ages, and above it in middle age. This is because income tends to rise with age over most of a person's career, but

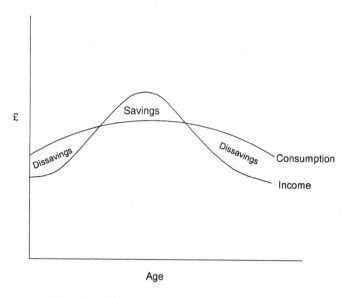

Figure 4.7   *Hypothetical income and consumption profiles of a life cycle saver*

then falls on retirement. When income is below expenditure, people must be borrowing or living off accumulated assets (dissaving), and when income is above consumption they are saving. The stylized consumption and expenditure profiles shown in Figure 4.7 indicate that the typical individual in early working life will have an expenditure stream higher than income, and so will have to resort to borrowing (in order for instance to buy a home). In later working life the excess income is used first to pay off the existing debts, and then to accumulate a stock of assets in anticipation of a fall in income in old age. Once income falls below expenditure these assets are used up to sustain consumption until death.

The most obvious implications of the model are that we should find evidence of assets being accumulated during prime earning years and decumulated in retirement. But there are behavioural implications too, since the model is based on the assumption that households make decisions about consumption over their entire life cycle, and in making these decisions take account of the resources they will have available over their entire lifetimes. This can only be done accurately in a world with perfect foresight and no uncertainty, a world more familiar to economists than other social scientists. It is, however, possible to introduce into the model a degree of uncertainty (for instance about length of life), and an element of learning from experience and adapting to new circumstances – in economists' jargon, reprogramming (for example Davies, 1981; Courant et al., 1984). These refinements, together with motivational amendments which allow for the desire to leave bequests to children rather than run down assets to zero at death, enable the theory to accommodate a wide variety of income and expenditure profiles. Even so, within the life cycle model the retirement decision is viewed as part of a life-long economic plan; the transfer out of work and into leisure is a goal towards which many years of saving are devoted, and the retirement decision is made only when the accumulated assets are considered by the individual to be sufficient to sustain an acceptable level of post-retirement consumption.

The life cycle theory therefore postulates that retirement is the result of individual choice, although this choice is obviously made within the context and constraints of a number of social and economic parameters such as wage rates, interest rates and family size. Given that we seldom have comprehensive and reliable data about retirement decisions, the retirement process, or of people's expectations of future income and expenditure streams, it would seem that the easiest way to find empirical support for the life cycle hypothesis is to look at the age–wealth profile of individuals to see if assets are indeed accumulated during prime working years and run down during retirement.

The findings of a number of US studies do not provide ready support for the life cycle hypothesis – cross-sectional microdata show no consistent decline of wealth with age (Mirer, 1979; King and Dicks-Mireaux, 1982). Cross-section data, however, cannot really provide a direct test of the life cycle hypothesis, because differences between the economic circumstances of successive cohorts may blur the picture. To test the hypothesis directly we need to know not whether today's 55 year olds have more wealth than today's 65 or 75 year olds, but whether today's 55 year olds will run down their assets over the next ten or twenty years. This can only be found out by tracing in some detail the savings behaviour of a number of individuals as they age. Recent analysis of just this sort of longitudinal data from the US Retirement History Survey finds, for instance, that there is no evidence of older people systematically reducing their housing assets as they get older; in fact housing equity tends to increase with age after retirement rather than decrease (Venti and Wise, 1989). Given the difficulty of assembling fully comprehensive data about present and expected household income, wealth and expenditure, it is certainly not possible to refute the life cycle model, but enormously ingenious attempts to demonstrate its behavioural validity have not produced convincing support. This will be of little surprise to non-economists who point to the large numbers of elderly people living in poverty as being a direct refutation of the life cycle model and the idea that people choose retirement on the basis of economic calculation. Very few people, it might be argued, will opt for leisured poverty if the alternative is employed affluence. But there may be sound economic reasons why individuals do choose retirement even though their savings are relatively low, reasons that derive from the rules and operations of occupational pension schemes.

In a typical occupational pension scheme an employee's annual pension on retirement is calculated according to a formula of the following sort:

$$P = N / K . W$$

where P is the annual value of the pension, N is the number of years of membership of the pension scheme, W is the wage or salary of the employee in his or her last year of work (or an average of the last several years or the maximum from the last several years), and K is a scaling factor, usually set at 60 or 80. This sort of pension scheme is called a 'final salary' or 'defined benefit' scheme, since the pension payout is defined at the outset of the pension contract as some proportion of the final salary achieved by the worker. Other occupational pension schemes, of much less common occurrence, are called 'money purchase' or 'defined contribution' schemes because the pension contribution is defined as a certain proportion of annual salary, and the pension benefit is determined by the value of an annuity that can be purchased on retirement with the accumulated pension fund. In the more common final salary schemes, forty years of service and a scaling factor of 60 allows an annual pension of two-thirds final salary, a scaling factor of 80 sets the pension at half final salary. The total expected pension income (Y) of the employee at retirement therefore approximates to:

$$Y = P . T$$

where T is the expected number of years until death. This is not quite the same as pension wealth, which is an estimate of the present value of expected pension income, calculated with reference to interest and time discount rates. Pension wealth is the appropriate variable to use in calculations of the retirement decision, but for the purposes of exposition the simplified formula given here for total expected pension income is adequate. Although at first sight the final salary pension is straightforward and fair, there are four distinct ways in which, depending on the specific rules of each pension scheme, this sort of pension formula can result in strong economic incentives for the worker to choose retirement at some particular age rather than continue in employment.

1 *Reduction of final salary*. We have already noted that in order to manage their internal labour markets, companies often pay older workers more than their marginal product, and are therefore keen for older workers to take retirement at a set age. If the employee wishes to continue to work beyond a normal retirement age, the company may say that employment can only be continued in a job with lower status and lower pay. Since the pension throughout retirement is determined by the final salary of the worker, a demotion in the final years of work (reduction of W) can lead to an enormous decline in expected total pension income (Y), and so provides a large economic inducement not to continue in employment.

2 *Limitation on length of qualifying service*. Many schemes set a maximum to the number of years of qualifying service that can count towards a pension – for example N may take a maximum value of 40. This means that someone who joined the scheme at age 20 will reach his or her maximum pension entitlement at 60. Thereafter, each extra year of employment can increase the annual value of the pension only in so far as it leads to a rise in W, but at the same time total expected pension income will be forced down because each extra year of employment reduces the value of T. Expected pension income will remain constant only if, for each and every year in which retirement is postponed, the proportionate increase in W compensates for the proportionate decrease in T.

3 *Reduction in length of retirement period*. If the wage rate remains fixed once the worker has reached the normal pension age, and even if each extra year of service is credited towards the pension entitlement (W constant, N increasing), there will still be an economic incentive to retire at some point, because of the fall in T, the number of years over which a pension will be drawn. In other words, compensating a 60 year old worker for an extra year's work by increasing N by one is normally not actuarially fair, because the value of total pension income will fall due to the larger relative decline in T.

4 *Actuarial inducements to retire*. The pension system may provide actuarial incentives to retire by giving a bonus to those who retire early. In a pension scheme designed to promote early retirement, workers who have reached a threshold age, say 60, with a given minimum length of service, say 30 years, may have their number of credited years of service made up to the maximum; i.e.

N may be arbitrarily raised from 30 to 40. This means the worker can retire early on a full pension, but cannot increase pension wealth by continuing in employment.

It is clear, therefore, that occupational pension scheme rules can give workers a very strong incentive to retire at a particular age *even if* their pension wealth is not sufficient to support them in a comfortable retirement, because further years of work will do nothing to increase the stock of pension wealth. Recent studies of company pension plans in the United States have shown that pension scheme rules do have a very large effect on the accrual of pension wealth and on employee retirement decisions (Kotlikoff and Wise, 1987, 1989).

How do these various theories and findings about the role of savings, assets and pensions relate to the retirement experience in twentieth-century Britain? It is clear that the average wealth of the population has risen over time, and that retirement rates have also risen, but this sort of casual correlation tells us nothing about causation. To demonstrate that rising wealth is the cause of increasing retirement, we would need to show that people have incorporated this secular trend in wealth into their life cycle financial plans, and at an early age decided that they would plan to save heavily in order to retire at an earlier age than older generations. There is little evidence that this has happened on the wide scale necessary to explain the trends in the labour force participation of older people outlined above. There has, for instance, been no secular increase in the aggregate savings rate in Britain over the course of the twentieth century; in fact personal savings rates have fallen sharply over the last decade when retirement rates have been rising rapidly, and personal wealth (including housing and other physical assets) has shown no increase relative to GDP (gross domestic product) for the last twenty-five years (HM Treasury, 1989b).

Nor does the pattern of occupational pension scheme membership lend ready support to wealth related explanations of retirement behaviour. The proportion of full-time employees in employer occupational pension schemes is shown in Table 4.4; the rising trend since the Second World War was reversed for men in 1967 and again in the mid-1980s when higher retirement and early retirement rates have been accompanied by a fall in the coverage of occupational pension schemes (Hannah, 1986: 67, 145; OPCS, 1989: 74–83). The primary reason for non-membership is that the employer does not operate a pension scheme, so it is obvious that some proportion of men and women who leave the workforce at or below the state pension age do so for reasons quite unrelated to pension scheme

Table 4.4   *Membership of occupational pension schemes in
Britain, percentage of total workforce, excluding unemployed*

	Number of members (millions)			Percentage employed who are members		
	Men	Women	Total	Men	Women	All
1936				–	–	13
1956	6.4	1.6	8.0	43	21	35
1963	9.4	1.7	11.1	63	21	48
1967	9.9	2.3	12.2	66	28	53
1971	8.7	2.4	11.1	62	28	49
1975	8.6	2.8	11.4	63	30	49
1979	8.3	3.3	11.6	62	35	50
1983	7.8	3.3	11.1	64	37	52
1987	7.2	3.4	10.6	60	35	49

Source: Government Actuary (1991: Table 2.1, p. 4)

rules, because they are not members of such schemes. Only in 1985 did the proportion of pensioners in receipt of an occupational pension creep above 50 per cent (up from 34 per cent in 1970 and 43 per cent in 1980), although coverage was higher among newly-retired pensioner couples, with 70 per cent receiving an occupational pension in 1985 (57 per cent in 1970, 66 per cent in 1980). Nevertheless, occupational pensions, which accounted for just 16 per cent of gross pensioner income in 1970 still made up only 20 per cent by 1985 (Dawson and Evans, 1987).

A further reason for questioning the role of rational economic calculus on the part of individuals contemplating retirement is that many workers do not know enough about the details of their specific pension scheme to work out the optimal time of retirement. Because the specifics of pension scheme rules vary so widely, workers who use a rule-of-thumb to decide on retirement may make very costly mistakes. One US study has found that for a 60 year old worker with 35 years service, one extra year at work can increase pension wealth by 12.8 per cent of the wage or decrease pension wealth by 0.6 per cent of the wage, depending on the rules of the particular pension scheme (Gustman and Steinmeier, 1988). Furthermore, pension schemes change their own rules quite significantly over time, so workers need to know the pension rules not just on entry to a scheme, but also in each successive year of membership (Mitchell and Luzadis, 1988). It seems simply implausible to believe that more than a handful of pension scheme members possess the knowledge of pension scheme rules and the actuarial abilities required to calculate their optimal date of retirement, and even if they manage this they need remarkable prescience and good fortune for their projections about interest, inflation and growth rates during their years of retirement to be a close approximation to reality. One recent piece of research into retirement behaviour uses highly sophisticated vector mathematics and the enormous power of a Cray supercomputer to develop a dynamic programming model of the retirement decision (Rust, 1989). However, as a sceptical commentator has remarked, the average reader will need persuading 'that the decision-making model provides a conceivable approximation to reality, as well as the best a consumer could do if he had a couple of hours on a Cray and the professional advice of a consulting economist' (Burtless, 1989: 403). The life cycle model itself does not depend on computing power, but it does demand a degree of faith in logical behaviourism. The model began as a heuristic device, a simple representation of the world 'as if' people behaved in a certain way, but it is now taken to be a valid behavioural postulate which should be verifiable by observational data; when examined in detail the data seem frequently to be wanting.

Yet it is clear that most people do make some financial plans for their old age, that many do have some degree of choice over when to retire, and that these saving and retirement plans are viewed as important issues rather than trivial decisions. As the data in Chapter Three showed, a significant proportion of retired people in Britain possess savings of some kind (often in the form of the home they own), which is an indication of prior accumulation during their peak earning years. Many retired people, however, are very poor, which suggests that the financial plans they made for old age were inadequate from the start or that other circumstances changed to such an extent (for instance, a rise in inflation) that their plans became inadequate. Until we can get a better understanding of why so many people seem unable to make adequate life-long financial plans, we have to remain sceptical about the general validity of the life cycle model. The spread of occupational pensions and other savings in old age has certainly provided more workers with a financial incentive to give up work, and may explain the increased popularity of retirement and early retirement among the rich, but it does not provide a satisfactory account of why so many manual workers with few savings and trivial or no occupational pensions give up work so young.

Social Security Pensions

A final factor that may act to lure workers into retirement is the receipt of a social security pension. Since in Britain state pensions have been paid, for most of this century, on a flat-rate basis, they are likely to have been a stronger inducement for low-paid manual workers to give up work than for better-paid white collar staff. Old age pensions were first paid in Britain in 1909 on a means-tested basis to people aged 70 or over. Eligible elderly people with an income below £21 a year received a pension of five shillings (25 pence) a week, those with an annual income above £31.10s. received nothing, and any one with an income between these lower and upper limits was entitled to a reduced rate pension.

This first old age pension represented (or replaced) about 17 per cent of the average weekly earnings of a male manual worker – a figure usually referred to as the pension replacement rate – and because the same pension was paid to both men and women, married or single, the replacement rate for a married couple was around 35 per cent. This was not enough to live on, and the pension was not intended to provide for all the necessities of life, but rather to supplement casual earnings, savings, and contributions from family, friends and charity. The need for this pension is shown by the high take-up rate; despite the severe means-test, by 1912 over 60 per cent of the 70 plus age group were regularly collecting their pensions (Hannah, 1986: 16). It is clear, however, that the availability of this pension did not precipitate a flight out of employment and into retirement by elderly workers. Figure 4.1 shows that the downward movement of the unadjusted labour force participation rate for men over 65 did not accelerate after 1908, and when adjusted for sectoral shifts in the economy this participation rate is found to be virtually constant between 1881 and 1921 (Johnson, 1991: 16).

From 1928 contributory pensions were paid under the national insurance scheme to insured workers over 65 who had paid the requisite number of contributions. There was no means-test for these insurance pensions and no retirement condition – payment was made irrespective of income or employment. This meant that the economic incentive to withdraw from the workforce was less than for the earlier means-tested pensions. In fact in the late 1930s 55 per cent of pensioners remained at work at age 65, and 12.5 per cent were still working at 75 (Beveridge Report, 1942: 197).

This widespread practice of continued employment beyond the state pension age was curtailed by the pension rules of the 1946 National Insurance Act, which required workers to retire from full-time employment in order to qualify for a pension. A retirement rule or earnings limit was applied to all recipients of state pensions until 1989, and this restriction almost certainly acted to promote retirement at 65 for men and 60 for women. However, the rule

Table 4.5   *Retirement pension as percentage of average male earnings, UK 1948–2050*

	As percentage male manual earnings	As percentage male earnings
1948	19.1	—
1955	18.4	—
1961	19.1	—
1965	21.4	—
1971	19.5	17.5
1975	21.5	19.6
1981	22.9	19.8
1985	22.5	19.2
1990	—	16.0
2000	—	14.0
2010	—	12.0
2020	—	10.0
2030	—	9.0
2040	—	8.0
2050	—	7.0

Note: Projections from 1990 assume the pension is updated in line with prices, and that real earnings grow at 1.5 per cent per annum.
Sources: Department of Health Social Security (1986: 262–3); Government Actuary (1990: 18)

existed for forty-three years during which time the participation rate for men over 65 fell from over 30 per cent to 8.8 per cent, so it does not appear to be an adequate explanation of post-war retirement trends.

Retirement decisions are likely to be affected not just by the rules governing the payment of the state pension but also by the value of this pension. If the pension replacement rate rises over time, then this could have a major impact on retirement propensities at age 65. A pronounced increase in the real value of state pensions may also increase retirement rates below pension age if people are careful life-time planners. An unanticipated increase in the value of the state pension after age 65 (60 for women) will allow the life cycle saver to begin using up private savings from an earlier age, and so will allow retirement to take place at a younger age than originally planned. In practice, however, as can be seen from Table 4.5, the replacement value of the state pension has not followed a simple upward trend since the Second World War, and the indexation of the basic state pension to prices rather than earnings since 1979 means that the replacement rate is now falling and is projected to fall in the future. Even so, an increase in other assets available to older people, in combination with a stable or declining state pension replacement rate, could have served to increase retirement incentives over time. It seems unlikely, however, that this has occurred. As Table 3.2 shows, social security benefits (primarily state pensions) provided about 59 per cent of pensioners' incomes in 1986, compared with 55 per cent in 1974, 51 per cent in 1970 and around 42 per cent in 1951 (Fiegehen, 1986; Dawson and Evans, 1987). Far from declining in importance, social security benefits have increased their share of pensioner incomes, despite the unimpressive performance of the state pension replacement rate.

Although, as was shown in Chapter Three, pensioners' real incomes have increased substantially since the Second World War, most retired people in Britain have neither high incomes nor luxurious lifestyles, and around one-third are so poor that they qualify for means-tested income support. In general the relative meanness of state pensions in Britain suggests that state pension entitlements will have less influence on retirement decisions here relative to other countries. Table 3.1 shows that the pension replacement rate between 1969 and 1980 was generally lower in the United Kingdom than in other developed countries yet, as Figure 4.2 shows, UK participation rates over this period have not been noticeably higher than for countries with much more generous pension systems.

This is not to say that state pensions have no impact on retirement rates – if there is any element of personal economic calculation in the decision to retire, then the qualification at a particular age for a state pension must influence the decision. This has been confirmed by a study of the labour supply decisions of the elderly carried out by Zabalza et al. (1980). Income effects associated with pension payments were significant in explaining which men under pension age retired early and which over pension age continued to be economically active, but the model could not explain the abrupt change in participation at age 65 solely in terms of changes in the budget constraint. The authors concluded that there appeared to be a shift at age 65 in the income/leisure preference of many men, and/or a sudden fall in the demand for workers at that age. The financial inducements of the British state pension therefore seem to have a positive impact on retirement decisions, a finding which has been replicated in detailed studies of the US and West German pension systems (Börsch-Supan, 1991). These financial inducements are not, however, a complete explanation; other important factors appear to be structural conditions of the labour market or non-economic elements of personal choice.

Assessing Alternative Explanations

This survey of the factors which may push or pull older people out of the labour force has shown that all the explanations advanced are potentially valid, but none of them can provide an adequate account of retirement behaviour on their own. This is perhaps not surprising; we know that older people are no more homogeneous than any other broad age group in society, that the social and economic circumstances of the elderly population vary across countries and have changed greatly over time, and that retirement is for many people a complex process of withdrawal from the labour force which is spread over a number of years, rather than a simple work/leisure trade-off. In these circumstances, it would be remarkable if any simple monocausal explanation of retirement behaviour were to be convincing; perhaps instead we should be looking for a ranking of the relative importance of the different explanatory factors for distinct groups of retirees.

Laczko et al. (1988) found that the early retired individuals they studied could be divided into two groups, the 'poor', who had few assets or pension rights and who had been driven into premature retirement by bad health, and the 'non-poor' who had chosen to give up work early in order to enjoy well-financed leisure. Johnson (1989b) looked at retirement rates for men by industrial sector for Census years between 1951 and 1981 and found that structural factors (proxied by trade union density) were the most important determinants of retirement at 65, that income and wealth were the key determinants of early retirement, and that unemployment and health were of little significance. On the other hand, Walker (1985), in his study of Sheffield steelworkers, found labour market conditions – the rate of unemployment and the availability of similar jobs – to be an important influence on the retirement decision. Warburton (1987) using a budget line analysis that focuses on the financial cost of retirement, found that the high pension replacement rates for low paid manual workers gave this group a much lower optimum retirement age than better-paid non-manual staff, though he noted that 'subjective attitudes to work must remain a major ingredient of the personal retirement decision'.

Why is there apparently no consistent ranking of the competing explanatory factors in these and other studies of retirement? There are three primary reasons: different investigators address different questions, they do so from different theoretical perspectives, and they attempt to provide some empirical resolution by applying different research methodologies. Many, but not all, of these differences stem from the individualistic focus of much economic research compared with the macro-social concerns of sociological investigation. The sort of questions economists tend to ask are: 'Why does A retire at 63 but B retire at 65?' or 'What inducements would A need to retire one year earlier or one year later?' or 'How large an incentive to retire is the provision of a state or occupational pension at a particular age?', and by extension 'What impact will a change in pension rules or the value of pensions have on A's or B's retirement decision?' These questions derive from an economic theory in which calculating individuals are empowered to take economic and social decisions which will maximize their (broadly defined) utility. Each individual's array of choices will be conditioned by many personal and social circumstances – health, wealth, human capital, employment opportunities, tax regulations, and so on – but retirement is conceived of as a personal decision, and retirement trends in a society are therefore no more and no less than the summation of personal decisions. This sort of explanatory framework requires detailed data about all the conditions which may influence an individual's retirement decision, from which models can be constructed which allow predictions to be made about the impact on retirement decisions of marginal changes in one or more of the determining variables.

By contrast, sociologists tend to ask why retirement rates have changed so dramatically over the course of the twentieth century and how these trends are related to the working of capitalist economies, why there is diversity in retirement rates between countries at similar stages of economic development, and how fashion, culture, ideology and politics affect retirement patterns. These questions derive from broad theories about the nature and causes of social change, about the structure and function of social institutions in market economies, and about the exercise of economic and political power by competing or collaborating interest groups.

Retirement is viewed as a social process, part of that formal age structuring of the life course which is apparent in all developed economies, in which entry into the labour force in youth is regulated by the legal requirements of education, and exit in old age is influenced or controlled by pension rules and retirement norms (Kohli, 1986; Hagestad, 1990). From this perspective, data relating to particular individuals and a particular time period cannot possibly provide a full explanation of current retirement behaviour, because retirement is a collective social expectation that has become normalized in the second half of the twentieth century. The research methodology tends to use long-run data sets and make international comparisons in order to identify the reasons for the development of this social norm. Although objective economic and structural factors have some part to play in this sort of explanatory framework, considerable emphasis is placed on social values, aspirations and cultural orientations (Inkeles and Usui, 1988).

The attraction of the sociological approach is its broad scope and enormous ambition to link retirement into a general model of socioeconomic development, but this can produce seemingly vague and imprecise conclusions. The individualistic tack taken by most economists, on the other hand, can give apparently precise answers to clearly specified questions such as 'What will be the impact on the labour supply of a typical 64 year old man of an unexpected 5 per cent increase in pension wealth?', but when changes in the key variables are non-marginal, precision gives way to speculation. Most of the very detailed studies of retirement behaviour carried out in the United States have used microdata relating to the 1970s and early 1980s when the crucial features (age thresholds, earnings tests) of the US public pension system did not change. As Allen (1988: 298) has noted, 'the only potential sources of exogenous variation in key parameters were changes in real benefits and payroll taxes'. This does not matter if the questions we wish to answer relate to marginal changes in financial parameters, and in the short run most questions about retirement behaviour will almost certainly be framed in this rather narrow way. But over the next two or three decades, as the age structure of the developed economies changes dramatically we can be less confident that retirement conditions will experience only marginal changes or that the social conception of retirement will maintain its current position. We may find that an understanding of the way in which social norms are created or reformulated is more useful than an ability to calculate the present discounted value of pension wealth.

The diversity of routes out of the labour market at older ages, and the variety of economic and social influences on the retirement process, suggests that both individual financial calculus and the pressure of social norms come to bear on the retirement decision, but in different ways and magnitudes for different people. Some older workers are undoubtedly pushed out of the labour market, others are lured by the attractions of a more leisured life, and their economic well-being in retirement is to some large extent determined by whether they jumped or whether they were pushed. The future welfare of the growing older population will, therefore, be intimately linked with changes in employment and pensioning practice, and this practice will itself respond to demographic pressures. Whether population ageing will in fact transform these socioeconomic relationships, rather than merely alter them at the margin, is something we will move on to consider in the next two chapters.

5

Public Pensions, Government Expenditure and Intergenerational Transfers

Public pensions and other welfare provisions can, as the previous chapter has shown, affect older people through the incentives or disincentives they provide for continued labour force participation and through the way they enhance the welfare of older individuals. However, they also have a much broader economic impact on people of all ages through the transfer requirements they place on the tax system. The cash transfers that constitute the public pension system, the services provided by publicly employed doctors and nurses, the housing and other welfare benefits enjoyed by some older people, all depend on other people paying for them. Who pays, how much they pay, and in what manner they make the payments will be the central issues of this chapter.

It has been claimed by some observers that in an ageing society the scale and nature of public provision for the elderly may generate devastating economic and social problems, culminating in economic stagnation and conflict between people of different generations. Others have suggested that public pension and welfare systems will require no more than minor adjustments to accommodate the developing requirements of an ageing society. In this chapter we will first consider why it has been argued by some that population ageing may generate real economic problems for the public sector, and then we will go on to examine the extent and nature of this public pension and welfare system, and consider how it is likely to respond in Britain and other countries to population ageing.

Pensions, Savings and Transfers

Arguments about the way in which public pension schemes should be financed, and about the costs and benefits that alternative systems of financing may impose on different cohorts, are not a creation of the 1970s and 1980s. Over fifty years ago, when social security pension systems were in their infancy, the twin issues of finance and transfers were addressed directly by policy advisers and politicians. In the United States in the 1930s there was considerable debate among insurance and social security experts about the long-run costs of public old age provision under the newly introduced system of Old Age and Survivors Insurance (Achenbaum, 1989: 116–21). The US Treasury (and President Roosevelt) wanted to accumulate a large reserve fund to cover future benefit liabilities and protect general government revenue from future claims from the social security account. Business leaders, on the other hand, feared that the accumulation of a large reserve would diminish consumer purchasing power and adversely affect the capital market (Quadagno, 1988: 119–21). In 1939 a substantial amendment was made to the original 1935 Social Security Act which widened the scope of benefits and increased their generosity without changing the level of contributions. This began the shift of the US social security system from being a fully-funded scheme, in which future liabilities were covered by a reserve fund, to being a pay-as-you-go scheme in which this year's contributions pay this year's benefits. Over the twenty years from 1940 the ratio of reserves to benefits fell from 33:1 to 2:1 (Weaver, 1982: 129).

Much the same happened in the United Kingdom. The social insurance system planned by William Beveridge (Beveridge Report, 1942) and adopted by the post-war Labour government in 1945 envisaged a contributory old age pension system in which benefits were actuarially linked to contributions, and in which a reserve fund would be built up in the early years to pay for later pension benefits. This plan required full pension entitlements to be deferred for twenty years while an adequate reserve fund was being accumulated, but in order to assist pensioners on fixed incomes who were struggling to cope with the after-effects of wartime inflation, the government began in 1946 to pay the full state pension to all retired people over pension age (60 for women, 65 for men). The Government Actuary expressed his concern at the size of future pension liabilities that were not being covered by adequate contributions; only by raising contributions without offering any improved benefits for two or three decades could the long-run financial solvency of the National Insurance scheme be re-established. Political pressures, on the other hand, were pointing in the opposite direction, for an increase in benefits which were falling behind earnings as real incomes rose in the 1950s. The way out of this problem was to abandon the idea of building up a fund to cover future pension liabilities, and instead use current contributions to pay current benefits. By 1958 the British National Insurance system, like US Social Security, had changed from being a funded to a pay-as-you-go system, with the insurance 'fund' aiming merely to balance income and expenditure over each year (Dilnot et al., 1984).

This shift through the 1950s away from the original social security conception of full funding towards pay-as-you-go financing received little by way of adverse comment. Rapid economic growth and relatively small cohorts of pensioners allowed benefits to rise faster than contributions; income security in old age was enhanced, poverty diminished, and overall welfare raised. The effect of social security on the economy appeared to be benign, or even positive, assisting governments in their counter-cyclical macroeconomic management. But the economic stagnation ushered in by the major oil price increase of 1973 inaugurated a much more critical analysis of economic performance and economic management in the developed countries. Social security systems which had been seen as the handmaidens of growth in the 1960s were now seen as obstacles to economic efficiency (Johnson, forthcoming). This critique of social security was broad ranging (OECD, 1981), extending well beyond the specifics of public pension systems, but with pensions typically consuming close to half of the social security budget in the OECD countries these public transfers to older people increasingly came under the scrutiny of economists.

This economic concern about the long-run cost of public transfers to older people has followed two distinct but related paths since the mid-1970s, one looking at macroeconomic effects, the other emphasizing microeconomic transfers. The macroeconomic approach was initiated by Martin Feldstein (1974) who was concerned not so much with the dynamics of population ageing but with the behavioural responses to social security pensions. He argued, initially on the basis of US data but later in a more generalized way with international cross-section data (Feldstein, 1977), that public pensions tend to lower the long-run rate of growth of the economy. The mechanics of this process derive from a life cycle model of savings behaviour. Feldstein argued that in a world in which retirement (or considerably reduced income) in old age is anticipated, and in which individuals can reasonably expect to live into old age, people will save during their working life in order to support themselves in retirement. If, in these circumstances, a public pension system is introduced which guarantees an income to elderly retirees, working-age adults will reduce their savings and aim to accumulate a smaller net wealth by the time retirement age is reached. If all individuals respond in this way, the overall rate of personal savings in the economy will fall, and, other things being equal, this will force up interest rates making borrowing more expensive and investment less profitable. A fall in the rate of net investment will reduce the long-term growth rate of the economy; Feldstein (1974: 923) estimated that if there had been no public pension system in the United States over the period 1937–71, national income in 1971 would have been 11–15 per cent higher than its actual value.

The depressive effect on saving rates will be avoided if government saving acts as a direct substitute for personal saving. This can happen if the government levies taxes on working age adults equal in value to the savings individuals would have undertaken in the absence of a public pension scheme (i.e. if it funds the pension scheme), *and* if the government then makes this tax fund available for private sector investment (or, in the case of perfect substitutability between public and private borrowing, reduces public borrowing). In practice, however, governments seldom behave in this way. Social security taxes are not used to accumulate a fund which can substitute for private savings, because virtually all public pension systems operate on a pay-as-you-go basis with this year's contributions (taxes) equalling this year's benefits. Furthermore, governments have tended to use surplus income from social security systems not to support new public or private investment or to reduce other public borrowing requirements, but instead directly to boost public expenditure and indirectly to boost private expenditure by means of transfer payments and tax cuts.

This life cycle view of the depressive effect of pay-as-you-go public pensions on personal saving depends on the behavioural assumption that individuals consciously plan their economic actions over their whole lifespan in order to maximize their lifetime utility. Current economic decisions relating to work and leisure, consumption and saving, are assumed to be determined by their anticipated impact on lifetime wealth, earnings and rate of return on savings. But other behavioural assumptions – that people adopt planning horizons either longer or shorter than their own life cycle – also need to be considered. The fact that some people deliberately make bequests has been interpreted to mean that they derive some benefit from the economic well-being of future generations – in other words they exhibit a multigenerational planning horizon (Barro, 1974, 1978). If, in these circumstances, a pay-as-you-go public pension is introduced, the windfall gain of present generations in being granted pension rights will be balanced by the losses (tax liabilities) of future generations who will have to pay for these pensions. Current generations will therefore find that they need to save *less* to finance their own old age, but need to save *more* in order to increase their bequests sufficiently to compensate their successor generations for their increased tax liabilities. These two effects will tend to cancel each other out, leaving overall saving rates unchanged.

Both the life cycle and multigenerational models of savings behaviour have attracted, and continue to attract, considerable attention from economists who appreciate their elegance and rational consistency. However, they have received criticism both from within and especially from outside the discipline of economics for their behavioural implausibility (Thaler, 1990). Although some professors of economics may consistently adopt rational lifetime utility maximizing plans, many other mortals do not. Instead they make use of shorter, and possibly variable, planning horizons, either because the cost of processing all available information about the future is too high, or because the future is too uncertain, or because they discount the future so heavily that events more than a few years ahead have little bearing on current decisions (Aaron, 1982: 23–6). In the context of the relationship between social security and saving, this short horizon model implies that younger workers perceive social security contributions simply as a tax which reduces their consumption, but that older workers begin to take account of the benefits as they approach retirement age, and increase their consumption slightly. The aggregate effect on savings, however, is likely to be minimal.

The theoretical indeterminacy of the impact of social security on savings has forced economists to resort to empirical assessments. This has spawned a vast literature which has greatly increased our understanding of the potential economic effects of social security but which has not been able to produce either conclusive support for, or conclusive refutation of, the argument that public pensions reduce savings and inhibit growth (for a survey see Aaron, 1982). It has, however, made people aware that social security pensions can offer very unequal benefits to people born at different times, and this has drawn attention away from macroeconomic effects to the microeconomic transfer functions of social security pensions.

Despite the frequent use of the term 'fund' in relation to social security financing, in practice most social security funds are little more than holding accounts used to balance out uneven flows of income and expenditure over the course of a year. Although today's retirees may *feel* that they have been saving for their public pension throughout their working life in the form of social security contributions or payroll taxes, there is no stock of assets, no pot of gold, to which they can turn for financial support in old age. They have to rely on the current workforce making sufficient contributions to pay today's pensions. In an entirely static world with no economic growth or inflation and no changes in fertility or mortality, this type of pay-as-you-go public pension system is no different in its operation from a fully-funded pension system – the amounts being paid in to and out of the pension scheme will be equal and the lifetime contributions and lifetime benefits of each birth cohort will be identical. But public pension schemes do not operate in a static world, neither are the pension systems themselves static institutions; changes in these conditions in the 1980s have had a profound impact on the workings of public pension systems.

For a pay-as-you-go pension system to be sustained in the long run, successive birth cohorts must accept that they will pass through a phase of net contribution during working life before entering a phase of net benefit during retirement. There exists, in effect, an implicit contract between birth cohorts or generations to honour transfer obligations which are codified in national laws, but the specific terms of which can be altered by the passage of new laws or by administrative amendments. Until the 1980s there was little incentive for people to quibble with this unwritten intergenerational contract because each successive birth cohort did rather well out of it, for a mixture of demographic and economic reasons. For most of the twentieth century the number of pension recipients has been quite small compared with the number of people of working age, so the current tax contributions required to pay current pensions have also been quite small. Furthermore, long-run economic growth has enabled successive generations to be relatively generous to their elders and pay out in pensions far greater sums than these pensioner generations themselves paid in contributions when they were of working age. This does not mean that pensioners have always experienced the same rate of economic improvement as that enjoyed by the working population, but it does mean that successive cohorts of pensioners have reaped some of the benefits of economic growth produced by the labours of their children.

By the 1980s, however, the favourable demographic and economic trends that underpinned the widespread support for unfunded pension schemes which appeared to offer successive generations far more than they had paid for began to turn sour. In most western countries large numbers of survivors from the high fertility birth cohorts of the early years of this century were entering retirement and living a longer retirement, while the size of the working age population was remaining fairly stable. This had the inevitable effect of raising the old age dependency ratio (see Figure 2.7), and hence the number of state pensioners who have to be supported by the productive effort and taxable capacity of the employed population.

The potential effect of a change in the ratio of contributors to beneficiaries in a hypothetical unfunded pension system in a static economy is illustrated in Table 5.1. In this example the first cohort (A) contains two people, and population grows over the next six generations before beginning to decline. Each member of each

Table 5.1   *The contributions and benefits of successive cohorts in a hypothetical pay-as-you-go pension system*

Cohort	A	B	C	D	E	F	G	H	I	J
Cohort size	2	3	4	5	6	7	8	7	6	5
Contributions	0	30	40	50	60	70	80	70	60	50
Contributions per capita	0	10	10	10	10	10	10	10	10	10
Benefits	30	40	50	60	70	80	70	60	50	40
Benefits per capita	15	13.3	12.5	12.0	11.7	11.4	8.75	8.57	8.33	8

generation contributes £10 to the social security system while working, and each generation draws a pension funded from the contributions of its successor generation (cohort B pays for cohort A's pensions, C pays for B, D pays for C, and so on). When the population is growing, each generation enjoys pension benefits greater than its pension contributions, and so the value of individual pension benefits is always higher than the individual contributions of £10 made during working life. Larger gains are enjoyed by the earlier cohorts because of their small size relative to the working population, and the greatest gains are captured by the initial generation which pays no contributions but receives windfall benefits. However, when population begins to decline (from generation G) the pension funds available for each generation become smaller than that generation's net contributions when working; per capita contributions now exceed benefits. When the transfer chain is increasing everyone gains, as each generation receives back more than it pays in, but when the transfer chain is decreasing everyone loses (Keyfitz, 1988).

It was just this sort of demographic effect on existing public pension systems, identified as a rise in the dependency ratio, which began to concern economists and policy analysts in the late 1970s and 1980s. Little attempt was made to analyse this crude demographic dependency ratio along the lines advocated in Chapter Two in order to see whether it was an economically meaningful measure; instead it was taken to imply that the elderly population was becoming an increasing economic burden on society, and one which perhaps could not be sustained in the long run.

This interpretation of demographic trends, therefore, was beginning to cast elderly people in the role of economic parasites. At the same time western economies were suffering an acute economic depression which put an end, at least temporarily, to the post-war experience of sustained economic growth, and this in turn began to affect the operation of the unfunded pension system in two ways. First, it brought into question the idea that pensioners could always receive in benefits more than they had paid in as contributions because of the benign impact of increases in real incomes. With stagnant incomes, there would be no surplus for generous working populations to bestow on their elders. Second, the widespread unemployment which was a consequence of economic stagnation meant that many people of working age could now no longer afford to support themselves, let alone make tax contributions towards the support of the retired elderly. The principle underlying the unfunded public pension system, that people of working age were in a stronger economic position than those past the age of retirement, appeared to be crumbling.

The implications of these demographic and economic trends for social security systems in general, and public pensions in particular, were examined first in the United States. The impetus came from a demographic analysis of the changing age structure of the US population and the likely future cost of an ageing population for a US social security system already perceived to be in a state of financial crisis. Population projections indicated that social security payroll taxes would have to rise sharply in the early years of the twenty-first century when the baby-boom generation began to retire if pension levels were to be sustained. In 1983 an amendment to the social security system was introduced to finesse this problem by increasing old age insurance contributions and by raising the pension entitlement age in steps from the current age of 65 to 67 between the years 2003 and 2027 (*Report of the National Commission on Social Security Reform*, 1983).

The immediate financial problem for the social security budget of an ageing population was thus avoided (or at least postponed), but debate about the working of the social security system was not curtailed. One particularly important contribution came from the demographer Samuel Preston (1984) in his presidential address to the Population Association of America. Preston pointed out that between 1970 and 1982 the incidence of poverty among US elderly citizens had fallen sharply while among children under 14 it had increased. These divergent trends, he argued, were a consequence of a social security system which was becoming increasingly generous to the elderly while at the same time adopting a more severe attitude towards the funding of public services and welfare payments for children or families with dependent children. The family, it appeared, was being expected to take an ever greater moral and financial responsibility for the welfare of children at just that time when it was losing its functional ability to do so because of high and rising rates of divorce and family disintegration.

Preston saw this dramatic change in the age profile of well-being in modern America as the unplanned result of a number of apparently unrelated private and public choices, and he suggested that society should consider whether it really wanted to redistribute resources away from children in the manner and to the degree experienced in the preceding fifteen years. He was very careful in his address to avoid any explicit suggestion that children and the elderly were direct competitors for a fixed sum of public resources, though he did note that 'transfers from the working-age population to the elderly are also transfers away from children, since the working ages bear far more responsibility for child rearing than do the elderly'.

Subsequent commentators have been less careful and less subtle in their analysis. Philip Longman (1987) in an influential book *Born to Pay*, has argued that younger generations in the United States are in inevitable conflict with their elders, and in particular with the baby-boom generation who show no sign of relinquishing their historical entitlements to social security transfers as they move through middle age and towards retirement. The old are getting richer at the expense of the young, says Longman, not because of an increase in the relative need of older generations, but instead because of the way automatic resource transfers from young to old have become enshrined in modern social security systems. Such transfers made sense when, in the early and mid-twentieth century, to be old generally meant to be poor, but they no longer do so when the average net income and wealth of the younger paying households is lower than that of the elderly recipients. 'We cannot afford', writes Longman, 'to promise today's elderly, or our future selves, that for the last 20–25 per cent of adult life we will all be automatically entitled to subsidized consumption and be free from labor' (Longman, 1987: 247). A rise in the normal age of retirement, and the means-testing of all social security benefits are his preferred solutions to the perceived problem of inequity.

Longman has been a key actor in a pressure group, Americans for Generational Equity (AGE), which has lobbied quite successfully to bring the issue of generational conflict into the political and electoral arena in the United States in an attempt to counter the political influence of old-age pressure groups such as the American Association of Retired Persons. The battle lines of generational warfare have been sharply delineated, and brought into striking relief by arguments that life extending health care for the elderly should be restricted in order to provide better life improving health care for young and old alike (Callahan, 1987). But in practice neither the scale and nature of the resource transfers that will be initiated by further population ageing, nor the implications for government expenditure and borrowing, are as straightforward as many protagonists in this debate have suggested.

Public Pensions and Transfers in Practice

The scale of the net intergenerational resource transfer that is created by the social security system is a crucial element in any assessment of the overall economic impact of social security. The fact that different generations receive varying treatment from a public pension system as a population ages may be of almost no consequence if the variation in contributions and benefits is small relative to their overall level. This is entirely an empirical question, which depends on both the scale and pattern of demographic change and the institutional structure of each particular social security system.

Detailed comparative studies of the financial effect of demographic change on social security systems in the developed economies have been carried out by the International Monetary Fund (Heller et al., 1986) and the Organization for Economic Cooperation and Development (OECD, 1988a). By applying demographic projections to current social security expenditure patterns, estimates can be derived of future social security costs. Table 5.2 shows the OECD projections of the impact of demographic change on the share of pension expenditure in national income, assuming that the ratio of pension benefit to national income per worker remains constant. It can be seen that population ageing is projected to drive up the cost of public pension provision in all countries over the next fifty years.

Although public pension expenditure is the major item in national social security budgets, it is far from being the only one, so a concentration on pensions alone will not give a balanced view of the total impact of population ageing on social security expenditure. In 1985 public expenditure on health care averaged 5.6 per cent of GDP in the OECD countries (OECD, 1988c: 42), and much of this was directed towards elderly people. In Britain the proportion of hospital and community health service expenditure directed to people aged over 65 rose from 43 per cent in 1974 to 51 per cent in 1983, and this was almost entirely due to an increase in the number of people aged 75 plus, who on average cost the service nine times as much each year as persons aged 16–64 (Johnson and Falkingham, 1988: 143–4). These high average health care costs for people aged 75 plus are common to all countries, and are a function of the high rates of physical frailty and mental impairment incurred at these ages. In the United States in 1978, for instance, the proportion of

Table 5.2   *Influence of demographic change on the share of pension expenditure in national income,*[a][b] *1984–2040*

	1960	1984	Projections 2000	2020	2040
Australia	3.8	6.0	6.7	9.1	12.4
Austria	10.9	16.5	17.6	23.7	31.7
Belgium	na	14.0[d]	13.8	17.0	22.7
Canada	3.2	6.1	7.6	11.6	15.2
Denmark	5.0	10.1	9.5	13.5	18.7
Finland	4.3	8.5	9.7	16.0	17.8
France	6.7	14.3	16.5	21.6	27.0
Germany	10.5	13.7	16.4	21.6	31.1
Greece	3.9[e]	10.8	13.0	15.7	19.5
Ireland	2.6	6.7	6.2	6.8	9.9
Italy	5.9	16.9	19.7	25.6	35.7
Japan	1.5	6.0	9.4	14.0	15.7
Netherlands	4.3	12.1	13.4	19.6	28.5
New Zealand	4.7	8.9	9.3	13.0	20.3
Norway	3.6	9.6	9.0	11.0	15.0
Portugal	1.5[e]	8.2	10.6	12.1	16.9
Spain	2.7[f]	10.0	11.7	13.6	20.4
Sweden	4.9	12.9	12.1	15.9	18.0
Switzerland	2.5	8.8	10.6	16.9	21.1
UK	4.3	7.7	7.5	8.6	11.2
US	4.6	8.1	8.2	11.3	14.6
OECD average[c]	4.6	10.3	11.4	15.1	20.2

[a] The projections show only the impact of demographic change. They assume constant benefit levels per beneficiary relative to national income per worker, constant labour force participation rates and constant proportions of elderly people in receipt of benefits
[b] OECD medium fertility variant
[c] Arithmetic mean
[d] Expenditure ratio for 1983
[e] Expenditure ratio for 1962
[f] Expenditure ratio for 1967

Source: OECD (1988b: 35, 138–41)

the elderly population suffering from dementia ranged from 2.1 per cent of people aged 65–69 to 8.0 per cent of those aged 75–79 and 17.7 per cent of people aged 80 plus (OECD, 1988c: 45–6). The financial implications of this steep age gradient in the use of health care services are considerable, because the very elderly population is projected to grow rapidly over the next fifty years (as is shown above in Chapter Two). Even if real per capita health expenditure for people of different ages remains fixed at its current level (an unlikely assumption since health care expenditures have risen considerably faster than real incomes over the last twenty-five years), there will be a substantial increase in the funding liability for contributors over the next fifty years because of the ageing of the population (OECD, 1988a: 63).

Some compensation for the higher pension and health care costs of an ageing population is likely to come from the education budget since, as was shown in Chapter Three, this is concentrated on the shrinking child and young adult populations (Pearson et al., 1989). However, the total *public* costs of support for children aged under 15 are considerably less than public costs of support for people aged over 65. In 1980 the per capita public outlays on those aged 65 plus exceeded outlays on those aged under 15 by a factor of between 2.1 (Belgium, Denmark and the United Kingdom) and 3.8 (Italy and the United States), with the OECD average standing at 2.7 (OECD, 1988a: 34). Taking the twelve major OECD countries together, it is estimated that over the period 1980–2040, demographic change will lead to an 18 per cent reduction in education expenditure and a 15 per cent reduction in family benefits, but health expenditures will rise by 40 per cent and pension expenditure by almost 80 per cent. The overall impact of demographic change will be to raise social expenditure by around 30 per cent (OECD, 1988a: 36).

This increase in social expenditure will coincide with a stagnation and then decline in the size of the potential working population aged 15–64 in the industrialized countries. This will increase what the OECD calls the 'financing burden' of social expenditure, which it calculates by comparing the projected changes in total social expenditure due to demographic factors with projected changes in the size of the population of working age. Table 5.3 shows the projected evolution of both social expenditure and the 'financing burden' from a 1980 base of 100. The implication of this table is that social security tax or contribution rates will have to rise in all the developed countries over the next forty years to pay for the higher social security costs of an older population.

Projections such as these are only as good, bad or plausible as their assumptions. Fertility rates may rise very rapidly in the future, mortality and morbidity rates at higher ages may decline sharply, current age specific patterns of labour force participation may be fundamentally altered, and the real per capita value of benefits may either rise or fall. The OECD projections in fact assume that there will be modest gains in life expectancy for older people, that fertility rates will converge towards a replacement level of 2.1 by 2050, and that labour force participation rates and real per capita benefits will

Table 5.3　*Impact of demographic change on social expenditure and financing burdens, 1980–2040[a]*

	1990	2000	2010	2020	2030	2040
Australia						
Social expenditure	116	130	146	166	190	207
Financing burden per head 15–64 age group	99	100	103	112	124	130
Belgium						
Social expenditure	98	96	98	101	104	102
Financing burden per head 15–64 age group	96	95	97	103	116	120
Canada						
Social expenditure	111	124	141	162	181	187
Financing burden per head 15–64 age group	100	103	109	125	143	145
Denmark						
Social expenditure	97	91	92	91	90	88
Financing burden per head 15–64 age group	94	88	95	103	115	126
France						
Social expenditure	106	109	116	124	130	128
Financing burden per head 15–64 age group	99	100	104	116	128	132
Germany						
Social expenditure	98	104	104	103	106	97
Financing burden per head 15–64 age group	95	106	113	124	149	154
Italy						
Social expenditure	103	103	108	111	113	107
Financing burden per head 15–64 age group	97	99	106	116	131	139
Japan						
Social expenditure	113	125	141	141	136	140
Financing burden per head 15–64 age group	103	115	137	142	140	154
Netherlands						
Social expenditure	105	111	115	119	123	121
Financing burden per head 15–64 age group	96	100	104	114	131	139
Sweden						
Social expenditure	101	98	101	107	111	109
Financing burden per head 15–64 age group	99	95	100	110	119	122
United Kingdom						
Social expenditure	98	97	101	105	113	110
Financing burden per head 15–64 age group	95	93	96	101	112	111
United States						
Social expenditure	107	112	125	147	162	165
Financing burden per head 15–64 age group	99	96	99	117	132	131

[a] Base year 1980 = 100
Source: OECD (1988a: 41)

remain at their current level. All these assumptions may be questioned, and the OECD has itself experimented with alternative mortality and fertility projections, although their overall effect is relatively slight. The crucial assumptions, however, are those which relate to labour force participation and benefit levels.

The 'financing burden' calculated by the OECD is a fairly crude economic use of the basic age dependency ratio, the limitations of which were discussed in Chapter Two. Schmähl (1990: 163) has demonstrated just how sensitive even a crude age dependency ratio can be to alternative definitions. Using identical demographic assumptions about fertility, mortality and migration, projections of the age dependency ratio for the Federal Republic of Germany from 1985 to 2030 show an increase of 100 per cent when the earnings age span is taken to be 20–65, 111 per cent when taken to be 20–60, and 127 per cent when taken to be 15–65. Furthermore, if the intention is to calculate the probable increase in tax or contribution rates necessary to cover the increased public costs of demographic change, then the relevant denominator is obviously not the total population aged 15–64 but rather the population contributing to the social security system.

As shown in Chapter Two, a plausible *economic* dependency ratio is one that uses age and sex specific participation and unemployment rates to determine the size of the contributor population, and age and sex specific rates of benefit receipt to determine the number of beneficiaries. Economic dependency ratios in the developed countries are consistently higher than age dependency ratios, because although crude age categories for children and pensioners approximate quite closely the total number of beneficiaries, the age group 15–64 significantly over-estimates the number of social security tax payers since it makes no allowance for the large numbers of women with unwaged domestic responsibilities. The difference in *levels* between alternative definitions of age or economic dependency ratios can be large. However, long-run projections of these various ratios show that the *trends* are very similar (Hagemann and Nicoletti, 1989: 65), reflecting the fact that unless age and sex specific participation rates change dramatically over the next fifty years, demographic change will increase the per capita funding requirements placed on social security contributors. It should be borne in mind, of course, that age and sex specific participation rates have changed considerably in all developed countries since the Second World War, and it is possible that they will exhibit very great changes in the future. Even so, the demographic impetus will be for higher social security contributions.

Whether this increase will be large or small depends almost entirely on what happens to benefits. Since the determination of benefit levels and eligibility is part of the political process, this means that the influence of demographic change on social security financing is likely to be secondary to political pressures. This has certainly been true in the past. Table 5.2 shows that between 1960 and 1984 the share of pension expenditure in national income grew rapidly in all the OECD countries – in fact at a rate somewhat faster than is projected for the next fifty years. Only about a quarter of this growth was attributable to demographic factors affecting the age dependency ratio, whereas one-third of the increase was due to increases in the generosity of benefits and almost two-fifths due to a widening of pension eligibility to groups hitherto not included in the public pension system (OECD, 1988b: 26). In the recent past, it seems, demography has played only a minor role in influencing overall pension expenditure, and this expenditure has grown very rapidly without precipitating funding crises and unfair intergenerational transfers of the sort predicted for the early decades of the next century. Why should the future be so different from the past?

Part of the answer to this question lies in the timing of demographic change. Population ageing throughout most of the twentieth century has been accompanied by a consistent increase in the size of the potential working population aged 15–64 . Each year there have been more new entrants entering the labour force at the bottom of the age pyramid than there have been older workers retiring at the top, so that although the *relative* size of the working age population has fallen in many countries, the *absolute* size of this working age population has continued to expand. As the hypothetical pay-as-you-go pension system in Table 5.1 shows, the relative expansion of the pensioner population will still enable successive generations to obtain positive returns from the pension system (i.e. benefits higher than contributions) as long as the contributor population is growing in absolute size. However, if the rate of growth of the contributor population is below the rate of growth of the pensioner population (as in Table 5.1), the excess of benefits over contributions will be lower for each successive generation. If, however, the *absolute* size of the contributor population declines, then the rate of return from the pension system will become negative (contributions exceed benefits) – no more free lunches. Figure 5.1 shows that between 1950 and 1990 the working age population has grown in all the major industrialized countries, but from 1990 it begins to decline in Germany, Italy and Japan, and from 2010 in France and the United Kingdom as well. This decline in the absolute size of the working population will not only raise the ratio of contributions to benefits for current generations of contributors, but will also impose a negative rate of return on future contributors who will receive less in benefits than they pay in contributions.

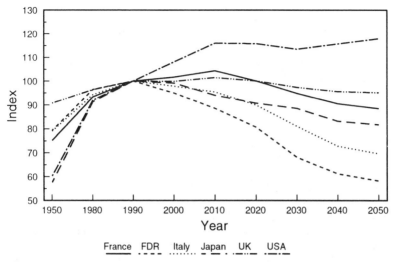

Source: United Nations, 1985

Figure 5.1   *Index of working age (15–64) population*

The impact of this change in the demographic ratios over the next three decades will appear to be more abrupt than shown in Figure 5.1, because two factors which have served since the Second World War to raise the growth rate of contributors above the purely demographic rate shown will diminish in importance. The first of these factors has been the substantial increase in the labour force participation rates of married women since 1945. In the case of the flat-rate British National Insurance scheme, the expansion of the female workforce has widened the contribution base of the national insurance system, but has done little to increase the pension liability of the scheme, because married women had already acquired pension entitlements through their husbands' contributions. To a large extent, therefore, the expansion of female employment has provided a windfall gain for the National Insurance system by increasing total contribution income without any alteration to the individual contribution rate. In earnings related pay-as-you-go public pension systems (such as the British state earnings related pension scheme – SERPS) the effect of an increase in female labour force participation rates is less beneficial to the financing of the scheme. Today's additional contributions create an entitlement to tomorrow's pensions, and therefore have the effect of transferring the funding liabilities forward onto future generations (Schmähl, 1989, 1990).

The case of SERPS is a good example of the other reason why the future will be different from the past – the maturing of pension schemes. When a new pay-as-you-go pension scheme is introduced or the eligibility of an existing scheme widened, the immediate effect is substantially to increase the aggregate income of the pension scheme (more contributors) while barely changing the aggregate benefit expenditure (few additional pensioners) since people close to or above retirement age have not paid sufficient contributions to qualify for benefits. As the pension scheme matures, the initial contributors will approach retirement with a full contribution record and so a full pension entitlement; the cost to younger contributors will rise as they have to pay for a growing proportion of fully entitled pensioners. In most developed countries the eligibility for public pensions (and liability for social security taxes) has been progressively widened since the Second World War. In general, this has kept pension scheme receipts rising faster than expenditure, thereby allowing the real value of pensions to be increased without, apparently, charging the contributors any more. But once the *entire* population is enrolled in the scheme, the scope for a further widening of eligibility disappears, and with it the opportunity to expand the tax base.

The immediate revenue gains for a pay-as-you-go pension system that emerge from a widening of eligibility are matched by longer-term costs. This is true of the SERPS scheme, introduced in Britain in 1975. The intention was to provide an earnings related pension for the 54 per cent of the working population not already enrolled in an occupational pension scheme. Reduced rate benefits were to be paid to retirees from 1978, and full pensions from 1998 – in other words the first cohorts of SERPS pensioners were to receive a full pension after only twenty years of contribution, though later cohorts would be expected to contribute throughout their working life. Just as in the hypothetical example of Table 5.1, there were to be windfall gains for the earlier generations of retirees. But by 2020, with the system reaching maturity as most people of pensionable age become eligible for full benefits (unless they had earlier opted out of SERPS and into an occupational or personal pension scheme), the ratio of contributors to pensioners would reach its long-run equilibrium level and contributions would rise to their real steady-state level.

Official estimates of the cost of SERPS made in 1975 did not extend beyond 2009, on the grounds that anything beyond that time-horizon would be very speculative, and they therefore failed to assess the likely steady-state costs of the scheme (they also, of course, failed to take account of the rapid growth in the size of the 65 plus population in the period 2010–30). However, Hemming and

Kay (1982) took a longer-run view, and showed that the true cost was likely to rise rapidly in the next century. In 1975 it was estimated that the long-run cost of SERPS would require an increase in National Insurance contributions of a mere 3–4 per cent, but Hemming and Kay found that the combination of system maturity and population ageing would require contributions equal to 13.4 per cent of qualifying earnings by 2030. They concluded that 'we have, in effect, secured the finance to impose lower rates of taxation on the working population now by selling promises that our children will pay more generous pensions than we are willing to pay to our parents' (Hemming and Kay, 1982: 314). Partly in response to this concern about the apparently unfair financial burden placed by yesterday's electors and legislators on tomorrow's workers (many of whom are as yet unborn), and partly to contribute to a general reduction of social security provision and expenditure, the SERPS scheme was substantially modified by the 1986 Social Security Act. From 2000 benefits will be reduced from 25 per cent to 20 per cent of maximum pensionable earnings, the entitlement basis will be changed to average lifetime earnings from best twenty years, and the long-run costs of the scheme will be approximately halved (Fry et al., 1990: 21–5).

The history of SERPS demonstrates why the future of public pension systems is likely to be different from the past. A stagnant and ultimately declining working age population, a high rate of female labour force participation with little scope for further extension, and almost full coverage of the eligible population together give few opportunities for expanding the contribution base, but as the proportion of former contributors reaching pension age rises, so will the overall cost of the scheme. The 1986 reform of SERPS also shows the crucial role of benefit levels and entitlements in determining the long-run liabilities of any pension scheme; at a stroke the expected costs of the scheme in 2021 were reduced from £16.4 billion to £7.1 billion (Fry et al., 1990: 24). As this example makes clear, changes in future benefits can be of such cumulative magnitude that they dominate the demographic determinants of pension expenditure, and since benefit levels and eligibility in public pension systems are set as part of a political process, it would be true to say that projections of future pension costs depend as much upon political as upon economic or demographic assumptions.

Despite this key role for political decisions, they are often ignored in the long-run projections of pension costs produced by the OECD, IMF and others, which are usually based on the (implausible) assumption that current policies will remain unaltered. For instance, in an attempt to calculate the rate of economic growth necessary to pay for the increased social security costs of ageing populations, the OECD assumes that the policy intention is to hold the ratio of social expenditure to GDP constant at the 1980 levels (OECD, 1988a: 39). Walker (1990) notes that this ratio in 1980 varied widely between countries (18.6 per cent in Australia, 22 per cent in the United Kingdom, 38 per cent in Belgium) and suggests that there may be good grounds for expecting it to change (increase) in the future as populations become older. But even without population ageing there might be other reasons to expect these ratios to vary in the future because of political pressures, since it was political decisions to increase benefit levels and expand coverage that were the main reason for the rapid growth of pension expenditure over the twenty-five years from 1960.

One of the key political decisions is how to index pension benefits to take account of changes over time in the level of prices and wages. One of two practices is usually adopted: either to adjust benefits in line with prices, or to adjust them in line with changes in real incomes. Price indexation maintains the real value of the pension at the level it was at when the indexation began, whereas income indexation maintains the value of the pension as a proportion of current average earnings. Since real earnings tend to grow over time, price indexation means that pension income gradually falls as a proportion of average employment income – pensioners become worse off relative to workers. Table 5.4 shows estimates made by the Government Actuary of the potential effect of these two alternatives on the value of pensions in the United Kingdom over a sixty year period from 1990. In the table it is assumed real earnings will grow at 1.5 per cent per annum, somewhat below the average for the post-war period of about 2 per cent. If the basic pension is uprated in line with earnings it will, quite obviously, maintain its value as a proportion of pre-retirement earnings, as shown in the first column (because men and women receive the same basic pension, but women's pre-retirement earnings are below men's, the pension is worth proportionately more to women). But as column 4 shows, if the basic pension is only uprated in line with prices, its value relative to earnings is more than halved over this period, falling to an almost trivial 7 per cent for men by 2050. For the SERPS pension the alternative indexation systems affect only contribution thresholds – the pension is, by definition, related to earnings – so there is little difference between columns 2 and 5. Note, however, how sharply the value of the SERPS pension rises up to the year 2000, at which point the more restrictive conditions of the 1986 reform begin to take effect, gradually lowering the value of the pension for subsequent retirees.

Table 5.4 *Pensions at award for men and women on average earnings as a proportion of earnings before retirement on the assumption of a growth in real earnings of 1.5 per cent per year, 1990–2050*

	Uprating in line with:					
	Earnings			Prices		
Year of award	Basic pension	Additional pension	Total	Basic pension	Additional pension	Total
Men						
1990	16	12	28	16	12	28
2000	16	21	37	14	21	35
2010	16	18	34	12	18	30
2020	16	18	34	10	18	28
2030	16	17	33	9	16	25
2040	16	16	32	8	14	22
2050	16	16	32	7	12	19
Women						
1990	24	11	35	24	11	35
2000	24	19	43	21	19	40
2010	24	16	40	18	17	35
2020	24	16	40	15	18	33
2030	24	15	39	13	17	30
2040	24	15	39	11	17	28
2050	24	15	39	10	16	26

Note: The table relates to pensions for single persons; for a married couple relying on the husband's insurance the basic pension would be sixty per cent higher.

Source: Government Actuary (1990: 18)

The choice of uprating system not only affects the future economic welfare of pensioners, but also has a direct bearing on the welfare of contributors. The Government Actuary (1990: 29–31) has calculated that if the basic and earnings related pensions are uprated in line with prices their combined cost will rise from £23 billion in 1990 to £47 billion in 2050, whereas if uprated in line with earnings the cost in 2050 will be almost £95 billion (in constant prices). When converted into projections of National Insurance contribution rates, as shown in Table 5.5, price indexation points to a fall in the level of worker contributions, whereas income indexation would necessitate a rise. Sensitivity analysis (Government Actuary, 1990: 35–8) shows that these projections are fairly robust with respect to alternative estimates of fertility and mortality, of labour force participation and of the rate of real earnings growth – political decision about how to index the benefits dominate all other factors.

Table 5.5   *Projected joint employer/employee National Insurance contribution rates*

| Financial year | Upratings and revaluation of contribution limits in line with: | |
	Prices %	Earnings %
1990/1	19.1	19.1
1995/6	18.1	19.2
2000/1	17.8	19.9
2010/11	17.4	21.3
2020/1	17.8	23.5
2030/1	18.4	26.4
2040/1	16.4	25.8
2050/1	14.1	24.5

Source: Government Actuary (1990: 31)

The abruptness of political decisions is in stark contrast to the gradual impact of demographic change. In Britain, for example, the basic state pension had been uprated in line with either prices or incomes, depending on which was rising fastest, until the Conservative government decided in 1980 to increase the pension in the future only in line with prices. The effect of this has been to reduce the expenditure cost of the basic state pension (and therefore the value of the pension for individual recipients) by about 20 per cent over the decade to 1990, with a further 20 per cent reduction anticipated in the decade to 2000. The Labour Party, meanwhile, has committed itself to restoring the more generous system of indexation. It seems that the economic fortunes of pensioners and contributors can swing with the short-term political cycle much more sharply than with the long demographic waves of baby-boom and baby-bust.

Public Pension Reform

One of the main objectives of the OECD and other proponents of pension reform is to moderate these swings by encouraging governments to balance the long-run pension costs of population ageing by gradual and long-run reductions in the generosity of benefits and the level of contributions. The case for reform is generally made by reference to two distinct arguments. First, it is claimed that high marginal tax rates on workers create strong work disincentives and increase labour costs, and so may reduce both the dynamism and the international competitiveness of the developed economies.

Although the rise in average tax/contribution rates in the United Kingdom is unlikely to be large, even if pensions are uprated in line with earnings (see Table 5.5), other countries with different demographic and social security regimes face some startling prospects. It was estimated in 1989 that the contribution rate in the West German social security system would need to rise from 18.5 per cent to 41 per cent of wage costs by 2030 in order to respond to the pension financing requirements of population ageing (Schmähl, 1989: 141). In France a similar rise in the contribution rate from 16.3 per cent in 1990 to around 40 per cent by 2040 has been projected (Vernière, 1990: 33). Increases in social security taxes of these magnitudes would undoubtedly have an impact on overall economic performance and competitiveness.

Second, it is claimed that in the absence of reform, social security pensions are unstable because younger cohorts will never receive in return from the system a sum equivalent to that which they have paid in, and so will have a large and growing incentive to abandon the entire social security system. Keyfitz (1985) has estimated the rate of return on social security pension contributions for successive birth cohorts in the United States. With fertility rates maintained at their 1979 level, the rate of return to generations born after 2000 will be negative. Lower fertility rates result in more strongly negative rates of return on contributions. Similar conditions apply in virtually all the developed economies and this has prompted David Thomson to observe that 'unless future generations of the young prove willing to pay taxes on a scale seen nowhere in the present century, the young adults of today cannot expect as they reach old age a treatment comparable to that which they are now giving the aged, let alone a return commensurate with their many times greater lifetime contributions' (Thomson, 1989: 54).

To preserve some semblance of equity in the treatment of successive generations and to avoid a substantial rise in social security contribution rates, three types of reform have been proposed, and variously implemented, for public pension systems. First, benefits can be reduced by lengthening the qualifying period for receipt of full benefits (as with the SERPS reforms) or by restricting the generosity of the indexing arrangements (as with the UK flat-rate pension system). Changes of this sort (usually quite minor adjustments to indexing arrangements) have been implemented in Austria, Belgium, Canada, Denmark, Finland, France, Germany, Greece, Spain, Sweden, the Netherlands and the United States, as well as in the United Kingdom (OECD, 1988b: 67–76). Second, the retirement age (or more precisely, the age of entitlement to a public pension) can be increased, thereby reducing the size of the pensioner population and probably increasing the size of the working population paying social security contributions. The 1983 amendment to social security in the United States legislated for an increase in the standard public pension qualification age from 65 to 67 in stages between 2003 and 2027, and the 1985 reform of the Japanese pension system will raise the age of eligibility for women from 55 to 60 by the year 2000.

The third type of reform attempts not to reduce future pension payments but instead to change the basis on which public pensions are paid for, by moving from pay-as-you-go to partial funding. In order to cushion relatively small generations of workers in 2020 from onerous pension levies, contributions could instead be increased immediately for all workers, allowing a reserve fund to be built up over the next twenty or thirty years, and then gradually run down as the baby-boomers retire and pension scheme expenditure exceeds pension income. This approach has been adopted in the United States, where since 1983 social security contribution rates have been set at a level designed to permit the accumulation of a social security trust fund which should reach $2 trillion (1988 prices) by 2020 before subsequently declining to zero by 2050 (Aaron et al., 1989). It is far from certain, however, that this move to partial funding in the United States will achieve its intended objective of reducing the future tax/contribution liabilities of workers in the third and fourth decades of the next century. In order to transfer real income over time, this social security fund needs to promote capital accumulation and additional economic growth. In practice, however, it is being used to fund the United States government's enormous public debt; the consequence is that instead of future workers being required to pay higher social security contributions, they will instead have to pay higher taxes so that the government can repay its loans from the social security trust fund. In fact it seems likely that there will be no substantial redistribution of the funding burden between generations.

Putting a social security trust fund into real capital accumulation rather than government loans may not, however, be as easy as it sounds for two reasons. First, the future liabilities of social security schemes are so large that even partial funding of the sort contemplated in the United States could swamp the capital market, having potentially large but uncertain influences on interest and exchange rates, capital formation, international asset flows and the pattern of foreign trade. Second, the past behaviour of politicians in using social security income to offer overly-generous benefits to current electors at the expense of future contributors suggests that it is difficult for the interest of future generations to be adequately represented in participatory democracies. The electoral pressures to make inroads into any long-term social security fund in order to meet current spending needs may prove to be irresistible.

The prospect of political interference could be reduced (though not eliminated) by simultaneously privatizing public pension systems and converting them to a fully-funded basis, so that benefits are strictly limited to the value of past contributions. Some move has been made in this direction in the United Kingdom by providing financial incentives for members of SERPS to opt out of the state scheme and into personal pension schemes. These personal pensions are essentially tax efficient savings accounts which are converted into an annuity on retirement. Since they are 'defined contribution' rather than 'defined benefit' pension schemes, they involve none of the disincentives to continued employment at older ages that can emerge in pension schemes based on the value of final salary, and since they are fully-funded they involve no intergenerational transfers from current workers to retirees. They cannot, however, 'solve' the existing pension problems of an ageing population.

It would certainly be possible to abandon public pensions for younger workers and compel them to save for their own old age via a personal pension. But for people within, say, twenty-five years of retirement, the cost of initiating a personal pension would be high and for those in their late 50s it would be prohibitive; the principle of compound interest imposes high costs on late entrants to any pension scheme. To abandon public pension schemes for workers who have already paid many years of contributions would be to break the implicit intergenerational contract on which the schemes are based, the blatant unfairness of which would probably mean that such a move would not be politically feasible. But to preserve public pension entitlements for current workers *and* to abolish them for future labour market entrants who will be expected to accumulate personal pensions would be to impose a *double* pension burden on new workers. They would be required to accumulate a fund for their own pensions and to make social security contributions to pay for the unfunded public pensions of current retirees. Far from solving the problem of public pension finance in an era of population ageing, this would exacerbate intergenerational inequity and would do nothing to eliminate the existing public pension liabilities created by relatively large cohorts today aged over 40 who already have accumulated substantial social security pension entitlements.

Furthermore, it is uncertain how far the funding of personal (or occupational) pensions can finesse the real economic difficulties caused by the succession of baby-boom by baby-bust. In practice, *any* saving for old age, whether public or private, funded or unfunded, involves the accumulation of a claim on the goods and services produced by future generations of workers. Loaves and fishes do not keep fresh in the larder for thirty or forty years – the food consumed by today's pensioners is produced by today's workers. If the ratio of pensioners to workers rises, but if the relative incomes of workers and pensioners remain constant, then this *necessarily* implies that the claim on current output exercised by pensioners will increase. In an unfunded public pension system this claim is exercised through the tax system, but in a funded private pension system it is exercised through the return to capital owned by the pension funds. If the alternative funding systems have no differential impact on overall national income, the *only* difference lies in the degree of social and political legitimacy attached to the alternative mechanisms for appropriating some of the output of current workers.

It is frequently argued, however, that during a period of population ageing, the temporary accumulation of assets in a funded pension forces down interest rates, encourages capital formation, and so induces a higher rate of economic growth than that enjoyed in an identical economy which has an unfunded pension scheme. This is true only to the extent that pension funds induce real capital accumulation (if they are used to finance government borrowing or speculative asset price inflation they may have no real economic effect), and only if the fall in interest rates caused by the additional pension fund accumulation does not induce an equal but opposite reduction in non-pension saving. If the net effect of funding during a period of population ageing is to raise the rate of growth of the economy, then both workers and pensioners in the future can enjoy real incomes higher than would otherwise be available. Whether both groups do in fact enjoy higher real incomes will still depend on how the claims of pensioners on national income are exercised. Economic growth does not necessarily lessen distributional competition.

It is possible, moreover, that far from permitting increases in real pension levels, funding might fail to maintain the income of the pensioner population. The similar demographic profiles of most developed countries means that the decumulation of the baby-boomers' pension funds would occur more or less at the same time throughout the world. As the baby-boomers save heavily in middle age in all countries, an excess of savings on world capital markets would tend to drive down the rate of return and stimulate asset price inflation. However, when the large baby-boom cohorts retire, pension funds in all countries will want to realize their assets, which will tend to drive down asset prices. Pension funds which have defined pension payments as a proportion of previous earnings may find that they cannot meet their liabilities; those which define pensions in relation to the capital value of past contributions may have to reduce the real value of pension payments.

This possibility highlights one of the weaknesses of funded pensions – with each cohort reliant on its own savings, it is difficult to insure against risks that affect any particular generation. These risks include variations in productivity growth, rates of return on capital and inflation, and variations which are themselves caused in part by fluctuations in the size of successive cohorts. Full insurance against these risks requires both intertemporal and intergenerational redistribution, and this can best be achieved through a public pay-as-you-go pension scheme (Green, 1988). Pay-as-you-go public pensions can provide this security because they can spread risks across generations; on the other hand, as we have seen, they do not necessarily spread risks equitably when the size of successive cohorts varies widely.

It has been suggested that these distributional tensions and the apparent intergenerational inequity inherent in current pensioning arrangements will be resolved not by changes to the social security system but through the fruits of future economic growth which will allow more resources for everyone (Midwinter, 1989; Macnicol, 1990b). This view is based either on false optimism or on a failure to understand the working of pension systems. Take the case of a pure pay-as-you-go pension system which operates according to the following accounting identity:

$$W.(t.w) = P.(p.w)$$

where W is the number of contributing workers, t is the average social security contribution rate, w is the average wage, P is the number of pensioners, and p is the pension replacement rate (i.e. the value of a pension as a proportion of the average wage). This is a reasonable approximation of the British basic National Insurance pension system. An increase in P, the number of pensioners, can be balanced by an extension of the tax base (W), an increase in the tax rate (t), or a reduction in the relative value of the pension (p). Economic growth – an increase in average real income (w) – will automatically affect both sides of the equation, leaving all other variables unchanged. In this formulation economic growth alters the absolute level of both wages and pensions, but not the relative value between the two which is defined by the pension replacement rate (p). If the size of the workforce is fixed, an increase in the value of pensions relative to wages or a rise in the number of pensioners necessarily involves an increase in the tax rate regardless of what is happening to real wages and economic growth.

The contention of those who see economic growth as the solution to distributional problems appears to be, therefore, that as long as the post-tax income of the working population – defined as $w-(w.t)$ – does not decline, there will be no difficulty in transferring a growing share of their pre-tax income to the pensioner population. Far from addressing the distributional question raised by an economic analysis of pension systems, this appeal to the benefits of economic growth simply ignores the issue, and it does so on grounds that seem implausibly optimistic and frankly unhistorical. A simple overview of economic development since 1945 shows clearly that four decades of rapid economic growth have done nothing to lessen disputes about how (and how much of) the income of tax payers should be redistributed to other groups in society. There is little sign that as the economic cake grows larger people care less about how the cake is cut.

If economic growth cannot provide a ready resolution of the distributional problems and inequities projected by many commentators for existing public pension schemes, then attention inevitably turns back to the internal rules of these schemes, especially to those setting pension levels and retirement ages. Changes to these parameters in public pension schemes can readily reduce the funding costs, but they may, at the same time, undermine some of the principle purposes of these schemes. Economic explanations for the intervention of government in old age pension provision which revolve around concepts of market failure, risk diversification, economies of scale, imperfect information, myopia and cognitive dissonance are not particularly convincing (Blinder, 1988; Kessler, 1989). More comprehensive explanations need to include the social and political objectives of poverty prevention and income redistribution which have been instrumental in the creation and development of modern social security systems.

Flat-rate public pension systems, such as that proposed by Beveridge in 1942 and introduced in the United Kingdom at the end of the Second World War, have an explicit aim of preventing poverty. Earnings-related public pensions place greater emphasis on facilitating the redistribution of an individual's income over his or her life cycle, from working years to retirement, but they usually also incorporate some special provision for basic income maintenance even if lifetime contributions have been minimal. There is no doubt that public pensions have been effective in reducing the proportion of old people living in poverty over the past thirty years (OECD 1988b: 44–8). It is also apparent, however, that among the major industrialized countries, only in Sweden has the pension system succeeded in eliminating poverty in old age. Elsewhere the number of elderly poor has been significantly reduced by public transfers, but typically around 10 per cent of older people continue to live in poverty (this figure varies, of course, according to the criteria used to set the poverty line). Furthermore, as the data presented in Chapter Three show, older people tend to be concentrated in the bottom half of the income distribution, with many of them being raised only just above the poverty line by their public pension. Any reduction in the value of public pensions which is introduced to serve the policy goal of reducing the level (or rate of growth) of public pension contributions may well undermine the different policy goal of preventing poverty in old age.

If pension reductions were targeted carefully on those groups of elderly people with incomes well above the poverty line, then this conflict of interests could be avoided. In the case of the United Kingdom, however, Chapter Three shows that the generally low level of pensioner incomes means that effective targeting would produce only modest expenditure savings, and would considerably increase administrative costs (Fry et al., 1990; Falkingham and Victor, 1991). The continued existence of pensioner poverty in fact provides a strong impetus for campaigns to increase the real level of the state pension (Midwinter, 1985). Social policy analysts tend to stress the needs and rights of current generations of elderly beneficiaries when discussing future pension policy whereas economists tend to give great weight to the actuarial fairness of public pension schemes for future generations of contributors and to the possibly depressive effects very generous public pensions might have on economic performance. Although both sets of views depend to some extent upon value judgements, assumptions and projections, the main reason for disagreement is the different conception of equity and fairness they adopt. Equity, however, is not a simple or unproblematic concept, and we will return in the final chapter to consider how alternative definitions of equity can be applied to the economic and welfare outcomes of population ageing.

6

Ageing and the Macroeconomy

The relationship between the age structure of the population and systems of public and private transfers has been, as the previous chapter made clear, an area of considerable discussion and disagreement among social scientists, with economists often appearing dismally unconcerned about the welfare of older people and mindful only of long-run distributional issues. But the nature of inter-generational transfers is not the only, or even the most important, locus for interaction between economic and demographic forces. Many other elements of our economic system – the scale and structure of demand, the creation and use of human capital, the savings and investment rate, the direction of international capital flows – may all in some ways be affected by changes in the age structure of the population. Furthermore, these interactions may be much more immediate than is the link between demography and social security because the relationship between, say, age structure and consumption or employment patterns responds to short-run changes in the relative size of different cohorts as well as to the longer-run ageing of one particularly large (baby-boom) cohort.

Short-term changes in past fertility rates mean that the number of people in different age groups is already changing very rapidly. Figure 6.1 presents some illustrative data for the United Kingdom, France, Germany and the United States for the ten-year period from 1990 to 2000. Over this decade the US population will expand by around 6 per cent, the French by 3.5 per cent, the United Kingdom's by a mere 1 per cent and the German population will show a very marginal decline in overall numbers. But these aggregate figures conceal very large movements in the relative size of different age groups. The United Kingdom, for example, will experience a 20 per cent decline in the number of 20–29 year olds with a corresponding increase among people in their 30s and in their 50s, while France will see a much smaller decline in the size of its young adult labour force, but a much greater proportionate increase in pensioners aged over 70. Although the total population in the United States will continue to expand through the 1990s, it will become considerably older, with a great increase of 40–60 year olds and a 15–20 per cent decline in the population aged 25–34. In a unified Germany the low fertility of the 1970s that was apparent in both East and West will manifest itself in a dramatic decline by over a third in the size of the young adult population.

The macroeconomic consequences of these quite abrupt shifts in age structure remain very much a matter for argument and speculation. This topic has received rather less attention from economists and policy analysts than has the issue of social security and ageing. This is partly because it poses greater technical problems of modelling, but also because it appears to be less immediate and less relevant to the government departments and international organizations that have pioneered much of the research on the social security side. Despite this relative research deficiency, enough work has now been done to show that the broader macroeconomic consequences of population ageing may be great, and may in fact overwhelm the consequences for social security systems alone. This chapter will review the somewhat patchy evidence by looking in turn at consumption, at human capital and the labour market, and then at savings and investment.

Ageing and Consumption

Population ageing will affect the structure and ultimately the level of demand within each economy, but the scale and nature of these changes can only be predicted on the basis of some heroic assumptions. Consumption projections are usually made by applying population projections to current age-specific expenditure patterns, but this procedure may not produce valid results. The expenditure patterns of today's elderly population are a consequence of the age of these individuals, of their lifetime socioeconomic experiences, and of the socioeconomic conditions now current in their country and place of residence. These three separate influences – the *age*, *cohort* and *period* effects – operate simultaneously and it is by no means obvious that age is the most important of these. The relatively low level of old age income and the limited variability in expenditure patterns among elderly people today may be a consequence more of lifetime employment and saving opportunities than of age itself. Future changes in both the mean and the variance of real income and wealth for the elderly population, together with possible changes in labour force participation and in morbidity, could easily alter current demand patterns.

Studies in both the United States and France (Musgrove, 1982; Serow, 1984; Ekert-Jaffé, 1989) suggest that, once household expenditure patterns are standardized for differences in income and household composition, age alone has very little impact on the

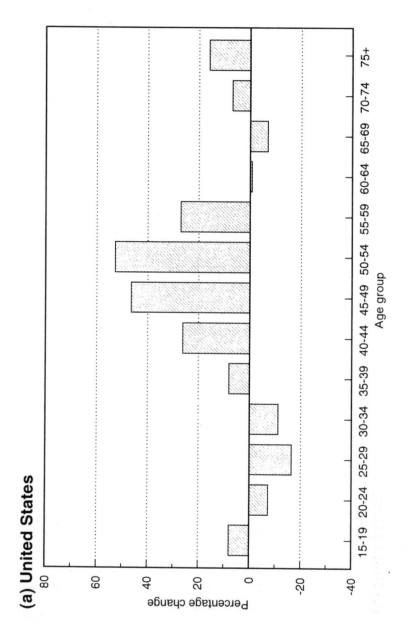

Figure 6.1   *Percentage change by age group 1990–2000, populations of: (a) United States; (b) United Kingdom; (c) France; (d) Germany*

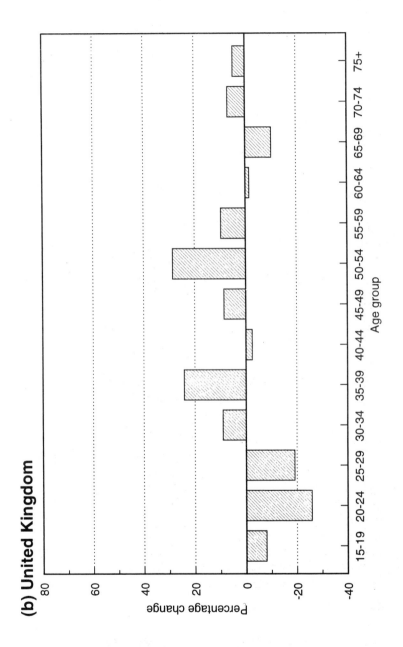

Figure 6.1 *continued*

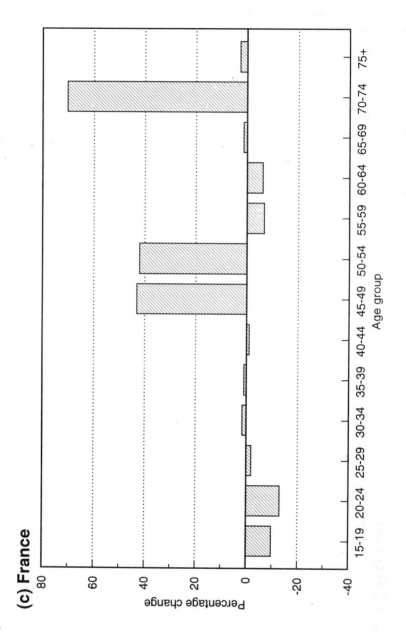

Figure 6.1   *continued*

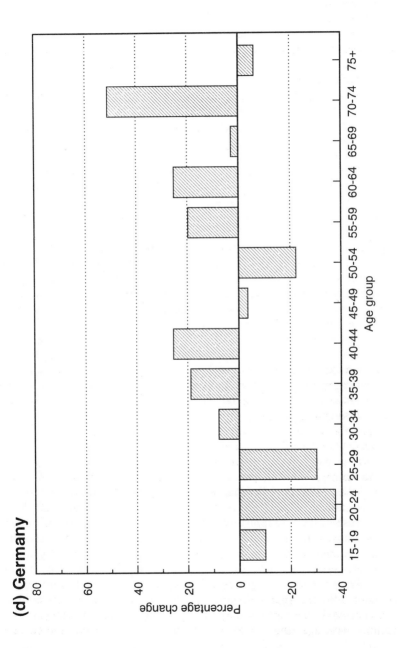

Figure 6.1 *continued*

overall structure of consumer demand. Even when the analysis is subdivided into over 100 different consumption sectors, few types of consumption expenditure appear to be closely related to age, although not surprisingly expenditure on domestic help rises with age from the mid-60s and expenditure on education and on personal (though not public) transport declines with age. Nevertheless, it is possible that a changing age structure among consumers may require non-marginal adjustments by producers in order to adapt to changing demand preferences *within* each consumption sector. Shifting from the production of prams to the making of wheelchairs may well require only a marginal change in the use of resources; it is less easy to see how schools or children's amusement parks can be recycled to meet the needs of an ageing population. Any goods or service sector which has a large and immutable capital stock may well suffer from the vicissitudes of short-run changes in the age structure of demand of the sort shown in Figure 6.1, with a consequent under or over provision of supply.

One market sector to which this obviously applies is residential accommodation, since the depreciation period of most houses stretches over several decades. As the baby-boomers move towards retirement, to be succeeded by smaller generations of their children and grandchildren, so the overall demand for housing will change. Smaller generations of smaller families will tend to reduce the demand for large houses, although an increase in the number of widows and widowers, rising divorce rates and high rates of solitary residence among young adults may increase the demand for single person units of accommodation. On the other hand, if real incomes continue to grow, then younger generations will be more affluent than the older ones, and so may seek qualitatively better (and larger) housing. The range of contingencies is such that it is difficult to draw firm conclusions about the effect of demographic change on the housing market, but some estimates are instructive. Mankiw and Weil (1989) predict that real housing prices in the United States could fall by 47 per cent from their current level by the year 2007 because of demographically induced changes in demand. Although they are cautious about putting too much weight on the specific results of their forecasting model, they note that 'even if the fall in housing prices is only one half what our equation predicts, it will likely be one of the major economic events of the next two decades'. This projected decline in prices, it should be noted, occurs despite the continued growth in the *total* US population; it is a consequence of a decline in the rate of household formation (directly related to the fall in the number of 25–34 year olds shown in Figure 6.1) and hence of housing demand.

Much larger effects might be anticipated in most European countries where total population will be stable or declining over the next two decades, although Börsch-Supan (1991: 123–9) controversially argues that increasing life expectancy will lead to a fall in the supply of homes being inherited by the young and so will create an overall housing shortage. For the United Kingdom, Ermisch has concluded that changes in the age distribution of the population alone increased the number of households (and hence housing demand) by between 80,000 and 90,000 per annum through the 1960s and 1970s, a rate which accelerated after 1982 to around 150,000 households per annum. But from a peak of age structure induced household formation of over 160,000 in 1989, the figure is projected to fall to little over 40,000 households per annum by 2003 as the maturing of the baby-boom generation is followed by the maturing of the much smaller baby-bust cohort. By 2025 the effect of age structure on net household formation is expected to be negative (Ermisch, 1990a, 1990b). Since the demographic boost to housing demand in the 1980s appears to have contributed to the increase in house prices over that decade, it seems likely that a weakening of this pressure in Britain over the next ten years will have a depressive effect on prices, thereby reducing the scope for older people to release housing equity. Overall housing demand, however, is driven not just by age structure but by a multitude of other factors such as changes in divorce rates, in the availability and cost of loans, and in the laws governing and regulating alternative forms of housing tenure, so the long-run determination of house prices cannot be inferred from purely demographic indicators.

The housing market will also be affected by changes in the location, as well as the size, of different age groups. As noted in Chapter Two, there is a well established pattern in most developed countries for a number of older people to move on retirement out of large cities and into provincial towns and villages. This is combined with a general drift of retired people to areas with warmer climates, a drift which has created quite distinct retirement enclaves in, for instance, Florida in the United States, the Gold Coast in Australia, a number of coastal towns in Southern England, and along the Mediterranean fringe of France. (Cribier, 1984; Vergoossen and Warnes, 1989). The converse of this drift of the old is the movement of the young to areas of rapid employment growth, and particularly to 'new towns' such as Milton Keynes in England and Créteil in France. This geographical concentration of particular age groups means that there may be pronounced local age-related effects on the structure of demand which are not revealed by national surveys. Within the European Community countries there is also increased scope for international migration, particularly by retired people who do not face the same functional language barriers as do migrant workers. Well established ex-patriot (mainly British) retirement communities have developed along the southern coast of Spain and Portugal, and with them have come demands for English-style goods and services.

This sort of highly localized and highly specific age related consumption effect undoubtedly is important in determining the market opportunities of particular producers and retailers, just as the more general change in the age structure over the next decade in all the developed countries will be of importance to the advertising and marketing strategies of all businesses. This can perhaps be seen most clearly by looking at the data for the United States in Figure 6.1. The consumer boom of the 1980s was driven by the baby-boom generation of yuppies, the high earners in their 20s and 30s. They were the target of advertisers and image makers who created the new icons of modern life – the filofax, the sailboard, the portable phone – but because of their cohort size and spending power this broad age group was also at the centre of rather more mundane sales efforts for cars, soap powders and margarines. Over the next decade, however, the purchasing power of the 20–40 age group in the United States will quite literally fade away as it shrinks by 10 per cent from 82 million to 74 million people. Meanwhile the number of Americans in their 40s and 50s will rise by over a third, from 56 million to 75 million, and marketing strategies will be forced, simply by weight of numbers, to give increased recognition to this older age group. Whether the baby-boomers will change their consumption preferences and propensities as they age is unknowable; what is certain is that their interests will continue to dominate the fin de siècle retail market.

Ageing and Production

Changes in the population age structure will also have a direct effect on production, in terms of the age structure of the workforce, the mix of skills and level of labour productivity in the economy, through changes in the recruitment, training and promotion policies of individual employers, and through possible changes in rates of international migration. Many of these factors will themselves influence the employment prospects and remuneration of different cohorts of workers, and so will feed directly into any changes in the age structure of consumer demand.

Since the Second World War all the industrialized countries have experienced positive, but declining, rates of population growth which have ensured that labour markets have been continually restocked with young, recently-trained workers. The low fertility rates of the 1970s and 1980s, as well as bringing about a net reduction in the total population in many countries by the third or fourth decade of the next century, will also inaugurate much more immediate shifts in both the age structure and the size of the working population, and these will have a direct effect on labour costs and productivity. The changing age structure will influence the size of the workforce because of the extent to which participation rates vary by age. The low labour force participation rates for older workers (shown in Figure 4.6) will tend to reduce the size of the workforce in the future before any overall reduction in total population size. This is because it is these older age groups which will see the fastest relative growth over the next thirty years. In other words, if age specific participation rates stay at their current level, the size of the active population will begin to fall slightly sooner and slightly faster than is shown by the simple demographic categories presented in Figure 5.1. If participation rates for older workers continue on the pronounced downward trend experienced over the last fifteen years, then the diminution of the active population will be even more noticeable. The International Labour Office (1986) estimates that, taking into account further small declines in the participation rates of older workers, the economically active population of Northern Europe (Scandinavia, Iceland, the United Kingdom and Ireland) will begin to fall from the year 2000, and that in Western Europe (Switzerland, Germany, France, Austria and the Benelux countries) this decline has been underway since 1990. The rate of decline will, however, be very slight until the second decade of the next century, and before then the most important labour market effects of demographic change will be felt in terms of the age structure rather than the overall size of the workforce.

The age structure of the workforce can influence both the economic prospects of people in different birth cohorts and the performance of the macroeconomy if it is the case that workers of different ages are not perfect substitutes for each other. There is very strong microeconomic evidence to support the contention that age is an important determinant of remuneration, and strong theoretical arguments that remuneration is related to productivity. Yet somewhat surprisingly the consistent empirical findings about the positive relationship between age and wage can be extrapolated to produce quite contradictory macroeconomic projections of the impact of an ageing labour force. At the root of these differences

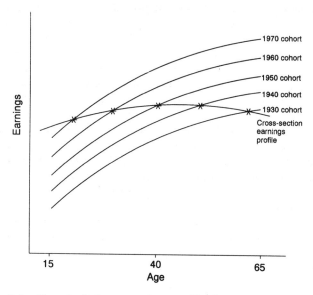

Figure 6.2   *Hypothetical age–earnings profiles for successive birth cohorts and for a population cross-section*

lies the empirical imprecision of alternative tests of human capital theory.

The theory of human capital has evolved as a means of providing a rationalistic explanation for the different earnings levels and trajectories of different workers in market economies. In a perfectly competitive market, it is argued, the wage of each worker will equal the value of the addition to total output that his or her labour has contributed (known to economists as the worker's marginal revenue product). This productive contribution of each worker will be some function of latent ability (a combination of physical, mental and cultural inheritance), of deliberate enhancements of this ability through formal training and education, and of less conscious enhancements acquired through work experience and on-the-job training. The most important common determinant of work experience is age (though this is less so for women, many of whom have an employment history interrupted by one or more periods of unwaged domestic responsibility), and studies of workforce remuneration consistently find that age is positively related to wage (Becker, 1964; Mincer, 1974).

This is often not immediately apparent from cross-section studies of the age–earnings profile, which often show a decline from middle age. Figure 6.2 gives a stylized illustration of why a cross-sectional analysis can give a misleading impression. For each birth cohort real earnings rise with age throughout working life though more slowly from the mid-40s until retirement at 65. However, because at each age the real earnings of successive cohorts are higher than preceding cohorts (a consequence of real earnings growth over time), the cross-sectional age–earning profile dips downwards after some point – in this example from age 40. Although the labour market is not perfectly competitive because of rigidities imposed by government legislation and by collective agreements between employers and workers, the very widespread finding across countries and industrial sectors that age is positively associated with remuneration indicates (within the context of simple human capital theory) that older workers are more productive than younger workers *because of* the greater employment experience they have gained with age. This might suggest that a relative expansion in the proportion of older workers and shrinkage in the proportion of younger workers would, other things being equal, increase overall labour productivity and therefore provide a positive stimulus to the macroeconomy.

Yet in 1949 the Royal Commission on Population issued a warning, often since repeated, that an ageing society might become 'dangerously unprogressive' with 'falling technical efficiency and economic welfare'. How can this interpretation be reconciled with the consistent evidence about age and earnings? Several possible explanations can be offered. First, in the hypothetical world represented by Figure 6.2 the rate of real income growth is faster for workers aged 20–40 than for those aged 40–60, so a shift in the age structure in this society towards workers aged over 40 will, in the absence of other changes, tend to reduce the rate of growth of labour productivity (although total labour productivity will, in an economy as represented by Figure 6.2, continue to increase). A second possibility is that technical efficiency is 'embodied' in each generation of young workers who are better adapted to the new technologies and production processes of each period than are older cohorts, because of their more modern and relevant cultural inheritance and their more recent education and training. If the supply of young workers declines it is possible that in the long run the technical efficiency of the workforce will fall (or grow less rapidly) unless older cohorts can be retrained as effectively as the young. It is commonly assumed (though, as will be discussed below, seldom demonstrated) that the costs of training for older workers are higher and the economic returns to training lower than is the case for younger workers, so that retraining middle-aged workers cannot fully compensate for a shortage of the young.

A further possibility, and one which challenges a fundamental assumption of simple human capital theory, is that remuneration is not strictly related to marginal revenue product, and that in fact labour productivity declines noticeably beyond a certain age threshold. If true, this would mean that population ageing unequivocally diminishes the rate of growth of labour productivity, and support for this interpretation comes from an analysis of the way in which companies organize their recruitment and promotion policies, or what have come to be known as their internal labour markets. In order to secure the long-run loyalty of their employees and to minimize the costs of labour turnover, companies tend to reward long service by paying older workers somewhat above their marginal product, and compensate by paying younger workers less than their 'real' worth (Lazear, 1981, 1990). Essentially this is a system of long-term deferred pay which is closely related to the deferred pay embodied in the occupational pension schemes discussed in Chapter Four, although it has been suggested that these seniority wage systems are much less effective in buying worker loyalty than is the deferred pay offered through an occupational pension (Ippolito, 1991). Nevertheless, under this interpretation the positive age–earnings relationship is an artefact of the employment contract rather than a representation of the marginal productivity of workers of different ages, so no direct inferences about the impact of population ageing on productivity can be drawn from age–earnings profiles.

Once it is accepted that the wage may not be closely related to the marginal product of labour, then it becomes very difficult to test the validity of human capital theory because for most workers there are few other direct measures of labour productivity, and many other potential influences on individual remuneration (for a brief review, see Strober, 1990). The complex and interrelated nature of most production processes in both the goods and services sectors makes it very difficult to identify the contribution of each worker to final output. In consequence, researchers investigating the relationship between age and productivity tend to resort either to indirect measures or to somewhat artificial laboratory experiments. In controlled conditions, psychologists can demonstrate that both physical reactions and mental retention on average decline from middle age (Rabbit, 1992). Yet they also point out that it is inappropriate to draw from these experiments simplistic inferences about the economic capacity of workers of different ages, and for three distinct reasons. First, they find that while average (mean) physical and mental performance declines with age, the variance does not alter with age. So while it is true that on average 60 year olds will exhibit slower mental and physical reactions than 40 year olds, a substantial proportion (though a declining proportion with age) of 60 year olds will have reaction times at least as good as the average of 40 year olds. Second, they find that many of the laboratory tasks at which older people perform less well than the young – such tasks as remembering or recognizing word or number sequences, have little relevance to the employment tasks encountered by most workers. Third, they find that older people can improve their performance in these laboratory tests through repetition or training – in other words they can compensate for some of the functional decrement of age by working harder at the task in question (Charness, 1985).

It is therefore very difficult to infer anything concrete about workplace performance from laboratory experiments, and an alternative approach is to observe in detail the actual workplace behaviour of workers of different age. A number of such enquiries were carried out in Britain in the 1950s (though little subsequent work has been done in this area) investigating the work performance of older men in a diverse range of employments such as mining, printing and bus driving (for details, see Davies and Sparrow, 1985; Thane, 1990: 299–301). They found that older workers were as efficient as younger workers in tasks which required skill, experience and self-motivation, but were less efficient at work carried out at an externally-set pace, for instance on a production line (Clark and Dunne, 1955; Welford, 1958). Given the relative decline in production-line manufacturing over the last three or four decades and the expansion of less closely monitored or strictly paced service sector employment, it might be thought that job opportunities for older workers would have increased significantly over time. The evidence of age related participation and unemployment rates suggest that this has not been the case, at least in the North American and West European economies (see Table 4.3). Older workers have borne the brunt of labour market adjustments during the recessions of the 1970s and 1980s, even in the United States where the Age Discrimination in Employment Act outlawed age discrimination in hiring and firing decisions. One researcher who has studied executive recruitment and employment practices in some of the larger British companies has noted that 'You are considered an old manager at 40, but to have great potential in your late thirties. So your life as a high-flying executive can be pretty short' (Sue Webb of the Industrial Society, quoted in *The Observer*, 21 April 1991: 38). It seems frankly implausible, given the findings of industrial psychologists and sociologists about the abilities of older workers, to believe that such a rapid decline in employment prospects for workers who reach middle age reflects the diminishing marginal productivity of this age group.

An alternative explanation is that there is a deep-rooted prejudice in western societies against older people who are *believed* to be slower, less adaptable and less productive than the young. Western ageism is often contrasted with a veneration for the aged which is said to exist in Japan, and which is reflected in both the high average age of Japanese executives and the continued high rates of labour force participation for male workers in their late 50s and 60s (Ono, 1989–90; see also Figure 4.6). In the 1950s it was found that some of the apparent conservatism and inflexibility of older workers in Britain was a product of socialization rather than any inevitable physical or mental consequences of biological ageing. Social expectations which categorize the young as dynamic and productive and the old as inefficient or redundant still prevail. If, however, the issue were simply one of cultural prejudice rather than economic incentive, then it needs to be explained why ageism in employment seems to have been sustained, and even enhanced, over the last three or four decades, while sexism has been gradually diminished, though not eradicated, as more employers have come to recognize the true productive potential of female workers. It is, of course, practically impossible to weight the restrictive and oppressive influence of employer prejudice towards women against employer prejudice towards older men.

The widespread existence of the positive age–earnings relationship, however, gives employers a strong economic incentive to shed older workers in times of retrenchment not because they are unproductive in any absolute sense, but because the employment of younger workers who are paid somewhat less than their marginal revenue product gives the employer higher unit profits. It is perhaps significant that in Japan, where employment rates for men aged 65 plus are four times higher than in the United Kingdom (35.8 per cent compared with 8.8 per cent), it is common for men to retire from their primary employment between 55 and 60, and then to embark on a 'second career', sometimes with the same employer though more usually with a small employer in the trade or service sector, and in a job with fewer responsibilities, lower pay, no automatic age increments and no pension rights (pension and health care cover having been acquired during the 'primary' career) (Martin and Ogawa, 1988; McCallum, 1988). It has not been demonstrated that the absence of a strict link between age and earnings in 'secondary' careers is the cause of the high participation rates of older men in Japan, but it seems reasonable to assume that it is a contributory factor.

In North America and Western Europe, traditional age related earnings profiles and cultural assumptions about the low productivity and low learning capacity of older workers reinforce each other in limiting the labour market opportunities of older workers. Where employers have been willing to set aside these commonplace beliefs they have found many older people to be highly employable. Older workers tend to have lower rates of absenteeism and job mobility than the young, and are often seen to be more 'responsible', requiring less supervision (Coates et al., 1990: 25). One case study from the United States is particularly revealing: in the early 1980s the Travelers Insurance Company started to recruit older people to fill the part-time and temporary vacancies formerly taken by juvenile or casual workers. The company found that the performance of its own retirees in temporary jobs was far superior to that of staff supplied by employment agencies, and in 1985 the company inaugurated 'un-retirement parties' to expand enrolments in its Job Bank of retirees willing to undertake temporary employment. Travelers also found, to its surprise, that many retirees are willing to be retrained in the use of new technologies, and that this training takes no longer than for younger workers. A senior vice-president of the company reports that:'the return on our training investment has been substantial. Far from being wasteful – the common attitude towards spending money to train older workers – this program has yielded a productive group of people not otherwise available to us at any cost' (Libassi, 1988).

With workers, particularly younger workers, becoming a shrinking resource over the next thirty or forty years, employment policies such as those adopted by the Travelers Insurance Company which harbour rather than waste older-aged labour may be increasingly attractive to employers. Rapid technological advance in both service and manufacturing sectors provides a further incentive to retain and retrain older workers rather than rely on new entrants for new skills. With job specific skills now sometimes depreciating so rapidly that even workers in their mid-30s can be considered to be technologically backward, it is no longer appropriate to view education and training as a stage of life to be completed by the late teens or early twenties. If the enhancement of human capital through employment training is viewed on a par with investment in physical capital, with a depreciation period of perhaps ten years, then in terms of pay-back it may make as much sense to train a 50 year old as a 20 year old. In fact it may make better economic sense to train the 50 year old, given the lower rate of labour turnover among older workers (Davies and Sparrow, 1985).

More retraining and improved employment prospects for older

workers are only likely to occur on a large scale, however, if employers alter their age related promotion and remuneration policies. There will be strong labour market pressures for them to do this. Shortages of juvenile workers are likely to narrow the differential between the juvenile and adult wage, and competition between employers for school-leavers may increase the level of juvenile job mobility and further reduce the incentive for employers to invest in general skills training for their young workers. At the same time the large baby-boom cohorts in their 40s and 50s will increase average employment costs and produce severe barriers to vertical mobility for younger workers as promotion prospects decline (Keyfitz, 1973). The economic incentive for employers to break the traditional link between age and earnings will be great, but opposition from employees is likely to be equally strong for two reasons, one structural and one political.

The structural reason relates to the nature of the occupational pension schemes which dominate in Western Europe and North America. As noted in Chapter Four, most public sector employees, and many private sector workers in large and medium-sized businesses, are enrolled in pension schemes in which the value of the pension on retirement is related to their pay in the final year of employment (or some other variant of the value of their final salary). Therefore any diminution of their salary as they approach retirement has an effect not just on current income but on future pension income as well; the real cost of a small pay cut in the last year of work is multiplied by the number of years of expected pension income. Final salary pension schemes, therefore, require a positive age–earnings profile for them to be attractive to the workforce. This is not true of the alternative, and less common, 'money purchase' pension schemes, in which a defined percentage of a person's salary paid as a pension contribution forms a personal fund which is used to purchase an annuity on retirement. Under a money purchase scheme, as long as an individual has positive earnings and is paying pension contributions, the value of the ultimate pension annuity will continue to rise, even if annual earnings for the worker are declining.

Figure 6.3 illustrates these two possibilities for a hypothetical worker whose earnings rise with age until 60 and then decline along the earnings function *EE*. If the worker is in a final salary scheme in which the pension paid equals 50 per cent of the final year's salary, the real value of his or her annual pension income (assuming no inflation) is determined by the pension function *PP*. The optimal retirement age for this worker is at age 60, since further employment will clearly diminish the annual value of the pension received.

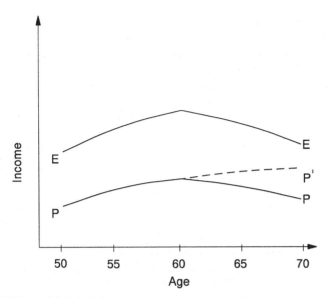

EE is employment income.
PP is pension income in a defined benefit scheme
where pension is 50 per cent of final salary.
PP' is pension income produced by accumulated
savings in a defined contribution scheme.

Figure 6.3 *Pension income for a hypothetical worker in
'defined benefit' and 'defined contribution' pension schemes*

If, however, the worker is in a money purchase scheme in which the
pension value of the final annuity exactly matches the value of the
final salary pension scheme up to age 60, then below this age the
annual pension value is also described by the pension function *PP*.
Above age 60, however, although the worker's annual salary is
declining, the value of his or her pension annuity continues to rise
(though at a slower rate than previously) because some fixed
percentage of the worker's diminishing salary continues to be paid
into his or her growing pension annuity fund. The annual value of
the worker's pension is described by the pension function *PP'*, and
optimal retirement age is not determined, therefore, by any immediate link between current salary and future pension levels. It is
apparent from Figure 6.3 that the reversal of the positive age–
earnings relationship at some earlier age could significantly reduce
the expected pension income of workers in final salary pension
schemes. Older workers are unlikely to accede to any weakening of
the positive association between age and earnings, even if it is likely

to increase their employment prospects marginally, unless it can be done without reducing their pension entitlements. If employers wish to change the traditional shape of the employment contract, they will first have to alter the pension contract.

The second, political, reason for employee opposition to non-age related earnings lies in the dominant numerical position the baby-boom cohorts have, and will continue to have, in trade unions and other employee associations. Public choice voting models suggest that in democratic, participatory organizations policy goals will tend to represent the interests of the dominant (age) groups (Buchanan and Tullock, 1962). As the workforce ages, unions are likely to shift their bargaining efforts away from the training and promotion of the young towards the income and pension preservation of middle-aged and older workers. This has already happened in US collectively bargained pension schemes which have been concentrated in declining industries with rapidly ageing workforces (Sass, 1989), and can be expected to occur in other countries and industrial sectors over the next two or three decades. Although younger workers might benefit from less age structuring in salaries and promotion, their's will be a minority voice in labour organizations.

The extent to which large cohorts can use their voting power to capture resources, whether in the social security system or the labour market, may have an important bearing on the relative welfare of different birth cohorts, and may act as a countervailing force against the economic costs of belonging to a large birth cohort. Richard Easterlin (1980) has suggested that being a member of a large cohort diminishes an individual's lifetime earnings because the extra competition for jobs reduces age specific wages (or slows their rate of increase). There have been a number of studies which confirm that the large youth cohorts that entered the labour market in the 1970s suffered both low relative earnings and high unemployment rates (US results are summarized in Bloom et al., 1987; UK evidence is examined by Ermisch, 1988b; Wright, 1991). Although the effect of cohort size on earnings appears to diminish as cohorts age and become more 'mixed up' (e.g. a five year age difference between a 19 and a 24 year old is far more significant in terms of employment and remuneration than a similar age difference between a 42 and a 47 year old), the surveys indicate that being a member of a large birth cohort depresses lifetime income. It does not, however, mean that baby-boomers are particularly poor.

Behavioural changes, such as acquiring more or better education, have enabled baby-boomers to avoid some of the competitive pressures in the juvenile labour market by postponing labour market entry through university enrolment and then by using the qualifications gained to leap-frog into jobs hitherto reserved for older and more experienced workers (Riboud, 1987). And, as Easterlin et al. have recently pointed out, baby-boomers have drastically altered their demographic behaviour relative to earlier generations 'by remaining single, by having fewer children, by doubling up with parents or others, by forming unmarried couple unions, and by coupling mother's work with childbearing. For the baby boom generation, altered demographic behaviour has been the key to transforming adverse labor market conditions into favorable living levels' (Easterlin et al., 1990: 287). Whether these behavioural changes have occurred as a *consequence* of the depressive lifetime income effects of large cohort size cannot, however, be demonstrated, nor even adequately tested. Nor can it be determined whether in the future the baby-boomers will use their voting power to appropriate some of the (higher) income of the small and economically favoured baby-bust generation which follows them.

Relative cohort size can, of course, be altered by net migration, and while it seems unlikely that the baby-boomers will emigrate in large numbers to less developed countries with younger age structures, it is conceivable that the scarce juvenile labour of the baby-bust generation will be supplemented by immigration. Since the Second World War labour shortages in the United States have been met by a substantial inflow of unskilled workers from Mexico and Puerto Rico, in Western Europe by similar immigrations from North Africa and the Eastern Mediterranean, and in the case of the United Kingdom from the Caribbean and the Indian subcontinent. It can be shown, however, that short-term attempts to use immigration to stabilize the ratio of workers to pensioners in the developed countries would create waves of immigration of increasing amplitude as immigration would need to oscillate inversely with the fertility waves created by baby-boom and baby-bust. Furthermore, the immigration would have to be on a scale far greater than that seen since the Second World War (Blanchet, 1988).

Whether labour market conditions in the future will be allowed to influence political decisions about immigration policy as they did in the 1950s and 1960s remains to be seen. The demographic pressure may be stronger, because in the early decades of the next century the economically active populations of developing countries such as Mexico, Pakistan and Nigeria will still be growing at over 2 per cent per annum, whereas the workforces of the developed countries will be stagnant or declining (International Labour Office, 1986), and this will tend to increase labour cost differentials. Political responses to immigration in developed countries have tended to be restrictive during the 1970s and 1980s when domestic unemployment has been high, but it is by no means certain that attitudes to immigration in the future will neatly reflect labour market conditions. The problems of assimilation encountered by both host and immigrant populations as a consequence of the post-war migrations may have altered fundamentally popular perceptions of the desirability of using immigration as a labour market policy (Höhn, 1987).

Two effects of population ageing on production and the labour market – an increase in average labour costs because of positive age–earnings profiles, and a depressive effect on cohort lifetime income for the baby-boomers because of more intense labour market competition – can be predicted with some certainty. However, the economic conclusions that can be drawn from these predictions are very tentative. Uncertainty about the real relationship between age and productivity makes it difficult to determine how much (if any) of the extra wages bill implied by population ageing will be matched by increased labour productivity. Furthermore, the magnitude of the behavioural changes exhibited by the baby-boomers, relative to older cohorts, means that the depressive impact on lifetime income of large cohort size may not be reflected in either economic measures of the living standards or more general indicators of the well-being of the baby-boom generation. Part of the reason for the vagueness of these economic predictions about productivity and living standards is that they are derived from a labour market analysis which says little about changes in the capital stock. Since labour and capital can, at the margin, be substituted for each other, and since the size of and changes in the capital stock are important determinants of labour productivity and economic growth, we need to include an analysis of saving and investment behaviour in order to develop a more complete picture of interactions between the economy and population age structure.

Saving and Investment

Changes in age structure are likely to affect the savings rate of a society to an extent determined by age specific savings propensities (this will occur independently of any impact on savings rates deriving from the intergenerational transfer functions of social security systems). A rise in the savings rate will, other things being equal, lead to a reduction in the real rate of interest which will itself promote more net investment, increase the size of the capital stock and stimulate future economic growth. However, in practice the scale, direction and macroeconomic consequences of any such demographically-induced change in the savings rate are difficult to determine. Two approaches are typically used to construct projections of future savings rates; the first incorporates demographic variables into life cycle models of aggregate private saving, and the second applies actual age specific saving parameters to population projections (this is essentially the same procedure as that described above for estimating the effect of demographic change on consumption, since that part of individual net income which is not consumed must, by definition, be saved). Heller (1989) has used both approaches to estimate the impact of demographic change on saving rates in the major industrialized countries which constitute the Group of Seven (G-7). He concludes that 'over the period 1980–2025, the models imply that demographic pressures could lead to a decline in G-7 private savings by 5 to 12 per cent of GDP' (Heller, 1989: 140).

This methodology does, however, have two obvious weaknesses. First, the application of current age specific consumption/savings rates to long-run population projections ignores the potential impact of period and cohort effects on savings. There is no particular reason to expect the baby-boomers to have the same savings propensities in 2015 when they reach the age of 65 as their 65 year old parents have today. Second, it is not clear that savings rates decline with old age as is assumed in the life cycle hypothesis. Analysis of US longitudinal panel data has shown, for instance, that elderly people do not decumulate housing wealth as they age (Venti and Wise, 1989). In a review of this US literature Hurd (1990) claims that on balance recent research supports the life cycle hypothesis that dissaving occurs in old age, but this finding is not conclusive. For instance Aaron et al. (1989) point out that savings rates for the retired population in the United States are little below those for people aged 45–64, and clearly above those for the 25–44 age group. In fact, because consumption expenditure tends to fall in old age, many older people find themselves saving out of their annuity or pension income rather than reducing their accumulated wealth (Börsch-Supan, 1991: 121). A recent survey concludes that

> One way to describe the current state of knowledge about savings is that a great deal is known at a theoretical level about savings determinants taken one at a time. Much less is known about the interactions of these determinants, and too little is known at an empirical level about the true causes of savings. As is often the case in economics, the theory seems to have advanced well beyond the empirical research. (Kotlikoff, 1989: 34)

Even if private savings rates in any country do decline because of population ageing, it is not inevitable that this will be to the detriment of that country's long-term economic performance. Other things being equal, slower labour force growth lowers the rate of capital accumulation necessary to maintain the capital/labour ratio in the economy, and so reduces the need for savings and increases consumption per capita. On the other hand, a demographically-induced rise in the proportion of the population not in employment lowers average output per capita, and so tends to reduce consumption per capita. To what extent the effect of lower investment requirements offsets the long-run dependency effect on per capita consumption depends on the specific economic and demographic circumstances of each country.

It also depends on the relationship between population structure and innovation, since technical change and innovation are usually considered to be important influences on the growth path of an economy. A number of possibilities have been discussed. Habakkuk (1962) suggested that incentives to innovate are strongest when population growth is slow and labour is scarce, since technical progress tends to be labour-saving. Simon (1977: 10, 1981:196–215), however, argues that technological progress is to an important degree *a function* of population growth, because a larger, denser and more rapidly expanding population experiences increasing economies of scale in both the production and the application of new technologies. It has also been suggested that because new knowledge is embodied primarily in the recently-educated cohorts of young adults, a declining proportion of younger people will produce a less technologically up-to-date workforce (van Imhoff, 1988), and that ageing leads to a loss of economic dynamism and innovative spirit (Wattenberg, 1987: 71–5).

The variety of possible interactions between changes in the rate of growth and age structure of the population and savings, investment and technical progress is so wide that a very broad range of macroeconomic outcomes can be postulated with some plausibility. This is particularly the case when economic models are extended from a purely national focus to incorporate some of the consequences of differential rates of ageing across the industrialized economies. It has been suggested, for instance, that because of differential ageing the United States will be able to import surplus capital from European countries from 2020 when the retirement of the American baby-boomers begins to create a shortage of domestic savings in the United States (Cutler et al., 1990). Economists have attempted to take many of these factors into account in dynamic general equilibrium models which simulate the economic effect of various policy responses to population ageing (Auerbach et al., 1989; Cutler et al., 1990). But these models are often sensitive to assumptions made about the real nature of savings behaviour or labour force participation or technical progress, and as Marchand

and Pestieau have recently remarked, 'most current models, even the most sophisticated, assume away uncertainty which is however at the heart of retirement decisions and intergenerational redistribution' (Marchand and Pestieau, 1991: 452). It is not surprising, therefore, to find that the normative implications of alternative modelling exercises can vary widely, or even be diametrically opposed. For instance, Aaron et al. (1989) conclude that America needs a massive rise in its domestic savings rate over the next two or three decades to cope with the long-run costs of demographic change. Cutler et al. (1990: 53), on the other hand, argue that 'recent and prospective demographic changes do not warrant increasing the national saving rate. These changes increase wealth in the short-run, reduce the rate of return to saving, and attract foreign capital. Holding all else equal, their net effect would be a *reduction* in the optimal national saving rate.'

Such a fundamental disagreement between economists over policy prescriptions might lead a sceptical observer to conclude that nothing of substance can be said about the relationship between population ageing and macroeconomic performance. But this would be both an inappropriate and an unfortunate conclusion. Inappropriate because the economic simulations demonstrate that demographic change has the potential substantially to affect the long-run economic performance of the developed economies, and unfortunate because it might encourage a degree of political, economic and social complacency about population ageing that could undermine attempts to develop positive policy responses to the changing demographic environment. Because most economic analysis of population ageing has concentrated on social security issues and the specific distributional problem of funding benefits for rapidly rising numbers of pensioners in the second decade of the next century, economists have sometimes been caricatured as promoting a wholly pessimistic view of population ageing. As this chapter has shown, the economic analysis of ageing is much more wide-ranging than this, and much less doctrinaire.

If economists are to be criticized, then perhaps the charge should be that they are too open-minded. They have asked the question 'Will the changing age structure of the developed economies over the next forty years affect economic performance?', and have concluded that this demographic restructuring has the *potential* to alter patterns of consumption, production, employment, savings, investment and innovation. But because of the interactions between these separate elements, it is impossible to be sure of either the scale or, in some cases, of the direction of the economic impact. Our understanding of the processes of economic growth and of innovation is really too primitive to permit confident long-run economic assessments to be made. On the other hand, shorter-run reactions to ageing in, for instance, the labour and housing markets, can be anticipated with greater certainty. The economic analysis shows that population ageing is *not* just a social security issue that affects the distribution of economic resources and which can be addressed by fiddling with pension levels and contribution rates. It is a demographic force that will impinge on all aspects of economic performance – on the way we work and produce, spend and save, invest, inherit and bequeath. We cannot be sure exactly how ageing will affect this broad range of social and economic behaviour, but knowledge of the possible effects gives us an opportunity to devise institutional and political responses that will maximize potential social and economic benefits and minimize costs. It is to these policy options that we turn in the final chapter.

7

Ageing and Public Policy

The majority of older people in Britain today live on incomes well below the average for the total population. According to the government's own data, 5.6 million pensioners have incomes so low that they qualify for means-tested benefits to raise their living standard above the poverty line (DSS, 1988). In this respect British pensioners fare significantly less well than their peers in many other West European countries. In France, for instance, the average equivalent income for a retired person is now above the average equivalent income for all adults (Rapports Officiels, 1991: 65). The current poverty of many British pensioners is the clearest evidence available of the failure of the British public pension system to provide adequate income in old age. There is a pressing need for public policy initiatives to enhance the welfare of older people but, as the foregoing chapters make clear, it is important that new policies be considered in the economic and social context of an ageing, and ultimately a declining, population.

Changes to pension rules can have a very long-run effect. Moves to improve the economic welfare of today's 80 year olds will have a direct impact on today's 30 year olds, in terms of both tax liabilities and expectations of future public income support. These expectations have a bearing on current pension decisions, and the pensioning choices that 30 year olds make today will carry welfare and financing implications into the second half of the twenty-first century. We should be wary of any quick fix for today's retired population which does not take proper account of the long-run implications for these pensioners' grandchildren, and for their grandchildren's grandchildren, the young adults of 2050.

As we have shown, taking account of future economic and demographic interactions is far from easy because of the uncertainties which surround most of the demographic, economic and policy parameters which relate to ageing and welfare. Small differences in initial assumptions about the scale of international capital flows or the age profile of savings or the interaction between demographic change and technical progress can produce widely divergent long-run projections of growth rates and funding liabilities. Similarly small differences in retirement ages and trends, or pension indexing arrangements, can be extrapolated into highly optimistic or gloomily pessimistic predictions of pensioners' living standards. In many cases we have no good grounds, either empirical or theoretical, for favouring one assumption over another, yet the power of compound growth over a forty or fifty year period makes even small differences in initial conditions matter a great deal in terms of projected outcomes and recommended policies.

There is, it seems, a tension between short-term public policy goals of ensuring that today's elderly population has an acceptable standard of living, and long-term goals of preventing public transfer systems from becoming grossly unfair or grossly inefficient. The tension itself reflects the divergent approaches to the study of population ageing taken by different social science disciplines. The methodological individualism that dominates in economics places great weight on the fairness of public transfer systems for all people who participate in them, on the harmful effects of disincentives to work or save that can be created by tax-financed state pensions, and on the efficiency of private, market-determined decisions about how and when to save or spend. When these concerns about inequity and disincentives are matched with projections which indicate that the elderly population throughout the developed economies will grow significantly over the next forty years while the number of 'prime age' adults will stagnate or decline, then clear policy imperatives emerge: the growth of public welfare expenditure and of tax rates must be curbed or reversed, labour supply must be expanded, and saving rates increased (OECD, 1988a). In most of the economic analysis of population ageing, the welfare of older people in the future appears (if at all) as very definitely subservient to the goal of effective macroeconomic management.

For social policy analysts, on the other hand, welfare is typically the dominant concern, and the relative poverty of most older people today establishes an a priori need for policies to improve the welfare of the elderly. The methodological individualism of economics militates against enforced interpersonal transfers (such as in public social security systems) because of the difficulty of comparing utility gains and losses across individuals. The welfare concerns of social policy, on the other hand, encourage or even require interpersonal comparisons and transfers. As long as poverty and welfare are measured by *relative* rather than *absolute* criteria, then the well-being of any group can be defined *only* by reference to other groups in society. Again clear policy imperatives emerge: immediate action should be taken to improve the relative living standards of poor elderly people today; uncertainty about the relative living standards of older people in the future means that the long-run welfare effects of current policy initiatives are incalculable and should be given little weight in any policy assessments.

Sociologists often take a longer-term view than social policy analysts, and rather than concentrate on the immediate welfare of older people they instead examine the processes by which different groups of people become categorized. They emphasize that the restructuring of the life course in the twentieth century and the evolution of retirement as a distinct (and lengthening) stage of life has had both positive (leisure) and negative (income) effects for older people. The new social norm of withdrawal from the labour force between the ages of 60 and 65 has not been matched by a compensating norm of adequate income support in retirement. Social pressures increasingly deny older people an opportunity to earn a living without providing them with an alternative. Short-term pension adjustments can ameliorate the immediate financial problems, but only fundamental change to the processes of social differentiation and to the distribution of power in society will permit some further reconstruction of the life course and an improvement in the socioeconomic status of older people.

The lack of consensus over how public policy should respond to the dual problems of current old age poverty and future population ageing is, therefore, a joint product of the difficulty of adequately incorporating long-run economic, social and demographic inter-actions into our predictive models and of the different disciplinary backgrounds and methodological preferences of the various commentators. Much of the discussion focuses on the *structural* attributes of alternative policy scenarios and their projected long-run outcomes. A vast array of (often conflicting) proposals can be found in the literature concerning pension finance, retirement policies, care provision and so on. These proposals relate to possible changes in current policy structures such as retirement rules or systems of pension finance, and are based on the implicit assumption that policy changes *now* can resolve long-run economic or welfare problems, even though we know that these problems cannot even be adequately identified, let alone solved, given the current state of knowledge. A more constructive approach is to regard public policy as a flexible *means* that can be manipulated over several decades in order to achieve a desired set of *goals*. There will always be disagreement over goals, but we think we can derive some generally acceptable objectives from the discussion in the preceding four chapters.

1   *Welfare*: The data discussed in Chapter Three demonstrate the tremendous heterogeneity of older people in terms of the level and sources of their income and wealth, their state of health and

level of functional ability, and their overall welfare. The data also show that there is some association between low income, low wealth and poor health, all of which are correlated with age, since the very old are both poorer and sicker than the recently retired. Some of the relative impoverishment of the very old may be a function of age, but much of it is a cohort effect, since people who retired in the late 1960s probably left work with at best only modest occupational pension entitlements, and may well have seen the value of other savings fall during the rapid inflation of the 1970s. The much more comprehensive pensioning arrangements available for large parts of today's workforce makes it probable that more people will in the future enter retirement with high incomes and substantial assets. On the other hand, the existence of many marginal workers in temporary and short-term employment makes it likely that large numbers of people will continue to reach the end of their working life having accumulated few pension entitlements and few other realizable assets.

This means that Titmuss's observation about 'two nations' in retirement (Titmuss, 1955), those with decent occupational pensions and those without, are more relevant to the 1990s than they were to the 1950s, and may be more relevant still to the early decades of the next century. Fifty years ago to be old and retired meant to be poor for nearly everyone. In the future, retirement living standards increasingly will reflect past labour market status and lifetime earnings trajectories, and the income and wealth distribution of the elderly population will more closely resemble that of the working population. Such changes in the economic circumstances of older people will alter the problem of old age poverty, but they will not eradicate it, and we believe that a fundamental objective of public policy should be to ensure that all elderly retired persons enjoy an adequate standard of living.

2 *Work*: Chapter Three showed that a person's previous employment record is a key determinant of his or her welfare in old age; Chapter Four showed that labour force activity has declined greatly at older ages over the course of the twentieth century. It is clear that some of this increased retirement has been imposed by retirement rules, poor health, and fluctuations in labour demand which have created high levels of unemployment. Part of the move towards higher retirement rates at earlier ages, however, is a consequence of the improving financial status of some older people which has allowed them to exercise their preference for leisure over work. There is little consensus about the relative strengths of these push and pull factors in the past, but this need not deter us from establishing objectives for the future: that no workers should be

compelled to retire because of their age, that the maximum possible range of employment opportunities should be available for those older people who wish to continue in employment, but, following the welfare objective, that no older person should be forced to continue in marginal and demeaning employment because of their poverty.

3 *Transfers*: The discussion in Chapter Five emphasized that public transfers to older people (whether in the form of pension payments, health care or other services) involve public transfers from (tax)payers. To prioritize the claims of elderly people above claims from other groups in society (whether defined by age or some other criteria) simply because older people have passed some arbitrarily defined age threshold is a form of ageism which we believe to be objectionable on grounds of inequity. In this sense a state age pension is undoubtedly ageist, whereas care for the physically frail elderly is not, because it is provided in response to functional incapacity. State pensions would be non-ageist only if they were provided in response to financial incapacity or if similar benefits were provided to all people regardless of age. As the number of wealthy retired people in the future increases, the idea of automatic transfers from taxpayers to pensioners on grounds of age will become less appealing. This will particularly be the case if those paying the taxes have lower discretionary incomes than those receiving cash benefits. Already in France the growing financial resources of older people has stimulated inter-familial transfers from retired parents to their working age children and grand-children, and these tend to counter public transfers from workers to pensioners (Cribier, 1989). This is, of course, the antithesis of social security since it makes income support and redistribution come to rest on the fortune of birth and family sentiment, highly variable conditions whose unreliability public welfare systems were designed to overcome. The objective, therefore, should be to ensure that public transfer systems achieve their welfare and social protection goals without being consistently unfair to certain social groups.

4 *Growth*: Chapter Six has shown that population ageing can have a major impact on the rate of growth of market demand, the labour force, productivity, saving and investment. Although the interactions between these separate elements of the macroeconomic system in the future can only be guessed at, the available evidence suggests that demographic change *could* precipitate a fundamental and long-run decline in economic growth rates. Not all the economic variables are obviously and directly amenable to policy intervention, but a sensible strategy for minimizing any deleterious effect of ageing on growth would be one that maximizes labour

supply, enhances the quality of human capital to compensate for restriction on quantity, and stimulates savings in order to boost the rate of capital formation.

The potential for public policy intervention to meet these broad objectives in the areas of work, welfare, transfers and growth is enormous, and we will do no more than highlight what we believe to be the most direct ways of achieving these objectives. In the labour market some expansion of employment opportunities for older people who wish to continue in employment is likely to emerge automatically in response to labour shortages caused by shifts in the population age structure. Already in Britain the home improvements company B & Q has adopted a policy of employing *only* persons aged over 50 in its store at Macclesfield, a hiring policy forced on the company by a shortage of young workers who are the usual recruits for retail jobs. This store has profits 18 per cent higher, absenteeism 39 per cent lower and staff turnover six times lower than in comparable stores. The company now intends to have 10 per cent of its national workforce aged over 50 – a case, it seems, of the profit motive dominating habitual age prejudice (*The Independent*, 2 October 1991). The abolition of age thresholds on all training schemes would be a positive move to allow those older persons who wished to re-enter (or stay in) the labour market to enhance their skills, and the prohibition of mandatory retirement on grounds of age (as in the United States) would encourage employers to think more carefully about the real productivity of older workers.

We should remember, however, that in the United States the Age Discrimination in Employment Act has had only a limited impact on the employment opportunities of older workers, many of whom are still levered-out of the labour force through a mixture of pension inducements and threats. In Chapter Four we showed how seniority wage systems and final salary (defined benefit) pension schemes interact to produce strong incentives for both employers and workers to choose retirement at a set age. In order to give workers real choice about when to retire, occupational pensions need to be converted from a defined benefit to a defined contribution basis, a move which would have the added advantage of facilitating mobility between pension schemes and protecting future pensioners' assets from the depredations of asset-grabbing takeovers or company 'pension contribution holidays'. The greater choice over retirement that defined contribution pensions would allow workers needs to be bolstered with further anti-discrimination legislation to remove gender differentiation in pension rules. EC (European Community) regulations have already brought pressure to bear on UK occupational pension schemes to provide equal treatment for men and women; the removal of gender specific provisions in all public or private pension schemes should be a matter of priority (Tompkins, 1989). EC attempts to facilitate labour mobility between the member states will also be promoted by a shift to defined contribution pensions which are readily portable across frontiers. In order to make the pension entitlements associated with all jobs as clear as possible, all salaries should have to be quoted both gross and net of (employer and employee) pension contributions.

The immediate aim of these proposals is to expand the labour market opportunities and choices of all older workers, but they have the additional advantage of enhancing the prospects for long-run economic growth. They do this in three ways; by expanding the total labour supply, by creating more incentives for older cohorts of workers to improve and update their work skills, and by creating incentives for a higher level of personal saving for old age. In Chapter Six we showed that the long-run impact of population ageing on necessary saving rates in the developed economies is impossible to determine, but there is a general consensus that saving rates in most developed countries are at present too low, (Heller, 1989), and a move to defined contribution pensions could stimulate private savings.

The objectives relating to welfare and transfers involve rather more contentious public policy issues because they can appear to be mutually incompatible. The demographic trajectories of the developed countries over the next fifty years means that a significant increase in public welfare provision for older people will necessarily involve proportionately greater increases in contributions from relatively small cohorts of tax paying workers if the real value of welfare benefits is to be preserved. Social security contribution rates of over 40 per cent, as have been projected for Germany and France for the fourth decade of the next century, certainly look untenable, but it is less clear that social security systems need to aim for strict equality of treatment between successive cohorts of contributors and beneficiaries. We suspect that the real rate of return enjoyed by successive birth cohorts for their contributions to public pension systems is of interest only to those economists or actuaries who spend their lives calculating real rates of return, and even among these experts there is considerable disagreement over key parameters such as the appropriate discount rate. For most people complex calculations about the equity of inter-cohort, intertemporal redistributions are of little immediate relevance.

The equity of public pension systems is, we believe, more likely to be judged by the perceived current living standards of groups of pensioners and of workers. Public pension systems will be deemed to have failed in their welfare functions if they leave many older people abjectly poor, and to have failed in their transfer functions if they leave contributing workers with dependent children in a significantly less advantageous financial situation than benefit-receiving retired people. An obvious way to overcome the tension between the welfare and transfer objectives is to target public pensions only on those people who qualify under the welfare criteria. There are, however, three common objections to the targeting of pensions: the administrative costs are high; the small size of the 'Woopie' population means that the expenditure savings are minimal; and the take-up rate of means-tested benefits among pensioners tends to be low; so that already very poor pensioners may end up with even lower incomes.

The small size of the immediate expenditure savings is not a major obstacle as long as the impact of targeting increases over time in order to create maximum expenditure savings in 2030 when the demographic ratios will be at their most adverse. However the imprecision, administrative complexity and low take-up of means-tested benefits, especially those for older people, makes this a far from ideal way of solving the welfare problems associated with old age, even though it can ameliorate the transfer problems associated with population ageing. Furthermore, targeting may undermine the transfer objective of treating different cohorts equitably if the targeting criteria become more strict over time.

We believe, however, that strict equality between cohorts in rates of return to social security contributions, or equality in terms of rates of tax levied or levels of benefits received, are impractical as well as undesirable transfer goals. A viable concept of intergenerational equity for social security systems to aim for during a period of rapid population ageing is that of a fixed ratio between the value of the public pension and average net real income. The determination of this ratio is, of course, a matter for debate, but in Britain there can be little doubt that the current level is too low, and that the projected further decline if the current indexation system is retained (see Table 4.5) would reduce pensioners with no other means of support to a state of abject want.

A fixed parity between the public pension and average net income offers three advantages over both the (diminishing) flat rate public pension payable to all older people in the United Kingdom and the earnings-related public pensions typical in other European countries. First, it ensures that pensioners share equally with the rest of the population in increases or decreases in real incomes over time. Second, it should prevent pensioners individually accumulating such large public transfer entitlements that they receive substantially higher state benefits than, for instance, families with dependent children. Third, a stable long-run ratio would allow all current workers to make coherent plans for their own old age. Repeated administrative and political interference with public pension schemes, such as has occurred in most developed countries since the Second World War, is not compatible with coherent individual retirement planning.

A fixed pension/income parity would involve a fundamental change to existing public pension systems. It implies the abandonment of all earnings related benefits and the redirection of any voluntary and individual old age saving to other (public or private) savings institutions. It would also make transparent the real nature of the tax transfers involved in public pension systems and make both contributors and beneficiaries better aware that, despite the use of insurance terminology, public pensions are based on other people's (implicit) promises to pay rather than the proceeds of an accumulated fund.

This system would nevertheless still face the problem that it would be ageist in nature, in that there would be an age requirement to be fulfilled before entitlement. An alternative would be to abandon the concept of an age related pension altogether, in favour of a benefit that was payable to *all* members of society regardless of economic status. In such a system, whether a person's non-participation in the labour market was due to retirement, ill health or unemployment would be irrelevant and the system would be age-blind. Such a strategy approximates a full basic income scheme (Williams, 1989). This would involve the abolition of the present dual system of separately administered state cash benefits and income tax reliefs, and their replacement by a new integrated system of personal basic incomes, which would convert automatically from cash benefit to tax relief and vice versa. All earnings rules would be abolished and individuals would be able to build on their basic incomes through employment earnings, subject to tax. Under a basic income scheme each individual in society would have the unconditional right to an independent, non-means-tested, tax-free income sufficient to meet basic living costs, irrespective of age, gender, occupation or marital status. The basis of entitlement becomes citizenship rather than chronological age. This solves the problem of intergenerational equity as all age groups are assured of the same treatment throughout different stages of the life cycle. By removing an age threshold of entitlement it also provides complete flexibility in choice of retirement age.

Furthermore, a basic income scheme would also meet the welfare objective that no elderly person, or any other member of society, need continue in marginal and degrading employment because of their poverty. If the distinction between earner and non-earner status is removed, so too would be the link between state income in later life and earlier contribution records. At present there are a significant number of elderly people in Britain who do not receive the full pension, either because they are dependent, or because of incomplete contribution records. In 1988 over 4 million elderly married women or widows were claiming on their husband's insurance rather than in their own right (DSS, 1990a: Table 13.34). Under a basic income scheme, income in later life would no longer be seen as 'earned', that is as a product of former work effort, but as something to which everyone is entitled. Means-tested benefits would be abolished, with the tax system acting like a means-test, clawing back the basic incomes of the well off. Problems of take-up would be avoided, while ensuring that goals of equity and redistribution could be achieved.

A flat rate basic income for all citizens may not be sufficient to meet the higher needs of some individuals resulting from their physical incapacity. The present benefits structure discriminates against elderly disabled people. Only persons below age 65 can initiate a claim for mobility allowance; the onset of disability after age 65 is seen as one of the risks inherent in old age and as such is not recompensed, whereas at younger ages it is. The present system recognizes increased need only to the extent that the level of basic pension is raised by £0.25 for pensioners aged over 80. However it is not necessary to associate disability payments (or lack thereof) to age. A basic income scheme could also incorporate an individualized disability costs allowance that would be available to all handicapped and disabled people regardless of age.

Obviously a full basic income scheme may not be realistic in the short-term. Much more research has to be conducted into the funding feasibility and political acceptability of such a scheme. This research is being vigorously pursued by other commentators, in particular the Basic Income Research Group (BIRG, 1985). However, we suggest that a basic income scheme may be one way to achieve both the *inter*generational equity and the *intra*generational welfare objectives. Basic incomes would achieve a greater equality between men and women, and married and single persons. They would also remove the stigma from unemployment and the compulsion from retirement.

The basic income approach unites the dual systems of social insurance and social assistance, and integrates this unified structure with the tax system in order to avoid many of the problems of poverty traps, non take-up of benefit, and of non-eligibility that exist in current practice. It does, however, involve an even greater role for the state in personal financial management and planning, and this may be considered objectionable by those who wish to see a reduction in the role of the state. It is quite possible, however, to devise a largely private and funded (rather than pay-as-you-go and public) solution to the problem of old age support, while still meeting the four objectives on work, welfare, transfers and growth. One such solution would be a Unitary Personal Pension System (UPPS).

In a UPPS all earners would be compelled to contribute a set percentage of their income into a personal retirement fund (PRF), with the contribution rate set so that over a forty year period, an individual on average income would accumulate a fund sufficient to buy an index-linked annuity providing an old age income of, say, 50 per cent of average income. Earners who desire a higher replacement rate can contribute a larger percentage of their income. People with no income, or with an income in any year so low that their contribution is below the minimum capital sum needed to build up the PRF to the required level would receive a capital transfer into their PRF at the end of the financial year. Financial institutions could compete to manage these funds, and would be required to provide annual personal statements of the annuitized value of each PRF, together with details of overall fund performance and management costs. Individuals would be allowed to transfer their PRF between institutions without charge, thereby rewarding the most efficient fund managers. This funded, personal pension system would replace both public tax/contribution-financed pensions and employer-provided occupational pensions, thereby creating a unitary pension system.

The UPPS would meet all four objectives relating to work, welfare, transfers and growth. Employment choice for workers would be maximized because, by being quite independent of the employer, a PRF would be fully portable between jobs. Furthermore, as a defined contribution scheme it would be fully compatible with an earnings profile that declines at higher ages, and so would encourage flexible retirement. The UPPS would also meet the welfare objective by guaranteeing all individuals a minimum annuity-based pension. Un-waged workers with caring responsibilities in the home would receive an appropriate capital transfer for each year's absence from the paid workforce. To ensure income security throughout retirement the annuity stream would need to be indexed (preferably to average net household income), and this indexation would need to be underwritten by the government in order to provide security against medium-term fluctuations in capital market performance.

The transfer objective would be met in two ways. First, because the UPPS is funded, any desire on the part of the current workforce to pay themselves higher pensions in the future could be met only by an increase in current contributions. It would no longer be possible to transfer the cost of generous pension promises onto future generations. Second, the intra-generational transfer – from today's rich to today's poor – would be made quite explicit in terms of the tax cost of providing the annual capital top-up for low earners. Finally, the growth objective would be met by increasing the savings rate. Moreover, a UPPS would have the positive effect of making clear to everyone just how costly retirement income provision really is. At present the real cost of both social security and occupational pensions is, in most countries, largely hidden from view by a combination of employer contributions and subventions from general public revenue. Considered discussion of, and reasonable expectations about, retirement incomes in the future can only be achieved if both the cost and the workings of the pension system are made as transparent as possible.

What we have tried to do in the foregoing discussion is to outline some of the important public policy questions raised by the issue of population ageing and to suggest some generally acceptable policy goals we should have in mind when trying to address these problems. Although the demographic impetus is similar in all the developed countries, differences in the timing and rate of population ageing, and differences in the administrative structure of the public pay-as-you-go pension systems make it unlikely that any single policy regime will be suitable for all countries. But it is equally unlikely that existing policy regimes will be able to live on into the third or fourth decades of the next century without fundamental restructuring. If we can first gain agreement over the public policy objectives relating to work, welfare, transfers and growth, then we will be in a better position to develop coherent and stable proposals for public pension reform.

Bibliography

Aaron, H.J. (1982) *Economic Effects of Social Security*. Washington, DC: Brookings Institution.

Aaron, H.J., Bosworth, B.P. and Burtless, G. (1989) *Can America Afford to Grow Old?*. Washington, DC: Brookings Institution.

Abrams, M. (1978) *Beyond Three Score Years and Ten: a First Report on a Survey of the Elderly*. Mitcham: Age Concern.

Achenbaum, W.A. (1989) 'Public pensions as intergenerational transfers in the United States', pp. 113–36 in P. Johnson, C. Conrad and D. Thomson (eds) *Workers Versus Pensioners*. Manchester: Manchester University Press.

Aldrich, J. (1982) 'The earnings replacement rate of old-age benefits in 12 countries, 1969–80', *Social Security Bulletin*. (US) 45/11: 3–11.

Allen, S.G. (1988) 'Discussion', pp. 297–311 in R. Ricardo-Campbell and E.P. Lazear (eds) *Issues in Contemporary Retirement*. Stanford: Hoover Institution Press.

Allon-Smith, R.D. (1982) 'The evolving geography of the elderly in England and Wales', in A.M. Warnes (ed.) *Geographical Perspectives on the Elderly*. London: John Wiley.

Altman, R. (1982) 'The incomes of the early retired', *Journal of Social Policy* 11: 355–64.

Anderson, M. (1971) *Family Structure in 19th Century Lancashire*. Cambridge: Cambridge University Press.

Arber, S. and Ginn, J. (1991a) 'The invisibility of age: gender and class in later life', *Sociological Review* 39: 260–91.

Arber, S. and Ginn, J. (1991b) *Gender and Later life: a Sociological Analysis of Resources and Constraints*. London: Sage.

Arber, S. and Ginn, J. (forthcoming) 'In sickness and in health: care giving, gender and the independence of elderly people' in C. Marsh and S. Arber (eds) *Households and Families: Divisions and Change*. London: Macmillan.

Atkinson, A.B. and Sutherland, H. (eds) (1988) *Tax Benefit Models* STICERD Occasional Paper 10. London: London School of Economics.

Atkinson, A.B. and Sutherland, H. (1992) 'Two nations in early retirement?: the case of Britain', in A.B. Atkinson and M. Rein (eds) *Age, Work and Social Security*. Basingstoke: Macmillan.

Auerbach, A.J., Kotlikoff, L.J., Hagemann, R. and Nicoletti, G. (1989) 'The economic dynamics of an ageing population: the case of four OECD countries', *OECD Economic Studies* 12: 111–47.

Barr, N. and Coulter, F. (1990) 'Social Security: solution or problem?', pp. 274–337 in J. Hills (ed.) *The State of Welfare: The Welfare State in Britain Since 1974*. Oxford: Oxford University Press.

Barro, R.J. (1974) 'Are government bonds net wealth?', *Journal of Political Economy* 84: 1095–1117.

Barro, R.J. (1978) *The Impact of Social Security on Private Saving: Evidence from the U.S. Time Series.* Washington, DC: American Enterprise Institute.

Basic Income Research Group (BIRG) (1985), *Basic Income.* London: BIRG.

Becker, G.S. (1964) *Human Capital.* New York: NBER.

Becker, G.S. (1981) *A Treatise on the Family.* Cambridge, MA: Harvard University Press.

Benjamin, B., Haberman, S., Helowicz, G., Kaye, G. and Wilkie, A.D. (1985) *Pensions, the Problems of Today and Tomorrow.* London: City University.

Beveridge Report (1942) *Social Insurance and Allied Services.* London: HMSO.

Binstock, R.H. and George, L.K. (1990) *Handbook of Aging and the Social Sciences.* 3rd edn. San Diego: Academic Press.

Blaikie, A. and Macnicol, J. (1989) 'Ageing and Social Policy: a Twentieth century Dilemma', pp. 69–82 in A.M. Warnes (ed.) *Human Ageing and Later Life: Multidisciplinary Perspectives.* London: Edward Arnold.

Blanchet, D. (1988) 'Immigration et régulation de la structure par âge d'une population', *Population* 43: 293–308.

Blinder, A.S. (1988) 'Why is the government in the pension business?', pp. 17–34 in S.M. Wachter (ed.) *Social Security and Private Pensions.* Lexington, MA: Lexington Books.

Bloom, D.E., Freeman, R.B. and Korenman, S.D. (1987) 'The labour-market consequences of generational crowding', *European Journal of Population* 3: 131–76.

Börsch-Supan, A. (1991) 'Aging population: problems and policy options in the US and Germany, *Economic Policy* 12: 104–39.

Bosanquet, N., Laing, W. and Propper, C. (1990) *Elderly Consumers in Britain: Europe's Poor Relations?* London: Laing and Buisson.

Bound, J. (1991) 'Self-reported versus objective measures of health in retirement models', *Journal of Human Resources* 26: 106–38.

Bourgeois-Pichat, J. (1979) 'La transition demographique' in *Population Science in the Service of Mankind.* Leige: IUSSP.

Brody, J.A. (1985) 'Prospects for an ageing population' *Nature* 315, London.

Buchanan, J.M. and Tullock, G. (1962) *The Calculus of Consent.* Ann Arbor: University of Michigan Press.

Burtless, G. (1989) 'Comment', pp. 398–403 in D.A. Wise (ed.) *The Economics of Aging.* Chicago: NBER/University of Chicago Press.

Bytheway, B. (1987) 'Redundancy and the older worker', pp. 84–115 in R. Lee (ed.) *Redundancy, Layoffs and Plant Closures: Their Character, Causes and Consequences.* Beckenham: Croom Helm.

Callahan, D. (1987) *Setting Limits: Medical Goals in an Aging Society.* New York: Simon and Schuster.

Campbell, C.D. and Campbell, R.G. (1976) 'Conflicting views on the effect of old-age and survivors insurance on retirement', *Economic Inquiry* 14: 369–88.

Casey, B. and Laczko, F. (1989) 'Early retired or long-term unemployed? The changing situation of non-working men from 1979 to 1986', *Work, Employment and Society* 3: 509–26.

Census of Population for England and Wales 1911, 1921, 1931, 1951, 1961, 1971, 1981, London: HMSO.

Central Statistical Office (CSO) (1984) *Social Trends 14.* London: HMSO.

CSO (1986) *Social Trends 16.* London: HMSO.

Charness, N. (ed.) (1985) *Aging and Human Performance.* Chichester: John Wiley.

Cigno, A. (1984) 'Consumption versus procreation in economic growth', pp. 2–28 in G. Steinman (ed.) *Economic Consequences of Population Change*. Berlin: Springer-Verlag.

Clark, F. le Gros and Dunne, A.C. (1955) *Ageing in Industry*. London: Nuffield Foundation.

Clark, R.L. and Spengler, J.J. (1980) *The Economics of Individual and Population Aging*. Cambridge: Cambridge University Press.

Clarke, L. (1984) *Domiciliary Services for the Elderly*. London: Croom Helm.

Coates, J.F., Jarratt, J. and Mahaffie, J.B. (1990) *Future Work*. San Francisco: Jossey-Bass Publishers.

Conrad, C. (1990) 'La naissance de la retraite moderne: l'Allemagne dans une comparaison internationale. (1850–1960)', *Population* 45: 531–62.

Courant, P.N., Gramlich E.M. and Laitner, J.P. (1984) 'A dynamic microeconomic estimate of the life-cycle model', pp. 279–313 in H.J. Aaron and G. Burtless (eds) *Retirement and Economic Behaviour*. Washington, DC: Brookings Institution.

Creedy, J. and Disney, R. (1988) *Population Ageing and Social Security* Research Paper No. 195 Department of Economics, University of Melbourne.

Creedy, J. and Disney, R. (1989) 'The new pension scheme in Britain', pp. 224–38 in A. Dilnot and I. Walker. (eds) *The Economics of Social Security*. Oxford: Oxford University Press.

Cribier, F. (1984) 'La retraite au bord de la mer: la fonction d'accueil des retraits des villes touristiques', *Bulletin de l'Association de Géographiques Français* 101: 133–9.

Cribier, F. (1989) 'Changes in the life course and retirement in recent years: the example of two cohorts of Parisians', pp. 181–201 in P. Johnson, C. Conrad and D. Thomson (eds) *Workers Versus Pensioners*. Manchester: Manchester University Press.

Cumming, E. and Henry, W. (1961) *Growing Old: the Process of Disengagement*. New York: Basic Books.

Cutler, D.M., Poterba, J.M., Sheiner, L.M. and Summers, L.H. (1990) 'An aging society: opportunity or challenge?', *Brookings Papers on Economic Activity* 1: 1–73.

Dalton, R.J., Flanagan, S. and Beck, P.A. (1984) *Electoral Change in Advanced Industrial Democracies: Realignment or Dealignment?*. Princeton: Princeton University Press.

Davies, D.R. and Sparrow, P.R. (1985) 'Age and work behaviour', pp. 293–332 in N. Charness (ed.) *Aging and Human Performance*. Chichester: John Wiley.

Davies, J.B. (1981) 'Uncertain lifetime, consumption, and dissaving in retirement', *Journal of Political Economy* 89: 561–77.

Dawson, A. and Evans, G. (1987) 'Pensioners' incomes and expenditure 1970–1985', *Employment Gazette* May: 243–52.

Department of Employment (DE) (1990) *New Earnings Survey 1989*. London: HMSO.

Department of Environment (DoE) (1983) *1981 English House Condition Surveys*. London: HMSO.

DoE (1988) *1986 English House Condition Surveys*. London: HMSO.

Department of Health (DoH) (1989) *Caring for People: Community Care in the Next Decade and Beyond*. Cmnd 849. London: HMSO.

Department of Health and Social Security (DHSS) (1984) 'Population, Pension

Costs and Pensioners' Income: A background paper for the inquiry into provision for retirement'. London: HMSO.

DHSS (1985a) *Reform of Social Security*. Cmnd 9517. London: HMSO.

DHSS (1985b) *Reform of Social Security: Programme for Change*. Cmnd 9518. London: HMSO.

DHSS (1985c) *Reform of Social Security: Background Papers*. Cmnd 9519. London: HMSO.

DHSS (1986) *Social Security Statistics*. London: HMSO.

DHSS (1988) *Community Care: Agenda for Action* (Griffiths Report). London: HMSO.

Department of Social Security (DSS) (1988) *Social Security Statistics 1988*. London: HMSO.

DSS (1989) *Supplementary Benefit Take-up 1985*. Analytic Services Division Technical Note.

DSS (1990a) *Social Security Statistics 1990*. London: HMSO.

DSS (1990b) *Abstract of Statistics for Index of Retail Prices, Average Earnings, Social Security Benefits and Contributions*. London: HMSO.

Dilnot, A.W., Kay, J.A. and Morris, C.N. (1984) *The Reform of Social Security*. Oxford: Oxford University Press.

Easterlin, R.A. (1980) *Birth and Fortune*. New York: Basic Books.

Easterlin, R.A., Macdonald, C. and Macunovich, D.J. (1990) 'How have American baby boomers fared? Earnings and economic well-being of young adults, 1964–1987', *Journal of Population Economics* 3: 277–90.

Ekert-Jaffé, O. (1989) 'Viellessement et consommation: quelques résultats tirés des enquêtes françaises sur les budgets des ménages', *Population* 44: 561–79.

Ermisch, J.F. (1984) 'Economic implications of demographic change', London: Centre for Economic Policy Research, Discussion Paper 44.

Ermisch, J.F. (1988a) 'Economic influences on birth rates', *National Institute Economic Review* 126: 71–81.

Ermisch, J.F. (1988b) 'Fortunes of birth: the impact of generation size on the relative earnings of young men', *Scottish Journal of Political Economy* 35: 266–82.

Ermisch, J.F. (1989) 'Purchased child care, optimal family size, and mother's employment: theory and econometric analysis', *Journal of Population Economics* 2: 79–102.

Ermisch, J.F. (1990a) 'The background: housing trends and issues arising from them', pp. 5–27 in J.F. Ermisch. (ed.) *Housing and the National Economy*. Aldershot: Avebury-Gower Press.

Ermisch, J.F. (1990b) *Fewer Babies, Longer Lives*. York: Joseph Rowntree Foundation.

Études et Conjonctures (1953) 'Evolution de la population active en France depuis cent ans d'après le dénombrements quinquennaux', 8: 230–88.

Eurostat (1989) *Labour Force Survey Results, 1987*. Luxemburg: Eurostat.

Evandrou, M. (1987) 'The Use of Domiciliary Services by the Elderly: A Survey', London School of Economics: Welfare State Programme Discussion Paper 15.

Evandrou, M. (1992) 'Challenging the Invisibility of Carers: Mapping Informal Care Nationally', in F. Laczko and C. Victor (eds) *Social Policy and Older People*. London: Gower.

Evandrou, M. and Victor, C. (1989) 'Differentiation in Later Life: Social Class and Housing Tenure Cleavages', pp. 104–20 in B. Bytheway (ed.) *Becoming and Being Old: Sociological Approaches to Later Life*. London: Sage.

Evandrou, M., Arber, S., Dale, A. and Gilbert, G. (1985) *Who Cares for the Elderly?: Family Care Provision and Receipt of Statutory Services.* Paper presented at the Annual Conference of the British Society of Gerontology, September, Keele University.

Evandrou, M., Arber, S., Dale, A. and Gilbert, G. (1986) 'Who cares for the elderly?: family care provision and receipt of statutory services', pp. 150–66 in C. Phillipson, M. Bernard, and P. Strang (eds) *Dependency and Interdependency in Old Age.* Beckenham: Croom Helm.

Evandrou, M., Falkingham, J. and Glennerster, H. (1990) 'The personal social services: everyone's poor relation but nobodys baby', pp. 206–73 in J. Hills (ed.) *The State of Welfare: The Welfare State in Britain Since 1974.* Oxford: Oxford University Press.

Evandrou, M., Falkingham, J., Hills, J. and Le Grand, J. (1992) 'The Distribution of Welfare Benefits in Kind', London School of Economics: Welfare State Programme Discussion Paper 68.

Falkingham, J. (1987) 'Britain's Ageing Population: The Engine behind Increasing Dependency?', London School of Economics: Welfare State Programme Discussion Paper 17.

Falkingham, J. (1989) 'Dependency and Ageing in Britain: A re-examination of the evidence', *Journal of Social Policy* 18/2: 211–33.

Falkingham J. and Gordon C. (1990) 'Fifty Years On: the income and household composition of the elderly in London and Britain', pp. 148–71 in B. Bytheway and J. Johnson (eds) *Welfare and the Ageing Experience.* London: Avebury.

Falkingham, J. and Victor, C. (1991) 'The myth of the Woopie?: incomes, the elderly and targeting welfare', *Ageing and Society* 11/4: 471–93.

Family Policy Studies Centre (FPSC) (1989) *Family Policy Bulletin* no. 6 (Winter 1989), London: FPSC.

Feldman, J.J. (1983) 'Work ability of the aged under conditions of improving mortality', *Milbank Memorial Fund Quarterly* 61: 430–44.

Feldstein, M.S. (1974) 'Social security, induced retirement, and aggregate capital accumulation', *Journal of Political Economy* 82: 905–26.

Feldstein, M.S. (1977) 'Social security and private savings: international evidence in an extended life-cycle model', pp. 174–206 in M.S. Feldstein and R.P. Inman (eds) *The Economics of Public Services.* London: Macmillan.

Fennell, G., Phillipson, C. and Evers, H. (1988) *The Sociology of Ageing.* Milton Keynes: Open Univesity Press.

Fiegehen, G. (1986) 'Income after retirement', pp. 13–18 in CSO *Social Trends 16.* London: HMSO.

Fields, G.S. and Mitchell, O.S. (1984) *Retirement, Pensions and Social Security.* Cambridge, MA: MIT Press.

Ford, G. and Frischer, M. (1991) 'Issues in predicting the health of the elderly', pp. 275–311 in W.J. van den Heuvel, R. Illsley, A. Jamieson, and C.P. Knipscheer (eds) *Opportunities and Challenges in an Ageing Society.* Amsterdam: North Holland.

Fries, J.F. (1980) 'Aging, natural death and the compression of morbidity', *New England Journal of Medicine* 303: 130–5.

Fries, J.F. (1989) 'The compression of morbidity: near or far', *Milbank Quarterly* 67/2: 208–32.

Fry, V., Smith, S. and White, S. (1990) *Pensioners and the Public Purse.* London: Institute for Fiscal Studies.

Gibbs I. (!991) 'Income, capital and the cost of care in old age', *Ageing and Society* 11/4: 373–97.

Glendinning, C. (1989) *The Income Needs of Informal Carers: Addressing the Invisible Costs of Community Care,* paper presented at the social Policy Association annual Conference, Bath, July.

Glennerster, H. and Low, W. (1990) 'Education and the Welfare State: does it add up?', pp. 28–87 in J. Hills (ed.) *The State of Welfare: The Welfare State in Britain Since 1974.* Oxford: Oxford University Press.

Government Actuary (1990) *National Insurance Fund Long Term Financial Estimates.* London: HMSO.

Government Actuary (1991) *Occupational Pension Schemes 1987.* Eighth Survey by the Government Actuary. London: HMSO.

Grad, S. (1990) 'Income change at retirement', *Social Security Bulletin* 53/1: 2–10.

Green, H. (1988) *Informal Carers,* OPCS Series GHS No. 15, Supplement A. London: HMSO.

Green, J.R. (1988) 'Demographics, market failure and social security', pp. 3–16 in S.M. Wachter (ed.) *Social Security and Private Pensions.* Lexington, MA: Lexington Books.

Grundy, E. (1984) 'Mortality and morbidity among the old', *British Medical Journal* 288: 663–4.

Grundy, E. (1991) 'Age Related Change in Later Life', pp. 133–56 in M. Murphy and J. Hobcraft (eds) *Population Research in Britain.* London: Population Investigation Committee.

Guillemard, A.M. (1989) 'The trend towards early labour force withdrawal and the reorganisation of the life course: a cross-national analysis', pp. 163–80 in P. Johnson, C. Conrad and D. Thomson (eds) *Workers Versus Pensioners.* Manchester: Manchester University Press.

Gustman, A.L. and Steinmeier, T.L. (1988) 'An analysis of pension benefit formulas, pension wealth and incentives from pensions', NBER Working Paper 2535, March.

Habakkuk, H.J. (1962) *American and British Technology in the Nineteenth Century.* Cambridge: Cambridge University Press.

Hagemann, R.P. and Nicoletti, G. (1989) 'Population ageing: economic effects and some policy implications for financing public pensions', *OECD Economic Studies* 12: 51–96.

Hagestad, G.O. (1990) 'Social perspectives on the life course', pp. 151–68 in R.H. Binstock and L.K. George (eds) *Handbook of Aging and the Social Sciences* 3rd edn. San Diego: Academic Press.

Hannah, L. (1986) *Inventing Retirement.* Cambridge: Cambridge University Press.

Hansard 25 July 1990, written Answers, cols. 307–10.

Heller, P.S. (1989) 'Ageing, savings and pensions in the Group of Seven countries: 1980–2025', *Journal of Public Policy* 9: 127–53.

Heller, P.S., Hemming, R. and Kohnert, P.W. (1986) *Aging and Social Expenditure in the Major Industrial Countries, 1980–2025.* Washington, DC: International Monetary Fund Occasional Paper 47.

Hemming, R. and Kay, J.A. (1982) 'The costs of the State Earnings Related Pensions Scheme', *Economic Journal* 92: 300–19.

Henwood, M. and Wicks, M. (1984) 'The Forgotten Army: Family Care and Elderly People', FPSC Briefing Paper. London: FPSC.

Henwood, M. and Wicks, M. (1985) 'Community Care, Family Trends and Social Change', *Quarterly Journal of Social Affairs* 1: 357–71.

Heuvel, W.J.A. van den, Illsley, R., Jamieson, A. and Knipscheer, C.P.M. (eds) (1992) *Opportunities and Challenges in an Ageing Society.* Amsterdam: North Holland.

Hills, J. (ed.) (1990) *The State of Welfare: The Welfare State in Britain Since 1974.* Oxford: Clarendon Press.

Hinton, C. (1990) *Using your Home as Capital.* London: Age Concern.

HM Treasury (1989a) *The Government's Expenditure Plans 1989–90 to 1991–92.* Cmnd 614. London: HMSO.

HM Treasury (1989b) *Economic progress report* 200 (February). London: HMSO.

HM Treasury (1990) *The Government's Expenditure Plans 1990–91 to 1992–93.* Cmnd 1014. London: HMSO.

Hockerts H.G. (1981) 'German Post-War Social Policies against the background of the Beveridge Plan' in W.J. Mommsen (ed.) *The Emergence of the Welfare State in Britain and Germany.* London: Croom Helm.

Höhn, C. (1987) 'Population policies in advanced societies: pronatalist and migration strategies', *European Journal of Population* 3: 459–81.

Holtzmann, R. (1989) 'Pension policies in the OECD countries: background and trends', pp. 821–43 in J.M. Eekelaar and D. Pearl (eds) *An Ageing World.* Oxford: Oxford University Press.

Huby, M., Lawson, D. and Walker, R. (1988) *Avoiding Financial Dependency in Old Age*, Social Policy Research Unit, York, Working Paper 416.

Hurd, M.D. (1990) 'Research on the elderly: economic status, retirement, and consumption and saving', *Journal of Economic Literature* 38: 565–637.

Hurd, M. and Boskin, M.J. (1984) 'The effect of social security and retirement in the early 1970s', *Quarterly Journal of Economics* 99: 767–90.

Inkeles, A. and Usui, C. (1988) 'The retirement decision in cross-national perspective', pp. 273–96 in R. Ricardo-Campbell and E.P. Lazear (eds) *Issues in Contemporary Retirement.* Stanford: Hoover Institution Press.

International Labour Office (1986) *Economically Active Population 1950–2025, vol iv: Oceania, USSR, N America, Europe.* Geneva: ILO.

Ippolito, R.A. (1991) 'Encouraging long-term tenure: wage tilt or pensions?', *Industrial and Labor Relations Review* 44: 520–35.

Jacobs, K., Kohli, M. and Rein, M. (1991) 'The evolution of early exit: a comparative analysis of the labor force participation of the elderly', in M. Kohli, M. Rein, A.M. Guillemard and H. van Gunsteren (eds.) *Time for retirement: comparative studies of early exit from the labor force.* Cambridge: Cambridge University Press.

Japan Institute of Labor (1986) *Japanese Working Life Profile: Statistical Aspects.* Tokyo: Japan Institute of Labor.

Johnson, P. (1989a) 'The structured dependency of the elderly: a critical note', pp. 62–72 in M. Jefferys. (ed.) *Growing Old in the Twentieth Century.* London: Routledge.

Johnson, P. (1989b) 'The labour force participation of older men in Britain, 1951–81', *Work, Employment and Society* 3: 351–68.

Johnson, P. (1991) 'The employment and retirement of older men in England and Wales: a long-run analysis 1881–1981', Working Paper in Economic History 154. Canberra: Australian National University.

Johnson, P. (forthcoming) 'The welfare state', in R. Floud and D. McCloskey (eds)

The Economic History of Britain Since 1700: volume III. Cambridge: Cambridge University Press.

Johnson, P. and Falkingham, J. (1988) 'Intergenerational transfers and Public Expenditure on the Elderly in Modern Britain', *Ageing and Society* 8: 129–46.

Johnson P. and Webb S. (1990) *Poverty in Official Statistics: Two Reports*, Institute for Fiscal Studies Commentary no. 24. London: IFS.

Johnson, P., Conrad, C. and Thomson, D. (eds.) (1989) *Workers Versus Pensioners: Intergenerational Justice in an Ageing World*. Manchester: Manchester University Press.

Kessler. D. (1989) 'But why is there social security?', pp. 80–90 in P. Johnson, C. Conrad and D. Thomson (eds) *Workers Versus Pensioners*. Manchester: Manchester University Press.

Keyfitz, N. (1973) 'Individual mobility in a stationary population', *Population Studies* 27: 335–52.

Keyfitz, N. (1985) 'The demographics of unfunded pensions', *European Journal of Population* 1: 5–30.

Keyfitz, N. (1988) 'Some demographic properties of transfer schemes: how to achieve equity between the generations', pp. 92–105 in R.D. Lee, W.B. Arthur and G. Rodgers (eds) *Economics of Changing Age Distributions in Developed Countries*. Oxford: Oxford University Press.

King, M. and Dicks-Mireaux, L.-D.L. (1982) 'Asset-holding and the life-cycle', *Economic Journal* 92: 247–67.

Kohli, M. (1986) 'The world we forgot: an historical review of the life course', pp. 271–303 in V.E. Marshall (ed.) *Later life: the social psychology of aging*. Beverley Hills: Sage.

Kohli, M. (1992) 'Labor market perspectives and activity patterns of the elderly in an aging society', pp. 167–96 in W.J. van den Heuvel, R. Illsley, A. Jamieson, and C.P. Knipscheer (eds) *Opportunities and Challenges in an Ageing Society*. Amsterdam: North Holland.

Kotlikoff, L.J. (1988) 'The relationship of productivity to age', pp. 100–31 in R. Ricardo-Campbell and E.P. Lazear (eds) *Issues in Contemporary Retirement*. Stanford: Hoover Institution Press.

Kotlikoff, L.J. (1989) *What Determines Savings?*. Cambridge, MA: MIT Press.

Kotlikoff, L.J. and Wise, D. (1987) 'The incentive effects of private pension plans', pp. 283–340 in Z. Bodie, J. Shoven and D. Wise *Issues in Pension Economics*. Chicago: University of Chicago Press.

Kotlikoff, L.J. and Wise, D. (1989) 'Employee retirement and a firm's pension plan', pp. 279–333 in D.A. Wise *The Economics of Aging*. Chicago: NBER/University of Chicago Press.

Laczko, F. (1988) 'Between work and retirement: becoming "old" in the 1980s', pp. 24–40 in B. Bytheway (ed.) *Becoming and Being Old*. London: Sage.

Laczko, F. and Phillipson, C. (1991) *Changing Work and Retirement*. Milton Keynes: Open University Press.

Laczko, F., Dale, A., Arber, S. and Gilbert, N. (1988) 'Early retirement in a period of high unemployment', *Journal of Social Policy* 17: 313–33.

Laing, W. (1991) *Empowering the Elderly: Direct Consumer Funding of Care Services*. London: Institute of Economic Affairs.

Laslett, P. (1972) 'The History of the Family', pp. 1–90 in P. Laslett and R. Wall. (eds) *The Household and Family in Past Times*. Cambridge: Cambridge University Press.

Laslett, P. (1977) *Family Life and Illicit Love in Earlier Generations*. Cambridge: Cambridge University Press.

Lazear, E.P. (1979) 'Why is there mandatory retirement?', *Journal of Political Economy* 87: 1261–84.

Lazear, E.P. (1981) 'Agency, earnings profiles, productivity and hours restrictions', *American Economic Review* 71: 606–20.

Lazear, E.P. (1990) 'Pensions and deferred benefits as strategic compensation', *Industrial Relations* 29: 263–80.

Le Grand, J., Winter, D. and Woolley, F. (1990) 'The National Health Service: safe in whose hands?', pp. 88–134 in J. Hills (ed.) *The State of Welfare: The Welfare State in Britain Since 1974*. Oxford: Oxford University Press.

Leat, D. and Gay, P. (1987) *Paying for Care*. Research Report No. 661. London: Policy Studies Institute.

Leather, P. (1990) 'The potential and implications of home equity release in old age', *Housing Studies* 5: 3–13.

Lee, C.H. (1979) *British Regional Employment Statistics 1841–1971*. Cambridge: Cambridge University Press.

Lee, R.D., Arthur, W.B. and Rodgers, G. (eds) (1988) *Economics of Changing Age Distributions in Developed Countries*. Oxford: Oxford University Press.

Libassi, P.F. (1988) 'Integrating the elder in the labor force: consequences and experience for insurance', *Geneva Papers on Risk and Insurance* 13: 350–60.

Longman, P. (1987) *Born to Pay: the New Politics of Aging in America*. Boston: Houghton Mifflin.

McCallum, J. (1988) 'Japanese *Teinen Taishoku*: how cultural values affect retirement', *Ageing and Society* 8: 23–41.

Mackintosh S., Means, R. and Leather, P. (1990) *Housing in Later Life: The Housing Finance Implications of an Ageing Society*. Bristol: SAUS.

McLoughlin, J. (1991) *The Demographic Revolution*. London: Faber and Faber.

Macnicol, J. (1990a) 'Old age and structured dependency', pp. 30–52 in M. Bury and J. Macnicol (eds) *Aspects of Ageing*. London: Royal Holloway and Bedford New College.

Macnicol, J. (1990b) 'Ageing and justice', *Labour History Review* 55: 75–80.

Maddox, G. (1992) 'Transformations of health and health care in aging societies', pp. 311–30 in W.J. van den Heuvel, R. Illsley, A. Jamieson, and C.P. Knipscheer (eds) *Opportunities and Challenges in an Ageing Society.* Amsterdam: North Holland.

Malthus, T.R. (1798) *An Essay on the Principle of Population*, reprinted in E.A. Wrigley and D. Souden (eds) (1986) *The Works of Thomas Robert Malthus, vol. 1*. London: W. Pickering.

Mankiw, N.G. and Weil, D. (1989) 'The baby boom, the baby bust and the housing market', *Regional Science and Urban Economics* 19: 235–58.

Manton, K.G. (1982) 'Changing concepts of mortality and morbidity in the population' *Milbank Memorial Fund Quarterly* 60: 183–244.

Marchand, M. and Pestieau, P. (1991) 'Public pensions: choices for the future', *European Economic Review* 35: 441–53.

Martin, B. (1990) 'The Cultural Construction of Ageing: or How Long Can the Summer Wine Really Last?', pp. 53–81 in M. Bury and J. Macnicol (eds) *Aspects of Ageing: Essays on Social Policy and Old Age*. London: Royal Holloway and Bedford New College.

Martin, L.G. and Ogawa, N. (1988) 'The effect of cohort size on relative wages in

Japan', pp. 58–75 in R.D. Lee, W.B. Arthur and G. Rodgers (eds) *Economics of Changing Age Distributions in Developed Countries*. Oxford: Oxford University Press.

Midwinter, E. (1985) *The Wage of Retirement: The Case for a New Pensions Policy*. London: Centre for Policy on Ageing.

Midwinter, E. (1989) 'Workers versus pensioners?', *Social Policy and Administration* 23: 205–10.

Mincer, J. (1974) *Schooling, Experience and Earnings*. New York: NBER.

Ministry of Labour Gazette (1949) London, HMSO.

Mirer, T.W. (1979) 'The wealth-age relation among the aged', *American Economic Review* 69: 435–43.

Mitchell, B.R. (1988) *British Historical Statistics*. Cambridge: Cambridge University Press.

Mitchell, O.S. and Luzadis, R.A. (1988) 'Changes in pension incentives through time', *Industrial and Labor Relations Review* 42: 100–8.

Moore, Rt Hon. John (MP, Secretary of State for Social Services) (1989) Transcript of address to Help the Aged Sheltered Housing Conference, 5 June 1989. London: Help the Aged.

Morrison, M.H. (1988) 'Changes in the legal mandatory retirement age: labor force participation implications', pp. 378–412 in R. Ricardo-Campbell and E.P. Lazear (eds) *Issues in Contemporary Retirement*. Stanford: Hoover Institution Press.

Murie, A. (1983) *Housing, Inequality and Deprivation*. London: Heinemann.

Murphy, M. and Sullivan, O. (1983) 'Housing Tenure and Fertility in Post-War Britain'. London School of Hygiene and Tropical Medicine: Centre for Population Studies Research Paper 83–2.

Murphy, M. and Sullivan, O. (1985) 'Housing Tenure and Family Formation in Contemporary Britain', *European Sociological Review* 1/3: 230–43.

Musgrove, P. (1982) *U.S. Household Consumption, Income, and Demographic Changes: 1975–2025*. Washington, DC: Resources for the Future.

New Society (1986) New Society Database: The State of the Elderly. 24 October.

Organization for Economic Cooperation and Development, (OECD) (1981) *The Welfare State in Crisis*. Paris: OECD.

OECD (1988a) *Ageing Populations: the Social Policy Implications*. Paris: OECD.

OECD (1988b) *Reforming Public Pensions*. Paris: OECD.

OECD (1988c) *The Future of Social Security*. Paris: OECD.

OECD (1990) *Labour Force Statistics, 1968–1988*. Paris: OECD.

Office of Population Censuses and Surveys (OPCS) (1982) *General Household Survey 1980*. London: HMSO.

OPCS (1984) *Census Guide 1: Britain's Elderly Population*. London: HMSO.

OPCS (1987) *General Household Survey 1985*. London: HMSO.

OPCS (1989) *General Household Survey 1987*. London: HMSO.

OPCS (1990) *General Household Survey 1988*. London: HMSO.

OPCS (1991) *National Population Projections 1989 Based* Series PP2 No.17. London: HMSO.

Oldman, C. (1991) *Paying for Care: personal sources of funding care*. York: Joseph Rowntree Foundation.

Olshansky, S.J. (1988) 'On forecasting mortality', *Milbank Memorial Fund Quarterly* 66/3: 482–530.

Ono, A. (1989–90) 'Labour cost in an aging economy', *Japanese Economic Studies* 18: 30–57.

Oppenheim, C. (1990) *Poverty: The Facts*. London: Child Poverty Action Group.

Parker, S. (1980) *Older Workers and Retirement*. London: HMSO.

Pearson, M., Smith, S. and White, S. (1989) 'Demographic influences on public spending', *Fiscal Studies* 10: 48–65.

Percheron, A. and Remond, R. (1991) *Age et Politique*. Paris: Economica.

Phillipson, C. (1982) *Capitalism and the Construction of Old Age*. London: Macmillan.

Phillipson, C. (1991) 'Inter-generational relations: conflict or consensus in the 21st century', *Policy and Politics* 19: 27–36.

Piachaud, D. (1986) 'Disability, retirement and unemployment of older men', *Journal of Social Policy* 15: 145–62.

Preston, S.H. (1984) 'Children and the elderly: divergent paths for America's dependants', *Demography* 21: 435–57.

Preston, S., Himes, C. and Eggers, M. (1988) *Demographic Conditions Responsible for Population Ageing*. Paper presented at the annual meeting of the Population Association of America, New Orleans LA.

Quadagno, J. (1982) *Aging in Early Industrial Society*. New York: Academic Press.

Quadagno, J. (1988) *The Transformation of Old Age Security*. Chicago: University of Chicago Press.

Quinn, J.F. and Burkhauser, R.V. (1990) 'Work and retirement', pp. 307–27 in R.H. Binstock and L.K. George *Handbook of Aging and the Social Sciences*. 3rd edn. San Diego: Academic Press.

Rabbit, P. (1992) 'Some issues in cognitive gerontology and their implication for social policy', pp. 233–74 in W.J. van den Heuvel, R. Illsley, A. Jamieson, and C.P. Knipscheer (eds) *Opportunities and Challenges in an Ageing Society*. Amsterdam: North Holland.

Ransom, R.L. and Sutch, R. (1986) 'The labor of older Americans: retirement of men on and off the job', *Journal of Economic History* 46: 1–30.

Ransom, R.L. and Sutch, R. (1988) 'The decline of retirement in the years before social security: U.S. retirement patterns, 1870–1940', pp. 3–37 in R. Ricardo-Campbell and E.P. Lazear (eds) *Issues in Contemporary Retirement*. Stanford: Hoover Institution Press.

Rapports Officiels (1991) *Livre Blanc sur les Retraites*. Paris: La Documentation Française.

Rein, M. and Jacobs, K. (1992) 'Employment trends of older workers in western countries', pp. 197–212 in W.J. van den Heuvel, R. Illsley, A. Jamieson, and C.P. Knipscheer (eds) *Opportunities and Challenges in an Ageing Society*. Amsterdam: North Holland.

Report of the National Commission on Social Security Reform (1983). Washington, DC: Government Printing Office.

Riboud, M. (1987) 'Labour-market responses to changes in cohort size: the case of France', *European Journal of Population* 3: 359–82.

Ricardo-Campbell, R. and Lazear, E.P. (eds) (1988) *Issues in Contemporary Retirement*. Stanford: Hoover Institution Press.

Riddle, S.M. (1984) 'Age, obsolescence and unemployment. Older men in the British industrial system, 1920–1939: a research note', *Ageing and Society* 4: 517–24.

Rogers, A., Rogers, R.G. and Belanger, A. (1990) 'Longer life but worse health? Measurement and dynamics', *The Gerontologist* 30: 640–49.

Royal Commission of the Distribution of Income and Wealth (1978). London: HMSO.
Royal Commission on Population (1949). London: HMSO.
Rust, J. (1989) 'A dynamic programming model of retirement behaviour', pp. 359–98 in D.A. Wise (ed.) *The Economics of Aging*. Chicago: NBER/University of Chicago Press.
Sass, S. (1989) 'Pension bargains: the heyday of U.S. collectively bargained pension arrangements', pp. 92–112 in P. Johnson, C. Conrad and D. Thomson (eds) *Workers Versus Pensioners*. Manchester: Manchester University Press.
Schmähl, W. (1989) 'Labour force participation and social pension systems', pp. 137–61 in P. Johnson, C. Conrad and D. Thomson (eds) *Workers Versus Pensioners*. Manchester: Manchester University Press.
Schmähl, W. (1990) 'Demographic change and social security', *Journal of Population Economics* 3: 159–77.
Schneider, E.L. and Brody, J.A. (1983) 'Ageing, natural death and the compression of morbidity: another view', *New England Journal of Medicine* 309: 854–6.
Scott, P. and Johnson, P. (1988) *The Economic Consequences of Population Ageing in Advanced Societies* CEPR Discussion Paper 263, July. London: CEPR.
Serow, W.J. (1984) 'The impact of population changes on consumption', pp 168–78 in G. Steinman (ed.) *Economic Consequences of Population Change*. Berlin: Springer-Verlag.
Shanas, E., Townsend, P., Wedderburn, D., Friis, H., Milhoj, P. and Stehouwer, J. (1968) *Older People in Three Industrial Societies*. London: Routledge and Kegan Paul.
Shragge, E. (1984) *Pensions Policy in Britain*. London: Routledge.
Simon, J.L. (1977) *The Economics of Population Growth*. Princeton: Princeton University Press.
Simon, J.L. (1981) *The Ultimate Resource*. Princeton: Princeton University Press.
Smeeding, T.M. (1990) 'Economic status of the elderly', pp. 362–81 in R.H. Binstock and L.K. George (eds) *Handbook of Aging and the Social Sciences*. 3rd edn. San Diego: Academic Press.
Smith, R. (1984) 'The structured dependence of the elderly as a recent development: some sceptical historical thoughts', *Ageing and Society* 4: 409–28.
Steinman, G. (ed.) (1984) *Economic Consequences of Population Change in Industrialized Countries*. Berlin: Springer-Verlag.
Strober, M.H. (1990) 'Human capital theory: implications for HR managers', *Industrial Relations* 29: 214–39.
Taylor, R. and Ford, G. (1983) 'Inequalities in old age', *Ageing and Society*, 3/2: 183–208.
Teitelbaum, M.S. and Winter, J.M. (1985) *The Fear of Population Decline*. Orlando: Academic Press.
Thaler, R.H. (1990) 'Saving, fungibility, and mental accounts', *Journal of Economic Perspectives* 4: 193–205.
Thane, P. (1989) 'Old Age: Burden or Benefit', pp. 56–71 in H. Joshi (ed.) *The Changing Population of Britain*. Oxford: Basil Blackwell.
Thane, P.M. (1990) 'The debate on the declining birth-rate in Britain: the "menace" of an ageing population, 1920s–1950s', *Continuity and Change* 5: 283–305.
Thompson, C. and West P. (1984) 'The public appeal of sheltered housing', *Ageing and Society* 4: 305–26.
Thomson, D. (1983) 'Workhouse to nursing home: residential care of elderly people in England since 1840', *Ageing and Society* 3: 43–69.

Thomson, D. (1984) 'The decline of social welfare: falling state support for the elderly since early Victorian times', *Ageing and Society* 4: 451–82.

Thomson, D. (1986a) 'Welfare and Historians', pp. 355–78 in L. Bonfield et al. (eds) *The World We Have Gained*. Oxford: Blackwell.

Thomson, D. (1986b) 'The overpaid elderly?', *New Society*. 7 March 1986.

Thomson, D. (1987) 'Incomes in Old Age – Rising or Falling?', unpublished paper. (January 1987).

Thomson, D. (1989) 'The welfare state and generation conflict: winners and losers', pp. 33–56 in P. Johnson, C. Conrad and D. Thomson (eds) *Workers Vesus Pensioners*. Manchester: Manchester University Press.

Timaeus, I. (1986) 'Families and Households of the Elderly Population: Prospects for those approaching old age', *Ageing and Society* 6: 271–93.

Titmuss, R.M. (1955) 'Pension systems and population change', *Political Quarterly* 26: 152–66.

Titmuss, R.M. (1958) 'The position of women', pp. 88–103 in his *Essays on 'The Welfare State'*, London: George Allen and Unwin.

Tompkins, P. (1989) *Flexibility and fairness: a study in equalisation of pension ages and benefits*. York: Joseph Rowntree Memorial Trust.

Townsend, P. (1981) 'The structured dependency of the elderly: a creation of social policy in the 20th century', *Ageing and Society* 1: 5–28.

Townsend, P. and Wedderburn, D. (1965) *The Aged and the Welfare State*. London: G. Bell and Sons.

Trades Union Congress (TUC) (1989) 'TUC Pensioners Committee: Report of the Inaugural Conference Held on June 30, 1989', London: TUC.

United Nations (1985) *World Population Prospects* Department of Economic and Social Affairs, Population Studies No. 86. New York: United Nations.

van der Wijst, T. (1987) *Developments in the Age Structure of the Labour Force by Industry and by Occupation*, Netherlands Interuniversity Demographic Institute working paper 74, The Hague.

van Imhoff, E. (1988) 'Age structure, education, and the transmission of technical change', *Journal of Population Economics* 1: 167–81.

van Praag, B.M.S. (1988) 'The notion of population economics', *Journal of Population Economics* 1: 5–16.

Venti, S.F. and Wise, D.A. (1989) 'Aging, moving and housing wealth', pp. 9–48 in D.A. Wise (ed.) *The Economics of Aging*. Chicago: NBER/University of Chicago Press.

Venti, S.F. and Wise, D.A. (1990) 'But they don't want to reduce housing equity', pp. 13–32 in D.A. Wise (ed.) *Issues in the Economics of Aging*. Chicago: NBER/University of Chicago Press.

Verbrugge, L.M. (1984) 'Longer life but worsening health? Trends in health and mortality of middle-aged and older persons', *Milbank Memorial Fund Quarterly* 62: 473–519.

Vergoossen, D. and Warnes, A. (1989) 'Migration of the elderly', pp. 129–143 in J. Stillwell and H.J. Scholten, (eds) *Contemporary Research in Population Geography*. Dordrecht: Kluwer Academic.

Vernière, L. (1990) 'Retraites: l'urgence d'une réforme', *Economie et Statistique* 233: 29–38.

Victor, C. and Evandrou, M. (1987) 'Does social class matter in later life?', pp. 252–67 in S. di Gregorio (ed.) *Social Gerontology: New Directions*. London: Croom Helm.

Wachter, S.M. (ed.) (1988) *Social Security and Private Pensions*. Lexington, MA: Lexington Books.

Walker, A. (1981) 'Towards a political economy of old age', *Ageing and Society* 1: 73–94.

Walker, A. (1985) 'Early retirement: release or refuge from the labour market', *Quarterly Journal of Social Affairs* 1: 211–29.

Walker, A. (1990) 'The economic "burden" of ageing and the prospect of intergenerational conflict', *Ageing and Society* 10: 377–96.

Walker R. (1988) 'The financial resources of the elderly', pp. 45–73 in S. Baldwin, G. Parker and R. Walker (eds) *Social Security and Community Care*. Aldershot: Avebury.

Walker, R. and Hutton, S. (1988) 'Costs of ageing and retirement', pp. 46–62 in R. Walker and G. Parker (eds) *Money Matters*. London: Sage.

Wall, R. (1982) 'Regional and Temporal variations in the structure of the British household since 1851', in T. Barker and M. Drake (eds) *Population and Society in Britain 1850–1980*. London: Batsford.

Wall, R. (1984) 'Residential Isolation of the Elderly: a comparison over time', *Ageing and Society* 4: 483–503.

Wall, R. (1989) 'The living arrangements of the elderly in Europe in the 1980's', pp. 121–42 in B. Bytheway (ed.) *Becoming and Being Old*. London: Sage.

Wall, R., Schurer, K. and Laslett, P. (1988) 'The Changing Form of the English Household 1891–1921: a four community study', Mimeo Paper Cambridge Group for the Study of Population History.

Warburton, P. (1987) 'Labour supply incentives for the retired', pp. 185–234 in M. Beenstock (ed.) *Work, Welfare and Taxation*. London: Allen and Unwin.

Warnes, A. (1982) *Geographical Perspectives on Ageing*. London: John Wiley.

Warnes, A. and Law, C.M. (1984) 'The elderly population of Britain', *Transactions of the Institute of British Geographers*, New Series 9/1: 37–59.

Wattenberg, B.J. (1987) *The Birth Dearth*. New York: Pharos Books.

Weaver, C. (1982) *The Crisis in Social Security*. Durham, NC: Duke University Press.

Welford, A.T. (1958) *Ageing and Human Skill*. London: Oxford University Press.

Williams, B.R. (1989) *Stepping Stones to Independence: National Insurance after 1990*. Aberdeen: Aberdeen University Press.

Wise, D.A. (1989) *The Economics of Aging*. Chicago: NBER/University of Chicago Press.

Wright, R.E. (1991) 'Cohort size and earnings in Great Britain', *Journal of Population Economics* 4: 295–305.

Zabalza, A., Pissarides, C. and Barton, M. (1980) 'Social security and the choice between full-time work, part-time work and retirement', *Journal of Public Economics* 14: 245–76.

Index

affluence and old age, 49–50, 58–9,
  64–5, 70, 78, 80, 131, 177
age allowance, 78
Age Discrimination in Employment
  Act (US), 101–2, 182
age of workforce, 4, 160–1, 163–5, 167
age prejudice, 102–3
age structure, 9–10, 14, 18–27, 40–2,
  47, 138–9, 152–7
  of elderly population, 25–8, 41–2, 47
  see also individual countries
ageing and
  consumption, 153–60
  economic growth, 4, 174–6
  housing market, 158–9
  innovation, 174
  labour costs, 162–72
  production, 160–72
  public policy, 179–81
  saving, 5, 172–5
AIDS, 40
American Association of Retired
  Persons, 132
Americans for Generational Equity,
  132
Australia
  age structure, 21
  social expenditure, 134, 136
Austria
  age structure, 21
  pension expenditure, 134

baby-boom, 1, 26
baby-boomers, 1–2, 131–2, 148–9, 173
Bangladesh, age structure, 47
basic income scheme, 185–6
Belgium,
  age structure, 21
  social expenditure, 134, 136
benefits in kind, 57–8
Beveridge, W.H., 100, 125
birth rate, see fertility rate

Brazil, age structure, 47–8

Canada
  age structure, 21
  pension replacement rate, 56
  social expenditure, 134, 136
  sources of pensioner income, 60
care
  age distribution of, 46
  cost of, 10, 36, 46, 49, 74–80, 133
  informal, 10, 15, 31–6, 75–6
  privatization of, 50, 75–8
  provision of, 10, 36, 75–8, 82
China, age structure, 47–8
cohort size and earnings, 170–1
consumption patterns and age
  structure, 153–60
compression of morbidity, 72–3, 97
co-residence, see household
  composition

death rate, see mortality rate
demographic time bomb, 2, 42
demographic transition, 22
Denmark
  age structure, 21
  pension age, 89
  social expenditure, 134, 136
dependency
  burden of, 30–1, 36, 42–3, 49
  ratios, 18, 43–7, 129–30, 137
disability and ill health, 14, 71–4, 76–8,
  79, 133–5
  and employment, 97–9, 106–7
  incidence by age, 72
  incidence by income group, 77
disengagement, 11–12
divorce, 29–35

early retirement, 6, 105–7, 120
  and ill health, 96–9
earnings of older workers, 161–9

economic growth, 4, 148–51, 174–6
economic welfare, *see* affluence and old
    age, living standards of older
    people, poverty
economics and ageing, 3–9, 121–3,
    178–9
education expenditure, 57–8, 135
elderly population, *see* older
    population
equity release schemes, 66, 70
    see also home ownership
equivalence scales, 61–2

Feigehen, G., 51–3
Feldstein, M., 126–7
fertility
    decline, 10, 24
    rate, 21–4, 26, 34, 40
France
    age structure, 9, 15, 21, 47, 139,
        151–6
    labour force participation, 87–91
    pension contribution rate, 145
    pension replacement rate, 56
    retirement income, 177, 181
    retirement migration, 39
    social expenditure, 134, 136
    unemployment and retirement, 103–5
Fries, J. F., 72–3, 97
functionalism, 11–12

Germany
    age structure, 21, 139, 151–7
    labour force participation, 87–91
    pension contribution rate, 145
    pension replacement rate, 56
    retirement age, 89
    social expenditure, 134, 136
    unemployment and retirement, 103–5
Gray Panthers, 15
Griffiths Report, 82

health care, 14, 42, 57–8
    cost of, 49, 133–5
home ownership, 49, 51, 64–71, 82
    by income group, 67–70
household composition, 31–6
housing
    demand and age structure, 158–9
    quality, 69–70
    stock, 35

human capital theory, 162–4

illness, *see* disability
implicit contracts, 129
income in old age, 51–66, 78–9
    alternative estimates of, 53
    distribution of, 61–3, 81
    source of, 55, 59, 60
India, age structure, 47
individual ageing, 5, 18
Indonesia, age structure, 47
informal care, 10, 15, 31–6, 75–6
institutional care, 31–2, 36
intergenerational conflict, 8, 50, 59,
    124, 132
intergenerational transfers, 5, 8,
    129–33, 145–7, 149, 183–4
internal labour markets, 101–2, 164
International Monetary Fund, 133
Italy
    age structure, 139
    pension replacement rate, 56
    social expenditure, 134, 136

Japan
    age structure, 9, 15, 47, 139
    labour force participation, 166
    mandatory retirement, 102
    pension age, 146, 166
    pension replacement rate, 56
    social expenditure, 134, 136
    sources of pensioner income, 60
    unemployment and retirement, 103–5
job release scheme, 105

kinship links, 14–15

labour costs and age structure, 162–72
labour force participation, 44–5, 84–96
    and age, 6–7, 161–2
    female, 76, 86–94, 139
    male, 86–95
life expectancy, 22–8, 34, 73
life-cycle theory, 5, 8, 109–16, 126–8,
    173–4
living standards of older people, 49,
    51–9, 64–5
Longman, P., 132
long-term care insurance, 79–80

Malthus, T., 3–4

mandatory retirement, 99–102
means-testing, 50, 78–9, 82–3, 151,
  184–5
Mexico, age structure, 47
migration, 26, 28, 34, 40–1, 171–2
modernization, 11
mortality rate, 22–4, 26–30, 34–5, 40–1,
  73

National Insurance pensions, 100, 139
  origins of, 125–6
  value of, 52, 55, 57, 117–19, 143–4
National Health Service (NHS), 50, 75
New Zealand
  age structure, 20–1
  pension expenditure, 134
Nigeria, age structure, 47
Netherlands
  age structure, 21
  social expenditure, 134, 136
Norway
  age structure, 21
  pension expenditure, 134

occupational pensions
  coverage, 60–1, 114–15
  defined benefit (final salary) 112–14,
    168–70
  defined contribution (money
    purchase), 112, 169, 182
  reasons for, 13, 101–2
  and retirement decisions, 112–16,
    168–9
  as source of income, 59, 63–5
  see also public pensions
Old Age and Survivors Insurance
  (US), 125
older population
  affluence of, 49–50, 58–9, 64–5, 70,
    78, 80, 131, 177
  consumption patterns of, 49, 153–60
  employment income of, 59–66
  home ownership, 49, 51, 64–71, 82
  living standards, 49, 51–9, 64–5
  marital status of, 28–31
  migration of, 37–8
  poverty of, 12, 50–2, 54, 150–1, 177
  sex ratio of, 27–30
older worker and
  earnings, 161–9
  informal labour market, 46

productivity, 7, 100–2, 162–5, 182
  skill, 163–4
  training, 163, 167
  unemployment, 102–9
Organization for Economic
    Cooperation and Development
    (OECD), 56, 126, 133, 137

Pakistan, age structure, 47
pension age, 7, 89, 99
  increase in, 131, 145–6
  normalization of, 99–100
  see also retirement age
pension contribution rates, 8, 144–5
pension expenditure, projections, 134
pension replacement rate, 56, 117–19,
  143, 184–5
pensions, *see* occupational pensions,
    public pensions, National
    Insurance pensions
pensions and income distribution, 8,
  59–64
personal pensions, 147
personal social services, 57–8, 75, 77–8
Phillips Committee, 47
politics and ageing, 15–16
population
  decline, 3–4, 26, 42, 138–9
  growth, 3–4, 161–2
  projections, 2, 9, 40–2, 138–9
Poor Law, 12, 31, 92
poverty
  and old age, 12, 50–2 150–1
  numbers living in, 54, 177
Preston, S., 131–2
privatization of care, 50, 75–8
productivity of older workers, 7, 100–2,
  162–5, 182
public pensions, 42, 116–19, 124–51
  cost of, 43, 49–50, 135–8, 140, 143
  coverage, 138–9, 145
  and economic growth, 148–51
  funded, 146–50, 187–8
  indexation of, 56, 142–6
  maturing of, 140–1
  methods of financing, 124–6, 128–33,
    146–50
  pay-as-you-go, 124–6, 146
  and poverty prevention, 150–1
  as proportion of national income,
    133–5

rate of return to, 129–30, 145–6
reform of, 144–51
see also National Insurance pensions,
   occupational pensions

residential care, 14, 78
residential clustering of older
   population, 36–9, 159–60
retirement, 6, 11–13
   by age group, 86–93
   by birth cohort, 92–3
   by occupation, 92–5
   definition of, 84–6
   explanations of, 96–119
   trends, 86–91
retirement age, 89, 92, 100
   see also pension age
Royal Commission on Population, 1, 42

savings and pensions, 8, 109–16, 126–8,
   148–9
seniority wage systems, 164
State Earnings Related Pension
   Scheme (SERPS), 43, 49, 52,
   139
   cost of, 140–1
   returns from, 142–3
Smith, A., 4
social expenditure
   levels, 142
   projections, 135–7
social policy and ageing, 13–15, 178–9
social product, 10, 46
social security, 5, 7–8, 12, 42, 63–4
sociology and ageing, 9–13, 121–3, 179
structured dependency, 12–13, 107–9
Sweden
   age structure, 21, 47
   social expenditure, 134, 136
Switzerland
   age structure, 21
   pension expenditure, 134

targeting, *see* means-testing
Titmuss, R., 66, 81, 180
Thomson, D., 53, 55, 145
training, 163, 167

unemployment and retirement, 102–9

United Kingdom
   age structure, 9, 15, 18–27, 40–2,
      139, 152–5
   dependency ratios, 43–6
   disability, incidence of, 71–80
   housing
      demand, 159
      tenure, 66–71
   labour force participation, 85–95
   life expectancy, 23
   marital status of older population,
      28–31
   median age, 19–20
   pension, value of, 55–6, 59–63,
      117–19, 143
   pensioners
      affluence of, 63–5, 70
      number of, 52, 117
      poverty of, 50–4, 177
   saving rates, 114
   sex ratio of older population, 27–30,
      41–2
   sources of pensioner income, 59, 63
   unemployment and retirement, 103–7
   see also National Insurance pensions,
      National Health Service, public
      pensions
United States of America
   affluence and old age, 49–50
   age structure, 9, 15, 21, 47, 139,
      152–4
   consumer demand, 158–60
   housing equity, 70
   labour force participation, 87–91
   pension age, 89
   pension financing, 125, 146
   pension replacement rate, 56
   retirement age, 89, 102, 131, 146
   saving rates, 173
   social expenditure, 46, 134, 136
   sources of pensioner income, 60
   unemployment and retirement, 103–5
USSR, age structure, 47

widowhood, 28–9
WOOPIE (well-off older person),
   50–1, 76–8, 81, 184
   characteristics of, 64–5
   definition of, 64